Forces in Modern French Drama

FORCES IN MODERN FRENCH DRAMA

Studies in Variations on the Permitted Lie

edited by JOHN FLETCHER

 Frederick Ungar Publishing Co., New York

First American Edition 1972
Copyright © 1972 by University of London Press, Ltd
Printed in Great Britain
Library of Congress Catalog Card Number 79-163144
ISBN 0-8044-2199-4

CONTENTS

Acknowledgments

The publisher wishes to thank the following French publishers
for permission to reproduce copyright material:
Editions Gallimard for extracts from *Théâtre Récits Nouvelles*
(Camus), and *Théâtre* (Montherlant); Editions de la Table Ronde
for extracts from *La Sauvage, Eurydice, Antigone, Médée,
Le Rendez-vous de Senlis, Le Bal des voleurs, L'Hurluberlu* and
L'Alouette (Anouilh).

The editor wishes to thank his wife, Beryl S. Fletcher, for her
invaluable work in proof-reading and indexing the text.

The cover photograph, depicting a scene from a recent Théâtre de
la Ville production of *La Guerre de Troie n'aura pas lieu*, is
reproduced by courtesy of the French Embassy, London.

'The theatre', Thornton Wilder once wrote, 'lives by conventions: a convention is an agreed-upon falsehood, a permitted lie'. Whenever we set foot in a playhouse we contract, in return for edification and delight, to subscribe *en pleine connaissance de cause* to the pretences on which all drama depends. This book tries to show how that willingly-accepted falsehood is created by an especially active and imaginative body of dramatists – those who, in our own century, have written plays in French. It deals, in other words, with a particularly interesting and fruitful moment in the long and magnificent history of the stage, with a development which we have ourselves been able to witness with our own eyes, and which in 1971 still seems to be maintaining its impetus.

In line with this aim, the various contributors to the volume have concentrated their attention on questions of technique and dramatic method, and have emphasised the originality of those playwrights who are clearly living forces in the French theatre of today. We have, inevitably, had to be selective – there is little mention, for instance, of Duras, Schehadé, Vauthier or Weingarten, to cite only a few recent examples – but the dramatists dealt with in some detail are of undoubted importance in their own right, as well as being lively presences in the contemporary theatre. Their works, at any given moment in time, are being staged in various places around the world, and cannot be ignored by anyone claiming to take an informed interest in the art of drama. This book sets out to define for the concerned reader and theatre-goer what it is that makes modern French drama both significantly unique and exemplary, in a general way, of all vital theatre.

Each contributor to our symposium has brought his or her own point of view to bear on this larger question, and I have not, as editor, sought to do much more than give the volume as a whole a certain shape and emphasis. Some of my critics have chosen to discuss the works of their playwright in chronological order of composition or performance, and write an extended commentary on a life's creation. Others, on the contrary, have preferred a more thematic approach. I have been pleased with the variety this produces, and I hope our readers will be too. They will, I believe, find that although the essays are written by different people (all of whom are eminent in the field of contemporary French theatre studies) they do interlock and interrelate, such is the basic unity of the subject. Various Ariadne's threads will be seen to guide us through the labyrinth. Dorothy Knowles refers in the opening pages of her chapter to the famous Fratellini clowns, for instance; towards the middle of the book W. D. Howarth discusses the art of Jean Anouilh; and then I myself have occasion to refer to one of Anouilh's telling insights, the remark he made linking the Fratellinis and Pascal in his description of Samuel Beckett's best-known play. Or again, Richard N. Coe connects Sartre and Genet not only by referring to the philosopher's study *Saint Genet*, but also by pointing out that Genet's first two plays were strongly influenced by *Huis clos*. Or, finally, it will be noticed how Dr Knowles's demonstration of the role played by prominent directors in bringing the dramatic talents of certain writers to birth is confirmed by those who in later pages discuss the same question from the point of view of Claudel, Giraudoux or Camus.

The pattern of the book is therefore, we hope, logical and straightforward. The first chapter is devoted to a survey of the vital contribution made by the leading producers and theorists of the period, and – appropriately – is written by Dorothy Knowles, author of the standard work on the subject, *French Drama of the Inter-War Years* (Harrap). Dr Knowles is Honorary Research Fellow at Bedford College in the University of London.

Dr Flower is Reader in French at the University of East Anglia, and has written an important study of François Mauriac's fiction; he here turns his attention to the work of another Catholic writer, Paul Claudel (1868–1955). Taking as his text Claudel's remark to Jean-Louis Barrault, 'ce n'est qu'au feu de la rampe qu'une œuvre dramatique commence vraiment à vivre', Dr Flower lays particular stress on the part played by Barrault in helping Claudel to find effective theatrical means of expressing his poetic vision.

The next chapter, by Dr Godin (Reader in French in the Queen's University of Belfast), shows how in his drama of persuasion and debate Jean Giraudoux (1882–1944) treats subjects often borrowed from the classics in a thoroughly modern way, especially in so far as the dialogue is concerned, which is witty, pert, sharp and characteristic of the inter-war years even when it has the density of a controlled diction; so that, Godin argues, while it is very much a product of its age, Giraudoux's work also has a timeless quality which should ensure its survival on our stages.

H. T. Mason is Professor of European Literature (with special reference to French) in the University of East Anglia, and is best known as a historian of ideas and eighteenth-century specialist. He here turns to one of the most austerely classical of modern French playwrights, Henry de Montherlant (b. 1896), who more than once reminds one of Corneille, and not just because they both share a fascination with the proud and aristocratic ethos of republican Rome and medieval Spain.

The fifth essay is contributed by W. D. Howarth, Professor of Classical French Literature in the University of Bristol and well known as an authority on the golden age of French theatre. He here shows a fine sympathy for the most technically gifted of modern French dramatists, Jean Anouilh (b. 1910). If Montherlant has affinities with the great Corneille, there is no question which of the classical French playwrights Anouilh is closest to – it is, of course, the exquisite, bitter-sweet Marivaux.

In the next chapter Philip Thody (Professor of French Literature in the University of Leeds) discusses patterns and politics in the theatre of Jean-Paul Sartre (b. 1905), an author on whom he is an acknowledged expert. B. G. Garnham, Lecturer in French in the University of Durham, follows this up with a judicious appraisal of Albert Camus's merits and demerits as a dramatist, and shows what the theatre lost when Camus was killed in a car accident in 1960 at the age of forty-six.

'Scandal and sincerity' are the twin poles of the paradox which Richard N. Coe, Professor of French at the University of Melbourne and Professor-Designate at the University of Warwick, sees in the plays of Jean Genet (b. 1910), taking as his text Barrault's remark 'il n'y a donc de scandale et de provocation possibles au théâtre que si la sincérité y est entière'. Those who know Coe's book *The Vision of Jean Genet* will find here an equally sensitive approach to our contemporary *poète maudit*.

James R. Knowlson (Lecturer in French, University of Reading) offers a balanced assessment of that *enfant terrible* of the Theatre of the Absurd, Eugène Ionesco (b. 1912). Dr Knowlson's interests, like Mr Garnham's, lie as much in the history of ideas as in modern French drama, and this enables them both to come to grips with playwrights who, despite their differences, share an intense belief in humane values.

The editor, who is Professor of Comparative Literature at the University of East Anglia and contributes the concluding essay, has attempted to draw on his work on Beckett and the so-called 'new writers' of the post-1950 period by offering a provisional assessment of three playwrights who like Genet and Ionesco have sought to establish a new concept of theatre faithful to the spirit (if sometimes in opposition to the letter) of the old. The moral of this closing chapter, as of the whole book, is the staggering inventiveness of the French genius, even where its exponents are not brought up on French soil and do not speak its language as their mother tongue. Giraudoux, whose Siegfried, as Godin and Howarth point out, is the archetypal cultural transplant, would (if he had lived to see it) have approved of their existence. Whether, as himself a consummate master of the craft of drama, Giraudoux would also have been disconcerted by the practice of these gifted newcomers, our readers will no doubt judge for themselves, and draw their own conclusions.

1

Introduction : PRINCIPLES OF STAGING   *Dorothy Knowles*

When Jean Vilar, the producer who made the Théâtre National Populaire in Paris one of the high places of the theatre world, declared in 1946 that the real poets of the stage in his own lifetime had been the producers, he was making a serious claim which could be substantiated. With the notable exception of Claudel, the dramatists were not poets; they were analysts and commentators on the contemporary scene, whilst fantasy, brio and the search for rhythms marked the work of the *metteurs en scène*.

Indeed, the manifesto of the modern theatre movement was written by a producer: it is Jacques Copeau's *Un Essai de rénovation dramatique* of 1913. Piecemeal schemes had been implemented before that time by André Antoine and Lugné-Poe, but it was Copeau's imagination that produced a plan for a complete renovation of the theatre, and it was his faith and enthusiasm that launched the Vieux-Colombier theatre in 1913. He chose the Left Bank, away from the Paris theatre-land, and set out to recruit an audience of students and of the less well-to-do, breaking completely with the idea that a night at the theatre was first and foremost an occasion for displaying one's jewels and eyeing other people through a lorgnette. To attract this new audience Copeau fixed the price of seats as low as possible, introduced helpful booking arrangements and abolished the system current on the Boulevard of tipping usherettes and programme-sellers. He founded an Association of Friends of the Vieux-Colombier, instituted lectures, literary and classical matinées, and issued programme booklets, all with the intention of establishing closer relations with the public by enlightening it on the problems that had to be faced when producing plays. He did not in fact succeed in creating a popular audience, but he did succeed in creating a new audience, a 'Left Bank' audience, prepared to grant new and serious writers its confidence.

The first world war interrupted Copeau's efforts. He was called up, and though soon released on account of ill-health, he was sent off on a cultural mission to the U.S.A. (1916 and 1917–19), where he had to put on shows of the very kind he had fulminated against as a dramatic critic. However, during a period of forced inaction in 1915, he established fruitful contacts with three other men of like mind, Gordon Craig, Adolphe Appia and Jaques-Dalcroze, and laid plans for the future.

Copeau's renovation of the theatre was, in the first place, concerned with the actor as interpreter. The aim of the old-type actor was to become a star and make of the various parts he acted a mere pretext for the display of his own person and talents. Copeau wanted masters of expression and looked upon Charlie Chaplin, the Japanese Noh players and circus clowns, particularly the Brothers Fratellini, as men who could teach the dramatic actor the deepest secrets of the art. He referred to the Fratellinis as the heirs of the divine commedia dell'arte and called them in when he founded an acting school, together with the mimes Jean Dorcy and Etienne Decroux, to teach his future actors the art of physical expression. He would have them perform on bare boards with nothing in their hands. Only after intensive training of the body did his actors proceed to the training of the voice and then to the use of the spoken language.

The direct effect of Copeau's teaching was best seen in the productions of the Compagnie des Quinze which performed plays by André Obey, Jean Giono and Armand Salacrou. This company was formed in 1931 by Copeau's nephew, Michel Saint-Denis, from Les Copiaus, the group which had worked with Copeau himself in Burgundy from 1924 to 1929, that is to say between the closing of the Vieux-Colombier and the date when he left the Copiaus to become a candidate for the post of Administrator of the Comédie Française, a position which he did not in fact obtain. The direct Copeau tradition was also continued in London at the London Theatre Studio (1935–9) and later at the Old Vic School (1945–53) where Michel Saint-Denis trained many actors, and subsequently at the school of the Centre Dramatique de l'Est at Strasbourg where he took up an appointment from 1954 to 1957. Michel Saint-Denis quotes Copeau in 'The Actor' (*World Theatre*, vol. IV, no. 1, p. 42) as saying that he did not attempt to form actors or individuals, but to discover the rules of ensemble playing and constitute a chorus with full command of the means of expression. It was statements such as these, emphasising the creative role of the producer, whose unifying imagination harmonises the whole collective work, that had prejudiced the Comédie Française against Copeau's appointment; the Comédie Française actors preferred their individual autonomy. All the same, the new theatre movement developed in Copeau's direction and away from the Comédie Française. The work of both Charles Dullin and Louis Jouvet, who were in Copeau's company to begin with, bore the unmistakable stamp of Copeau's training, and that of Jean-Louis Barrault and Jean Vilar who served their apprenticeship with Dullin at the Atelier theatre which was also a drama school, reflects Copeau's influence to this day.

In addition to creating a school of acting, Copeau created a school of staging. *Mise en scène* he defined as the whole of the technical and artistic operations by means of which a dramatist's text develops from a potential existence to an actual one in space and time on the stage. The essence of the play was in the text, and in the text alone; a truly dramatic work contains within itself what is required to create the dramatic illusion for the spectator, but its potential must be actualised. This belief led him to champion the greatest economy in setting and in production methods, and in 1930 he was still as firm a believer in the virtues of bare boards for acting as he was in 1913. It was in fact his insistence on the superiority of *le tréteau nu* that led to his being called a dramatic Calvinist, Jansenist and even Benedictine. It was on *le tréteau nu* that the works of great dramatists should be performed by actors worthy of them. Copeau's choice of plays was at the opposite extreme from the naturalistic plays favoured by André Antoine. This fact necessarily implied a non-realistic conception of staging, and instead of a 'photographic image' in the manner of Antoine, Copeau sought to evoke an image for the intelligence to interpret by some simple detail, an electric-light bulb hanging in a single tree to create the impression of suburbia, for instance. The *trompe l'œil* painted drop was just as anathema to Copeau as was the realistic set, and was rigorously excluded from the stage of the Vieux-Colombier when this theatre was reconstructed under his direction in 1920. The stage was given instead a fixed architectural lay-out which was easily modifiable by the addition of mobile elements. The removal of the picture-frame (proscenium arch) and the continuation of the architectural design from stage to auditorium, the suppression of the footlights and the extension of the front stage with steps leading down into the auditorium, proclaimed the now quite widely accepted principle of a joint 'theatrical space' occupied by actors and audience alike, instead of a dual space with a strictly segregated stage and auditorium.

The whole effort of Copeau's theatre and school was directed towards setting the French theatre on the path of creative interpretation of works of the past and subsequently on the path of modern *poetic* creation, as Vilar says. Copeau did, in fact, succeed in creating a *poetic* climate in the Paris theatre. What he also did was to convert authors, who till then had remained aloof from the theatre, to the idea of dramatic writing. The literary prestige of the modern drama was greatly enhanced in consequence.

In the years that followed the closure of the Vieux-Colombier, Copeau undertook a number of individual productions in various theatres, including four at the Comédie Française, of which he finally became the Administrator in 1940, though only for a few months. But it was the production of a mystery play, *Santa Uliva*, which he undertook with the help of André Barsacq in the cloister of Santa Croce in Florence at the request of the Italian government, for a popular religious festival in 1933, that gave him the opportunity, had he been able to exploit it, of realising his own dream of 'public' theatre. Such a production, addressed to large popular audiences, had nothing in common with the 'little theatre' movement, offering luxury intellectual and aesthetic pleasures to an elite, which Copeau had sparked off in 1919 while attempting something else, and with which he had become reconciled as 'technical laboratories', but not as the real thing. The mystery play was much nearer in spirit to his Burgundy experiments when, together with Les Copiaus, playing in barns, on village greens, at harvest festivals and the like, he had sought contact with a popular audience. His mistake had been to think that the theatre could be transformed from the inside by purely aesthetic and moral means. Only later did he come to the conclusion that a transformation of the theatre was impossible without a radical transformation of society, and that a popular theatre could not be imposed on a nation, but could only be achieved by a vast popular movement such as the October Revolution of which he had heard Taïrov and even Stanislavsky speak with enthusiasm, or the Front Populaire movement, unfortunately abortive. In an address (reproduced in *Théâtre populaire*) delivered to the Volta Congress in Rome the year after his experience in Florence, Copeau said, 'I believe that the question is now whether the theatre will be Marxist or Christian, because the theatre must be alive, that is to say popular. To be alive it must give reasons for living, hoping, fulfilling oneself. The nature of the public, its size, its spirit, is the first datum in the problem of the theatre.'

From the technical point of view Copeau achieved a type of theatrical presentation with *Santa Uliva* towards which he had been straining for years. The play required multiple acting areas, music, choruses with a scope ranging from the ordinary spoken word, through rhythmic declamation and intoning to music and song proper. Florence and Santa Croce had given him a taste for space, and he did not see himself working easily in the future within three walls. Two years later, in the Piazza della Signoria, he staged Rino Alessi's *Savonarola*, using massive crowd movements (a thousand strong) to heighten emotion in the massive audiences. *As You Like It* followed in the Boboli Gardens in 1937 and then in 1943, in the courtyard of the Hospices de Beaune, he put on his own work, *Le Miracle du pain doré*, which he offered as a model for a religious rite. This and *Santa Uliva* he believed to be his best productions, in fact the only ones which realised his ideal, and which, as far as externals are concerned, thus foreshadow the movement which has gathered great momentum in France since the second world war, and is one aspect of the new popular theatre.

While Copeau was working towards this aim, the Cartel des Quatre, officially formed in 1927 by his two disciples, Dullin and Jouvet, together with Pitoëff and Baty, were continuing the work of renovation initiated by him at the Vieux-Colombier. They sought the 'retheatricalisation' of the theatre so as to make of it a place for 'dreams and imagination', as they put it. The Cartel showed the same scrupulous regard for the written text as Copeau, and like him, Dullin, Jouvet and Pitoëff made the actor's art the medium of its interpretation, with settings reduced to an accessory role. Dullin even founded a school to give training similar to that which he had himself received from Copeau. Pitoëff said that it was only after seeing a play acted, either in the flesh or in his imagination, that he was able to decide how it should be staged and in what setting. Baty, however, not being an actor himself, but originally a scholar who had spent several years on theatre research in Munich and Berlin and had acquainted himself with the work of Fritz Erler, Georg Fuchs and Max Reinhardt before himself embarking on production, placed less emphasis on the actor and more on visual and sound effects, making the actor the vocal element of a dramatic complex with the producer as prime mover. Baty's ideas on production methods thus differed from those of the other members of the Cartel, who followed Copeau's line and opted for the greatest simplification of staging possible. For his part Dullin extolled the merits of *le tréteau nu* as against technical and mechanical developments in staging which detracted from the dramatic illusion. The producer's task was to put forward suggestions which would lead to a real collaboration with the author, but on no account should he take precedence over the author. Jouvet sought stylised realism; conscious artistry and perfect finish were evident in every element of his productions. Though he roundly denounced the picture-frame stage as a *boîte d'illusion*, he nevertheless restored the footlights. The most simple and the most evocative of all settings were Pitoëff's. His son, the producer Sacha Pitoëff, said of him that, towards the end of his life, he considered stage settings to be a distraction, a diversion, useful merely for helping the spectator to swallow the bitter pill of the text. Pitoëff made little use of them, in fact he carried simplification in staging to the extreme limit, favouring black velvet curtains or other heavy draperies; for instance, in Henri Lenormand's *Le Mangeur de rêves* (1922), he used lengths of coloured ribbon to outline a tent or to suggest the sea's horizon. Even Gaston Baty constantly defended himself against the accusation of using the text as a pretext for staging. The splendour and multiplicity of his sets were responsible for the accusation, but Lenormand, who had four plays produced by Baty, testified to the fact that the text retained its prime importance in the hierarchy of theatrical values in Baty's productions, and Baty himself stated this publicly. However Baty's own ill-starred criticism of 'His Majesty the Word' (*Sire le Mot*) in 1921, which he reproduced in *Le Masque et l'encensoir* in 1926, made his claim ambiguous, and it must be said that his desire to 'serve the theatre according to Saint Thomas', and his criticism of the French classical tradition as being Cartesian and Jansenistic and limited to the verbal art, justify the doubt. Baty's ideas were different from Copeau's. He wanted to integrate man into history as had been done in Romantic drama, to integrate him into his social and material environment as had been done at the Théâtre Libre, and, what is more, into nature itself. Drama being, to Baty's way of thinking, a universe in miniature, the elements and inanimate objects, sun and sea, factories and ships, and even invisible presences beyond the physical world all have their place on the stage in so far as they all mould man. To call up these non-human elements the seven chords of the 'lyre of drama', painting, sculpture, drama, prose, verse, song and music, all need to be plucked. These seven complementary arts have to be 'organised' round the text, which is like the kernel of a fruit, and they have to take up from the point where words become inadequate, because words can only express notions and feelings in so far as the intelligence can analyse them. Total drama achieved by a synthesis of all the arts, through which could be presented a total vision of the world, was Baty's ideal. He confessed to being particularly attracted to works in which the author left much to be said outside the text. By creating the tone, climate, atmosphere, which go beyond the text, the producer really becomes the author's collaborator. He 'sets' the text as a jeweller sets a jewel. Such a conception of theatre made Baty the natural champion of playwrights like Lenormand, Jean-Jacques Bernard and Simon Gantillon, and he sought by his *mise en scène* to convey the element of the subconscious which permeates their works.

With a course set from the beginning towards a deliberately escapist theatre and a declared belief in the stage as a spring-board of dreams, it is not surprising, particularly in 1943, that Baty should have decided to escape from the live theatre into the world of puppets. He set up his own puppet theatre, the Théâtre Billembois, and ran it until 1949. His interest in puppets actually dated from his childhood and had led him to publish a number of articles on their history, together with collections of texts for puppet performances. 'There are things', Baty said in a radio interview given in 1948, 'which cannot be expressed in the theatre because the flesh and blood actor on the stage is too real to be able to interpret a dream.' He did not however burn all the bridges that linked him to the live theatre, but staged some plays at his old theatre, the Théâtre Montparnasse, then in the hands of his former partner, the actress Marguerite Jamois. He also undertook a number of productions at the Comédie Française to which he had been invited as a visiting producer along with Copeau, Dullin and Jouvet after the Comédie's reorganisation of 1936. Their policy at the Comédie had been to rejuvenate the classics and introduce new modern authors, just as it had been at their own theatres.

One member of the Cartel, Pitoëff, specialised on the production of foreign plays, many of them little known previously. The first French production of Pirandello's *Six Characters in Search of an Author* was by Pitoëff. But he also staged several of Lenormand's plays, Cocteau's *Orphée*, Gide's *Œdipe* and Anouilh's *Le Voyageur sans bagage* and *La Sauvage*. Dullin staunchly championed the work of Armand Salacrou, and in 1943 produced *Les Mouches* by Jean-Paul Sartre. Jouvet, to whom one owes the revelation in 1947 of Jean Genet with *Les Bonnes*, at first, in his early enthusiasm for the commedia dell'arte, staged a number of Jules Romains's plays, becoming almost identified in the public mind with the hero of *Knock*. He then entered on his famous partnership with Jean Giraudoux, a partnership which is perhaps responsible for the striking resemblances between his views on the theatre as expressed in *Prestiges et perspectives du théâtre français* (1945), and those expressed by Giraudoux, namely, that great drama is first and foremost good writing. Language's power of expression and suggestion is what matters, not the theme or the action. The aim of the theatre is to make the spectator feel something, not understand something. In *L'Impromptu de Paris* Giraudoux makes Jouvet, in his own name, say that the word 'understand' does not exist in the theatre. Giraudoux then makes another of his actors say that to wish to understand at the theatre is not to understand the theatre at all. The point of a play is to appeal to the imagination and the senses, not the mind, and style is the means by which this is achieved. The actor, according to Jouvet, had therefore to learn to 'breathe the text' – '*un texte est d'abord une respiration*' – and in producing a play by Giraudoux, he often directed the actors to slow down their speech so as to bring out the full effect of the text, both auditory and emotive. He also resorted to a kind of incantation, and at times even to verbal orchestration. This concentration on the stylistic qualities of the text led Jouvet to demand of his cast an unusually static type of acting. By a curious about-turn as compared with his early days, it would seem that, if Jouvet had not died before completing the production he was preparing of Graham Greene's *The Power and the Glory*, he might well have moved away from the Romantic type of participation of the spectator in the performance through an appeal to his sensibility, and opted instead for 'something approaching what Brecht calls "the theatre of alienation" ', as he put it in a letter to one of his actors. Such theatre entailed detachment on the part of the actor, and judgment and a clear appreciation of issues on the part of the spectator. In this Jouvet seems to have anticipated developments one was to see in the French theatre from the late nineteen-fifties onwards.

    Like Copeau, the Cartel had gradually come to the realisation that the renewal of the theatre – which they had hoped to achieve in every domain of theatrical activity – had in fact been restricted to a purely formalistic renewal of the scenic language. They realised too that if a true revolution were to be brought about, if the theatre were to become the indispensable instrument of aesthetic enrichment that they believed it to be, then it would have to burst the narrow bonds of the Paris experimental theatres directed towards a privileged elite, and reach out towards a much wider audience. No individual theatre manager could undertake such a task; the State alone could establish the theatre on a truly popular basis and make it readily accessible to all. As early as 1937 Dullin had presented a report to the Minister Jean Zay on the need for the decentralisation of the theatre, and the creation of popular theatres in the provinces and the Paris suburbs. There was a change of minister and the report was shelved, but the lines on which the reorganisation of the theatre was pushed forward from 1946 onwards by Mlle Jeanne Laurent, Sous-Directrice des Spectacles et de la Musique au Ministère de l'Education Nationale, were already contained in Dullin's report, which she had read. Dullin died in 1949, after having himself tried, without much success, to run a popular theatre in Paris from 1941 to 1947, in the large Théâtre Sarah-Bernhardt, renamed by the Germans during the occupation the Théâtre de la Cité. Renamed (once again) the Théâtre de la Ville, and entirely redesigned and rebuilt in the inside so as to provide a 'democratic' auditorium with equally priced seats, all equally good, the old Sarah-Bernhardt reopened in October 1968 under the management of the actor-producer, Jean Mercure. It is intended by its owners, the Paris Corporation, to be a municipal popular theatre presenting plays of worth as well as concerts and even music-hall shows. Baty, who had left Paris in 1949, because of ill health, founded the Centre Dramatique at Aix-en-Provence, in 1951, with the help of Jeanne Laurent. It was the fifth centre to be established, the others being at Saint-Etienne, Strasbourg, Toulouse and Rennes. For his part, Jouvet had come to believe that the future of the theatre lay in the hands of the new generation of producers in these centres, and he helped to make them known by lending his theatre to them. He also expressed a wish to work in them. So interested was he, in fact, that he even missed the first night of his own production of Sartre's *Le Diable et le Bon Dieu* (1951) at the Théâtre Antoine in order to discuss a production with Maurice Sarrazin at the Centre Dramatique de Toulouse (established 1949). Two days before he died Jouvet was nominated general adviser and inspector of the centres. It was however left to Jean Vilar to realise this new dream of a theatre for an audience other than a bourgeois elite.

Antonin Artaud, like Vilar, was a product of Dullin's school but the path he chose was different. 'It is strange', he wrote to Yvonne Gilles in 1921, 'that I should have landed up in an enterprise where the outlook is so much in keeping with my own.' This statement, and what he has to say about the work in Dullin's school, are indicative of the lines on which he was later to attempt to revolutionise the theatre. 'We act with our deepest hearts, we act with our hands, our feet, all our muscles and all our limbs. We feel the object, we smell it, we handle it, see it, hear it . . . and all the time there is nothing there, no accessories. The Japanese are our immediate masters, our inspiration, and so is Edgar Poe. It is wonderful' (Letter to Max Jacob, 1921). However, despite the early enthusiasm for Dullin and his methods, and despite the apparent parallel between Baty's opposition to the Word and Artaud's hostile attitude to the articulated language, together with the notion of 'Total Theatre' held by both, there are few real points of contact between Artaud and the Cartel, whose members he irreverently dismissed, as early as 1927 in a letter to Jean Paulhan, as 'pourritures branlantes . . . fantômes anti-représentatifs'. Jean Vilar, whose approach to the theatre is entirely different from Artaud's, nevertheless in 1946 underlined the originality of Artaud's ideas as contained in *Le Théâtre et son double* (1938). In that work Artaud says he found the theatre's 'double' in metaphysics, the primitive myths, cruelty, the plague; for example, the plague, like the theatre, helps to drain abscesses collectively by forcing men to drop their masks and see themselves as they really are; the drama and the plague both bring about a crisis which ends in a cure or in death. The double of the theatre is the dangerous reality from which modern man deliberately shies away (Letter to Paulhan, January 25, 1936).

Besides providing a revolutionary theory of drama, Artaud worked as an actor in both the theatre and films. He was also a producer, though his creations are limited to the five productions of the Théâtre Alfred Jarry (1927–9) which he founded together with the surrealist dramatist Roger Vitrac, and the single production of the still shorter-lived Théâtre de la Cruauté (1935), *Les Cenci*, his own savage tragedy of a rebel who is a prey to his own demons and who knows himself to be the sport of his political enemies.

In between Artaud's two ventures in theatre management and production, came the visit of the Balinese theatre to the Colonial Exhibition in Paris (1931). These performances helped Artaud to crystallise his ideas on the theatre and, broadly speaking, his appreciation of the mimo-drama *Autour d'une mère* (1935) adapted by Jean-Louis Barrault from William Faulkner's novel *As I lay dying*, and performed by him, sums them up. 'This is what theatre really is,' he said, because the performance was organised 'in relation to the stage and on the stage, and had no existence apart from the stage.' This phrase 'had no existence apart from the stage' holds the key to Artaud's conception of theatre, and in its ordinary sense it is so obviously true that one wonders that anyone should ever have thought otherwise – we should deem it impertinent for a dramatic critic to talk of a play he had not seen. But Artaud means more than this – he means that a dramatic performance *starts* from the stage, it does not *reach* the stage, and this principle makes of mimodrama the essential theatre. The production of *Autour d'une mère* was the first of its kind in France, and was given with Dullin's blessing in Dullin's theatre where Barrault and Artaud had worked alongside each other. Barrault had also taken part in the rehearsals but did not appear in the production because of a disagreement with a member of the cast; he however readily acknowledged Artaud's influence on him, and this influence was again apparent in Barrault's production of *Numance* (1937) adapted by him from Cervantes, and in *La Faim* (1939) adapted from Knut Hamsun.

The title of one of the chapters of *Le Théâtre et son double*, 'En finir avec les chefs-d'œuvre', defines clearly Artaud's starting point. He sees former masterpieces as no longer valid for us in our new times, and as leading to the 'superstition of the text and of *written* poetry in the theatre'; written texts contain some pre-determined meaning, but what has been given a name is dead, and it is dead because it has been given a name. Written texts are objects, secondary products expressing the individuality of their authors, and thus have a causal structure. In the theatre of the West, where primacy is given to the written text and theatre is only a branch of literature, the actor becomes the servant of a system of thought which is not his own. In the Oriental theatre the actor is a moving hieroglyph; he is not the servant of a pre-existing text; the text has to be written by him, with his whole body, on the stage and under the gaze of the spectator, and is effaced even as it is written. It is on the stage through the 'affective athleticism' of the actor, the integration of sounds and of all stage effects, that real theatre takes shape. The material elements of production, body, gesture, sets, lights, sounds of all kinds whether vocal or other, which take second place when the theatre is considered as a mirror of life, or as offering social or psychological studies, become the determining elements of the performance, indeed the performance itself: 'the domain of the theatre is not psychological but plastic and physical'. Such is the materialistic thesis propounded by Artaud. It is even more materialistic than Brecht's, where the central existence of a theme and plot is maintained.

What then is to become of grammatically articulated language in a conception according to which it is the *mise en scène* that is theatre, much more than the written text, and the director no longer plays second fiddle to the author? Is it to be suppressed? Not so, but it is not to be allowed to retain the 'abusive supremacy' attributed to it in the West. The importance given to it is to be that which it has in dreams, and no more. Spoken language is but one of the elements of acting, and has to be fixed on the stage in relation to the other elements of acting, and also in relation to the various elements that constitute the dramatic language. This language is a concrete language, a language in space and in movement, and is without meaning except in the circumstances of the stage. It is a language addressed, in the first instance, to the senses instead of being addressed primarily to the mind, as is the language of words. Apart from its conceptual content articulated speech has sound value, an affective value, which should be exploited to the full. Artaud talks of manipulating speech like a physical object, of extending the voice, using its vibrations and modulations and of juxtaposing words in an incantatory and truly magical way, thus restoring the spell-binding power of speech. As early as 1934 in *La Machine infernale*, with his spell-weaving Sphinx, Jean Cocteau had thought for a moment on similar lines, and earlier still in 1922 with *Les Mariés de la Tour Eiffel*, had worked in terms of concrete imagery offering 'poetry of the theatre' instead of 'poetry in the theatre', or, to use Artaud's terms, 'poetry in space' instead of 'poetry of language'.

Artaud envisages a performance which is addressed to the entire organism, with all the means of direct action on the nervous sensibility being used in their totality, and which penetrates through to the mind as the result of the effect it has produced on the organism. To such theatre Artaud gives the name Total Theatre. Instead of the 'chemical analysis' which is provided by present-day psychological or social studies, Artaud demands a kind of 'alchemical theatre' aimed at the thorough involvement of the spectator and having a therapeutic value. With his Théâtre de la Cruauté, through which he hoped to 'restore to the theatre a passionate and convulsive conception of life', Artaud sought actively to pierce the protective crust under which modern man chooses to *exist* rather than live intensely, and he aimed at bringing about, by the end of the frenzied ritual that each of the performances was intended to be, a complete transformation of spectators and actors alike, both 'victims burnt at the stake, signalling through the flames'. There was no question here of the kind of anarchical fete provided by companies such as the Living Theatre because though Artaud announced that no written text would be staged by the Théâtre de la Cruauté, and that the whole performance would arise directly from the stage itself, the performances were to be rigorously determined beforehand and worked out down to the last detail. Neither have they anything to do with Copeau's improvisations (he says this very specifically); they are not left to the 'caprice of the wild and thoughtless inspiration of the actor, especially the modern actor who, once cut off from the text, plunges in without any idea of what he is doing' (Letter to Jean Paulhan, September 28, 1932).

It is in Jean Genet's plays that Artaud's conception of theatre has been the most fully realised so far, except perhaps for Pierre Bourgeade and Girolamo Arrigo's *Orden*, staged by Jorge Lavelli in 1969 at Avignon, and in 1970 in a market hall at the old Halles. In *Orden*, incantation merges into oratorio and mime into dance, the whole orchestrated by a political theme, namely the beginning of fascist repression in Spain. Artaud's influence has also been felt in England, and Peter Brook's experiment, entitled Theatre of Cruelty and undertaken with LAMDA (1964), was directly inspired by his ideas, particularly in the scenario *The Public Bath*, which depicted Christine Keeler and Jacqueline Kennedy. Peter Brook's subsequent production of *Marat/Sade*, by Peter Weiss, follows on from Artaud's unfilled intention of staging a tale by the Marquis de Sade in which 'the eroticism would be transposed so as to create a violent exteriorisation of cruelty'.

Since he envisaged the spectators as coming to the theatre to take part in a creative activity, and not merely to look and listen, Artaud wanted them to be seated in the centre of the hall where they would be physically enveloped by the dramatic action. Artaud's plan, put forward in the manifestos of the Théâtre de la Cruauté in 1932 and again in 1933, to abolish the separate stage and auditorium of the conventional Italian-type theatre, and replace them by a single area without partition or barrier of any kind, the better to establish direct communication between the spectators and the spectacle, puts him, along with architects and scenographers of the nineteen-twenties and nineteen-thirties, such as Walter Gropius of the Bauhaus and the Pole Simon Syrkus, in the forefront of a campaign waged against the divided worlds of the players and the audience, and in favour of a 'single theatrical space' encompassing both. Artaud's references to mobile chairs for the spectators, to the dramatic action being deployed in the four corners of the hall and at all levels, scaling the walls from the ground even to the catwalks, and also to the performance of several actions simultaneously or of several phases of a single action, have a curiously contemporary ring about them. Indeed, his influence has been acknowledged by the theorist and playwright, Michel Parent, in the experiments he carried out in an improvised 'théâtre à scènes multiples en contrepoint' in Dijon from 1962 to 1966 as part of the festival of the Nuits de Bourgogne, the essential difference being, however, that whereas Artaud sought to bind his audience with a magical spell, Michel Parent's emphasis, like that of the scenographer Simon Syrkus, was laid on the simultaneity of the phenomena of modern life.

A criticism that can justifiably be levelled against Artaud is his failure to examine properly the element of theatre that is the audience, together with his insistence on participation by the audience without any real enquiry into the nature and role of that participation. A further justified criticism is his insistence on a kind of primeval theatre to the exclusion of all others, in an age when there is nothing primeval in the theatre or its organisation, and theatre-going is a sophisticated pastime for a sophisticated public. One can say, thirdly, that a good dramatist always imagines the words he writes as being spoken on a stage; so Artaud's distinction between play and stage is exaggerated, to say the least of it. But worse than Artaud's own shortcomings is a certain 'artaudism' hastily drawn from his teaching, such as the reduction to simple mime of the whole scale of physical and vocal gesture (*le gestuaire*) of the 'affective athlete', or the diminution of Artaud's vision of Total Theatre to a mere marriage of all the arts. Before the war, under Artaud's influence, Barrault had the idea of constructing a dramatic action on Daniel Defoe's *Journal of the Plague Year*, but on learning in 1942 that Albert Camus was writing a novel on the plague, he gave up the idea and suggested to Camus that they should create a theatrical work on the subject in which every possible type of dramatic expression would be called into play. The work, *L'Etat de siège*, was designed to break all existing dramatic moulds, termed by Barrault 'partial theatre', and provide the first modern example of Total Theatre. Out of this fruitful failure arose finally Barrault's production of Claudel's *Le Livre de Christophe Colomb*, the most complete of his attempts at Total Theatre as well as the production in which his theory of theatre was most fully applied, and not merely because cinema was added to the usual elements of *mise en scène*. In fact, as the next chapter will show, Barrault found in Claudel's drama excellent material for the realisation of his conception of Total Theatre. Himself no mean theorist of the stage, as the collection *Mes idées sur le théâtre* proves, Claudel was delighted to co-operate with Barrault. They found that they suited each other perfectly, even where their notions did not always precisely coincide.

Barrault's most recent production, *Rabelais* (1968), demonstrated how Total Theatre can arise when the whole of the cast, by its very stance on a solidly motionless platform-stage in the middle of a huge sports hall, and by bodily movement, evoked a violent storm at sea and the pitching and tossing of a ship on wild waves. It is good fun, but, as Boileau would have said, one can be excused for preferring *Le Misanthrope*.

The theatre has always been seen by Barrault as being essentially a 'sensual' art, an art of flesh and blood, not a branch of literature, and he has always maintained the essential identity of words and gestures, a word being in fact a physical gesture, a voiced emission of breath controlled by muscular contraction. These ideas, set out in detail in *Réflexions sur le théâtre* (1949, 1959) as well as in articles and commentaries in the *Cahiers Renaud-Barrault*, contain more than an echo of Artaud's teaching.

Barrault's career has been an eventful one. After working with Dullin and Artaud, he spent six years at the Comédie Française where he produced *Le Soulier de satin*, *Le Cid*, *Phèdre* and Montherlant's *La Reine morte*. Then in 1946, together with his wife Madeleine Renaud formerly of the Comédie Française, he formed a company of his own and installed it in the very 'parisian' Théâtre Marigny on the Champs-Elysées, taking up the heritage of the Cartel, but without its popular ambitions. He tried to provide for smart Paris a modern Comédie-Française, as it were. After 1956 he was without a permanent theatre until he was called upon by André Malraux to run the Odéon-Théâtre de France where he remained until he was dismissed after the student revolt of 1968. His production in these theatres includes *Pour Lucrèce* by Giraudoux, *Bacchus* by Cocteau, *Les Nuits de la colère* by Armand Salacrou, Montherlant's *Malatesta*, *Le Procès* which he and Gide together adapted from Kafka, *Rhinocéros* and *Le Piéton de l'air* by Ionesco, and Genet's *Les Paravents*. After his dismissal from the second national theatre Barrault emigrated to Montmartre where, in a boxing stadium, he triumphed with *Rabelais*, his first real success before a popular audience. Never, said a local café proprietor to the present writer, had he seen such crowds fighting to get in, even for the most important boxing events. With this production Barrault achieved a complete renewal, or rather retempering of his style, and took his first step in the direction of the popular theatre movement.

The work of all these producers had been carried out in the narrowly artistic field, and Vilar, who pointed this out as early as 1946, maintained that theatre that looks no further than this is moribund. To remain truly alive it must be given a central place in the activity of the community. His conception of theatre as a 'public service just as much as gas and electricity are', is well known. Except for Copeau's five years in Burgundy, no contact was ever established by the Cartel or their disciples with any but the middle-class theatre-going public, both because of the lack of good plays with sufficient appeal, and because, in the existing social structure, theatre was an industry like any other, existing for profit, or at least expected not to make a loss. The socialist dream of a Théâtre du Peuple, born of the French Revolution, had never been realised. The efforts of men like Romain Rolland had come to very little, and the Théâtre National Populaire, created by the government for Firmin Gémier in 1920 in the old Trocadéro, was deformed from the outset by the conditions under which it was expected to function. It was only in 1951, when Jean Vilar was appointed director of the T.N.P. (in the Palais de Chaillot) by the far-seeing Jeanne Laurent, that it established itself as a vital element in the French theatre. The success of this venture – together with the theatre festivals run since 1947 by Vilar in the immense courtyard of the Palais des Papes at Avignon – consolidated a movement begun as early as 1945 in the provinces by Jean Dasté, Copeau's son-in-law, the first of a new generation of producers. This new generation founded permanent residential companies in various cities, and later obtained the co-operation of the municipalities. Dasté formed his group in Grenoble and then migrated to Saint-Etienne (1947) where the municipality was prepared to support his work. Shortly after this Toulouse offered help to Maurice Sarrazin, who had founded the Grenier company there in 1945 — sad to say, the support was withdrawn in 1969. In Alsace-Lorraine, on the other hand, an intercommunal syndicate called on Roland Pietri in 1947 to provide the area with good-quality performances. Before this movement started, all the provinces together could muster only fifty-one theatres, as against fifty-two in Paris, and these fifty-one opened only periodically to house tours arranged by Karsenty-Herbert or Baret. In 1947 support was offered by the Government and, progressively, various theatre-groups were given the title of Centre Dramatique and a subsidy, on condition that they served specific areas. The creation of Troupes Permanentes in individual towns by the Government together with local authorities further stimulated the creation of more broadly-based audiences. Roger Planchon's Théâtre de la Cité in Villeurbanne (1957) was the first to obtain this status; the Villeurbanne company now has an international standing and played at the Aldwych in 1969.

For a time after 1961 André Malraux, the Minister for Cultural Affairs, promoted the founding of a number of Maisons de la Culture, where drama was one of the cultural activities and interests. In the working-class suburbs of Paris the creation of theatre centres with municipal support began only in 1961, but as early as 1946 Vilar had declared that the theatre would do no significant work until the theatres themselves were no longer situated on the Paris boulevards or inside the triangle Madeleine–Opéra–Saint-Lazare, but at Aubervilliers, Billancourt and Saint-Denis, that is to say in the working-class suburbs. In these 'peripheral' and provincial theatre centres many of the most gifted producers of to-day are to be found, in Aubervilliers Gabriel Garran, in Saint-Denis José Valverde, in Sartrouville Patrice Chéreau and at Nanterre Pierre Débauche. In Lyon there is Marcel-Noël Maréchal, in Strasbourg Hubert Gignoux, and in Bourges from 1963 to 1968 there was Gabriel Monnet, who has now gone to Nice. In Paris itself Guy Rétoré directs the Théâtre de l'Est Parisien, a sort of second T.N.P. in the working-class area of the twentieth *arrondissement*. Most of the original work in production methods since the war has been done in these new centres, and so has most of the research in theatre design. The Maison de la Culture in Grenoble containing three theatres (one of them a circular hall with a central revolving auditorium and a peripheral revolving stage), is the most adventurous so far. It is for these theatres that a new repertory has been provided by Arthur Adamov, Armand Gatti, Roger Planchon, Gabriel Cousin, Michel Vinaver and Pierre Halet; foreign playwrights such as Brecht, O'Casey, John Arden, Arthur Miller, Peter Weiss, Max Frisch and Friedrich Dürrenmatt have also been played there. Dürrenmatt, and more recently Zavattini, have been particular favourites of Hubert Gignoux at the Centre Dramatique de l'Est, because at the present time what is needed is *un théâtre dénonciateur* after the manner of Aristophanes.

The T.N.P. first began to function in the industrial suburbs of Suresnes, Clichy and Gennevilliers and in a circus at the Porte Maillot, a place of popular resort near the Bois de Boulogne. Vilar here tried out his plan for 'cultural week-ends' which he later adapted to the conditions of the Palais de Chaillot, though the latter had not the advantage of being in a working-class area. In Suresnes, at the first of Vilar's 'week-ends', an incredibly low-priced inclusive ticket secured admission to a musical matinée, a performance by Maurice Chevalier, a production of *Mère Courage*, and one of *Le Cid* with Gérard Philipe. The spectators could also take part in open discussions with the actors and each other. This was real 'audience-participation'. At Suresnes, as later at the Palais de Chaillot, a restaurant in the basement of the building also provided good cheap meals between performances, so as to make of the whole week-end a treat. At one such 'week-end' Laurence Olivier's film of *Hamlet* was shown alongside Barrault's production of the same play. Programmes of this kind catered for everyone's taste, and at the same time introduced people who had never set foot inside a theatre before to Corneille, Shakespeare and Brecht. 'I never realised there was anything like this in life', said a factory clerk as he enrolled in the 'Association des Amis du Théâtre Populaire' after attending the week-end at Suresnes and, embarrassing as this remark may be to the sophisticated theatre-goer, it was because Vilar took it to be literally true of millions of people, that he had at least some success in attempting to make the T.N.P. live up to its name. The clerk went to the theatre because the theatre had first gone to him. Vilar's theatrical revolution was thus accomplished not only on the stage, but in the auditorium where people with all levels of education were to be found together. Here were the beginnings of a completely new public. The pleasures of good theatre were no longer to be the prerogative of the Paris middle class.

On the production side, whether at Avignon or in the Palais de Chaillot, Vilar completely broke with the tradition of the picture-frame stage, and played without sets when the play did not specifically call for them, as some of course obviously do – *Uncle Vanya* for instance. His experience in 1941 with La Roulotte, a travelling company playing in barns, dance halls and cafés, had not only brought him into contact with a type of public quite unlike the sophisticated Paris audiences, but had also taught him how to create the atmosphere of the house or area where the action was supposed to take place. He applied his experience in the courtyard of the Palais des Papes at Avignon, under the night sky, and up against the vast unadorned walls of the palace. His actors situated the play without a set, relying only on costume and manners, with the help of lighting; a simple circle of intense light provided, for instance, the prison walls in *Le Prince de Hombourg*, and four vertical columns of light formed the pillars of the Commander's tomb in *Dom Juan*. This type of staging, with purely functional accessories, soon became known as 'le style Vilar'.

Vilar first sought to establish a 'rallying point at the highest level for the greatest number' by means of French and foreign classical works. There was no attempt to create a specifically working-class drama. In any case, said Vilar, no playwright could afford to write for one. Later, by choosing plays which reflected political preoccupations of the moment, Vilar made it clear that the theatre should take an active part in political issues, and his own 'modern transposition' of Aristophanes's *The Peace*, for instance, had a deliberately topical application. Vilar was not however prepared to stage a militant play unless it was a good play, and though one critic, Robert Kanters, mocked 'this worthy Robespierre of Chaillot who had taken upon himself to give lectures on freedom', and other critics protested against the 'public of a State theatre being metamorphosed into a political gathering', and still others, like Thierry Maulnier and François Mauriac, demanded the banning of *Mère Courage* (1951) and *La Paix* (1961), Vilar never at any time put on a play which was not at least the artistic peer of the commercial products of the Boulevard. The culminating point of Vilar's political theatre was the production of *Le Dossier Oppenheimer*, his own *pièce-document*, in a commercial theatre in Paris in 1964–5. With this play he aimed at 'un théâtre-prise-de-conscience-contemporaine', which is how he envisaged the function of the theatre in general. One might call it 'modern awareness drama'; its aim was to extend the awareness of the spectator in face of the modern world, and such an aim is undeniably an aesthetic aim. This is how Georges Wilson, his successor at the T.N.P. since 1963, also sees the theatre. After the staging of Brecht, Dürrenmatt, O'Casey and Gatti's *Chant public devant deux chaises électriques*, meaning those in which Sacco and Vanzetti died, Wilson's attitude was clearly defined by his proposed production of Gatti's *La Passion du Général Franco*, which the Government banned at the last minute (December, 1968), despite nation-wide protests and despite the 35,000 seats already booked for the production by the public. Suffice it to say that this play is not political in the sense of being a direct attack on fascism; it is a play about Spain in the minds of Spanish exiles and only indirectly condemns the fascist regime in Spain. It acquaints the spectator imaginatively with a certain perspective on the Spanish question.

Of the Théâtre de la Cité at Villeurbanne, which its director Roger Planchon sees as a 'public service' and compares with the schools, as Vilar had compared theatre with gas and electricity, one could say that it is a T.N.P. serving a truly proletarian community, for Villeurbanne is a working-class town with a communist local authority. Its repertory includes Brecht, Gatti (*La Vie imaginaire de l'éboueur Auguste Geai*), Michel Vinaver (*Les Coréens*), Adamov (*Paolo Paoli*), and is as 'committed' on the working-class side as the Boulevard theatres are on the side of bourgeois values, which they always take for granted as 'human' values. From the time of his discovery of Brecht in 1954, and his subsequent meeting with Brecht to discuss his own production of *La Bonne Âme de Sé-Tchouan*, Planchon was open to Brechtian influence. Like Brecht he believed that the theatre should provide the people with the pleasure of seeing and also assessing the artistic presentation of its own destiny. Since its destiny is that of a social order, it is right that the people should put up the same fight for its culture as for its wages. As regards the technical side, Planchon said that having come, like other producers, to the theatre through literature, he had believed that staging was an incomplete art, being restricted to not overloading or underplaying a dramatic text. The lesson taught by the theorist Brecht was that a performance was at one and the same time 'dramatic writing' and 'scenic writing', and that the full responsibility for the 'scenic writing' was the producer's. Planchon admits to having copied Brecht's style in production methods, but declares that with his first play, *La Remise* (1962), he shook off Brecht's tutelage and became independent. Nevertheless in *La Remise*, as in Brecht's plays, the individual adventure is 'inscribed in the historical venture'. The psychology and personal relationships of the character, as Planchon himself says, are of no interest to him unless set against a social and historical background. This same principle is applied in his production of Molière's *George Dandin*, in which he does not portray an imprudent man, a possible 'everyman' and worthy of some sympathy on that account, even in the cuckoldry he has brought upon himself, but an unlikable, hard-hearted, pretentious peasant, grown rich and anxious to get into the family of the local gentry. He is shown as rejected by the peasants and despised by the 'quality' who are as unlikable as he is, with the possible exception of the young wife who has been sold to him. The staging is made use of in order to supply this background, and Pierre Marcabru called it correctly the first Marxist production of a Molière play. The producer's task is to interpret, and Planchon interprets Molière for the modern man, not for the seventeenth-century gentleman.

Planchon knew that his public had been formed by the cinema, so he sought to create a theatre that could make use of their experience. He therefore turned for inspiration to the techniques of the cinema; in *Schweyk* (1961), for example, he achieved an almost filmic mobility by his use of the revolving stage. In some of his productions the mobility is achieved by scenery that can be wheeled about on the stage. But he is not obsessed by novelty or gimmicks. He has demonstrated with Racine's *Bérénice* that he can produce an effect of 'modernity' by artistic means as subtle as those used by traditional producers.

There are a number of free-lance directors working usually in Paris but also for theatre festivals in the provinces. Of one of these, Nicolas Bataille, it could be said that he launched the 'theatre of the absurd' with his production of *La Cantatrice chauve* in 1950. Subsequently Jacques Mauclair, with *Victimes du devoir* in 1953 and particularly with *Les Chaises* in 1956, helped to establish Ionesco in the theatre. In the meantime, in 1954, Jean-Marie Serreau staged *Amédée ou comment s'en débarrasser*, and then in 1966 Ionesco made his entry into the Comédie Française with Serreau's production of *La Soif et la faim*.

Roger Blin, who studied mime in the first instance, began his stage career with Artaud in *Les Cenci*, and with Barrault in *Numance* and *La Faim*. He then formed an association with Samuel Beckett rather like Barrault's association with Claudel, or Jouvet's with Giraudoux. He produced *En attendant Godot* in 1953 after a three years' campaign to persuade a theatre to take on the play, then in 1957 put on *Fin de partie* in

French in London at the Royal Court, because Paris managers would at first have none of it, despite the world-wide success of *Godot*. He acted in both productions. He also produced Beckett's *La Dernière Bande* for the T.N.P. (Récamier) in 1960, and *Oh les beaux jours* for Madeleine Renaud at the Théâtre de France in 1963. In Blin's opinion, the best type of stage decoration is that which goes unnoticed by the spectator, though he agrees that this axiom does not apply in the case of certain unusual plays like Genet's *Les Nègres*, which he produced in 1959. Blin's attention was also claimed by the early Adamov plays, and so was Mauclair's and Serreau's though Serreau soon turned towards a more committed theatre of the Left, staging for example Michel Vinaver's *Les Coréens* (1957) which suffered concerted boycott by the press, except for infuriated demands for it to be banned. Serreau was satisfied, however, because the Renault car workers booked a whole performance. His declared aim was, in fact, a truly popular theatre drawing its public from the factories. Serreau was a friend of Brecht and it was Serreau's production of *The Exception and the Rule* that started Brecht's career in France in 1947. Serreau has followed the Brechtian general line to this day, though always in a personal and spontaneous manner. He said recently, for instance, 'To-day the major event is the awakening of the *tiers monde*. To be a Brechtian to-day one must speak of the *tiers monde*. If Brecht were alive now he would doubtless have written plays on the subject.' This particular way of being Brechtian stirred up trouble for Serreau on more than one occasion. In 1958, during the Algerian war, he tried to stage Kateb Yacine's *Le Cadavre encerclé*, but was forced to transfer it to Brussels after the 'Biaggist' commandos (later called O.A.S.) had threatened to wreck the theatre. In 1963 his production at the Salzburg festival of *La Tragédie du roi Christophe* by Aimé Césaire, a native of Martinique, provoked some opposition and as a result was accorded only a few private performances at the Théâtre de France in 1964. Césaire's *Une Saison au Congo*, centred on Patrice Lumumba, was also staged by Serreau (Théâtre de l'Est Parisien, 1967), then in 1969, first at Hammamet and then in Paris, he staged *Une Tempête*, underlining, by his production, Césaire's reinterpretation of Shakespeare's comedy based on the situation of the Negro. With a few changes here and there Césaire made it into the story of the white coloniser – Prospero is a totalitarian, said Césaire – and presented the dispossessed and subservient though rebellious native, with Ariel and Caliban embodying the two aspects of resistance, the one attempting to lead Prospero to a full awareness of the plight of the colonised, the other representing the force that will one day crush the exploiter. On the technical side Serreau seeks to demystify the theatre of illusion, or, in concrete terms, the Italian-style theatre with the spectator having always a frontal view, and opts for a theatre in tune with the 'infantile world of the present', a theatre that is 'circus, barbarous, festival, carnival', utilising a simple, barbarous, primitive, audio-visual form of staging: it is only by bombarding the spectator with images and sounds that he can be aroused from his usual state of passivity. Such views made Serreau the obvious producer for the first of the Dijon experiments in 1962 in 'simultaneous theatre'. There, in a sports club, not built as a theatre, he staged the first play to be written specifically for such a form of presentation, *Gilda appelle Maë West* by Michel Parent, the theme of which is the effect of the dropping of the first atom bomb both on the pilot himself who was detailed for this duty, and on the outlook of the whole of the human race which has to live with the knowledge of it.

The last to date of these experiments, of which one aim was to contest the 'offensive segregation of audience and actors', was undertaken by Victor Garcia with Arrabal's *Le Cimetière des voitures* in 1966. Garcia staged the play the following year in Paris, where an attempt was made in an ordinary theatre to integrate the stage and the auditorium by continuing the stage round the four walls of the auditorium in the middle of which the spectators could swing round on swivel chairs. But Garcia seemed to forget, when in Paris, the reason for this particular lay-out of the acting space, except towards the end of the production when the audience was hemmed in by a hallucinating procession which made its way round it on the continuous stage. What the spectators followed was a Way of the Cross of Arrabal's shanty-town Christ stretched across a motorcycle which was used for his crucifixion. Garcia was clearly interested in the creation of remarkable visual images and violent effects, including almost unbearable noise.

Like Victor Garcia, with whom he had at times had occasion to work, Jérôme Savary did not hesitate to mould the text to his desires. In his London production of Arrabal's *Le Labyrinthe* (1968), though not in his previous production of the same play in Paris, Savary treated the text as mere raw material, and concentrated on integrating the stage and auditorium by having his actors seat themselves where they would among the audience, or invite the members of it to get up and, for no special reason, dance a tango up and down the aisles while Savary himself beat a big drum at the back of the hall.

Producers and actors have so effectively asserted their presence in the drama that a new kind of dramatic author is necessary to supply such verbal effects as are required. It is doubtful whether the older dramatists can bring themselves to accept this function, but the new generation will. However, would it not be a pity to reduce the dramatist to this role? Is not the dramatist's imagination just as capable as the producer's of the grasp and insight into the contemporary world that secures the unity of the dramatic work? Some producers certainly think so, and Planchon is one of them; so, for that reason, it is to be hoped that he, rather than Garcia or Savary, will be listened to.

Select Bibliography

ANDERS, FRANCE   *Jacques Copeau et le Cartel des Quatre*   Paris, Nizet, 1959

ARTAUD, ANTONIN   *Œuvres complètes*   Paris, Gallimard, 1956 etc.

BORGAL, CLÉMENT   *Metteurs en scène*   Paris, Lanore, 1963

COPEAU, JACQUES   *Théâtre populaire*   Paris, Presses Universitaires de France, 1941

COPFERMANN, ÉMILE   *Le Théâtre populaire, pourquoi?*   Paris, Maspero, 1969   *Roger Planchon*   Paris, La Cité, 1969

KNOWLES, DOROTHY   'Michel Parent and Theatrical Experiments in Simultaneity' Research, XI, no. 1 (1971), 23-41

LEBESQUE, MORVAN   'Le Théâtre National Populaire' *Le Point, revue artistique et littéraire*, no. 52, March 1957

MADRAL, PHILIPPE   *Le Théâtre hors les murs*   Paris, Editions du Seuil, 1969

SERRIÈRE, MARIE-THÉRÈSE   *Le T.N.P. et nous*   Paris, Corti, 1959

VILAR, JEAN,   *De la Tradition théâtrale*   Paris, L'Arche, 1955   'Le Metteur en scène et l'œuvre dramatique' *La Revue Théâtrale*, no. 3, 1946

CLAUDEL   J. E. Flower

Although Paul Claudel was hailed by T. S. Eliot as the greatest poet-dramatist of the century, the fact remains that only a handful of his plays have withstood the acid test of regular theatrical production. It may also be argued with some conviction, if not so much justice, that had it not been for a number of fortuitous collaborations with several leading theatrical producers of his day – Lugné-Poe, Jacques Copeau and Jean-Louis Barrault, for example – and for the influences of various foreign playwrights both at home and abroad, this number might have been even smaller. As it is the most regularly produced plays are *L'Annonce faite à Marie, Partage de midi, Le Soulier de satin* and the historical trilogy *L'Otage, Le Pain dur* and *Le Père humilié*; others such as the early *Tête d'Or* or *La Ville* and the later experimental *Le Livre de Christophe Colomb* or *Jeanne d'Arc au bûcher* tend to appear rather as curiosity pieces or as evidence of producers' virtuosity than for any intrinsic or long-lasting theatrical appeal that they may possess.

To dismiss Claudel in such a summary fashion would, of course, be both harsh and unfair, but it does remain true that his plays have met with opposition and are not readily accepted by all even today, a situation that is largely the result of two important factors: the first Claudel's inexhaustible readiness to experiment with new theatrical techniques and to revise standard practices, and the second his Catholicism.

It is to some extent ironic that his many innovations should have fallen, at least initially, on such stony ground. The generally held view that for two hundred years or so French dramatists had given little evidence that they could recapture the unchallengeable position of supremacy held by their seventeenth-century ancestors was justifiable enough. Certainly there had been some exceptions, but by the late nineteenth century the French theatre was once again in the doldrums. The symbolist writers had discovered that the uses they could make of association and atmosphere in the short form of the lyric poem were not to be extended to the larger genres of play and novel in which, traditionally, their audiences looked for something firmer and more substantial around which to focus ideas. With Claudel the situation was to change. Certainly he adopted some of their techniques and characteristics – his use of light, of colour or of particular objects for example – but at no time do his plays have that amorphous quality that is a feature of Maeterlinck's work or of Villiers de l'Isle-Adam's *Axel*. Instead they are based very firmly on his religious faith and on the tension that is created when the absolute values which this dictates come into conflict with the shallow and transitory pleasures of this world, creating not only a complex network of ideas but a corresponding system of symbols as well. At the same time, however, Claudel's particular brand of Catholicism has hindered as much as helped his reputation as a dramatist. His conversion on Christmas Day 1886 marked the beginning of an attitude to life that was henceforth to stand as a value in the light of which all other events, whether personal or public, would be judged. Inevitably both his faith and the conclusions to which it led were as unpalatable to some as they were attractive to others, and the same simplified dualistic approach which they inspired is also frequently characteristic of reactions to him as an imaginative writer. In many cases, and in England in particular, the result has been harmful. All too frequently his work has been rejected even by those to whom it is known in the most superficial manner, if at all, on the grounds that Claudel's personal views or political stances were unacceptable, and even critics whose admiration for and understanding of his writing are unquestionable have, on occasions, allowed themselves to be led astray by irrelevant considerations. What we are faced with is a man whose work deserves to be judged on grounds that apply to other playwrights whatever their personal creed. François Mauriac's view that he is a novelist who happens also to be a Catholic is, with the necessary adjustment, just as applicable to Claudel. We may not share nor agree with the religious views of these two writers (and indeed they were themselves in dispute on several occasions), but we must accept their integrity as artists and attempt to judge and evaluate their work as it stands and not with continual reference to a set of values external to it. This is not to deny the importance of their Catholicism, and as we shall see, Claudel argues that only the Catholic play can provide a true dramatic reflection of life. It is our duty to allow his values and ideas to stand within the context of the play, however, no matter how violently we may disagree with them outside the theatre; as Richard Griffiths remarks in his introductory chapter to *Claudel, a Reappraisal*, 'the audience must suspend judgement, and accept for the duration of the play that its suppositions are true'. Then, and only then, are we giving him a chance.

Claudel's views on the relationship between religious faith and imaginative writing are to be found throughout his work, and in spite of what
he may have said in the later years of his life, it is clear that he considered
his duty as a writer to be to act as a moral guide. In 1905, for example, he
wrote to Andre Gide in the following terms:

> Quelle responsabilité surtout pour nous, écrivains, qui sommes des
> meneurs d'hommes et des conducteurs d'âmes! Par le fait même que
> nous sommes éclairés, nous répandons de la lumière. Nous sommes
> délégués par tout le reste de l'univers à la connaissance et à la
> vérité, et il n'y a pas d'autre vérité que le Christ, qui est la Voie et
> la Vie, et le devoir de le connaître et de le servir s'impose à nous plus
> qu'aux autres avec un caractère d'urgence terrible.

And nine years later, at the time of his famous dispute with Gide over
Les Caves du Vatican, he underlined his belief that literature necessarily
exerted a moral influence on the young. For Claudel, the problem of
reconciling art with religious faith that had tormented Mauriac in the
late nineteen-twenties and that had also been largely responsible for
prompting Maritain to write *Art et scolastique,* was as yet non-existent.
He was arguing from a position of personal conviction; faith for him was
an accomplished fact necessary if life was to be understood and lived to
the full. Moreover, he maintained, the Christian situation provided the
perfect prototype for dramatic action. Writing to Stanislas Fumet in
1923 he remarks: 'J'ai de plus en plus l'idée que tous les sentiments, tous
les événements humains, même universels, ne sont que des paraboles du
drame qui se joue éternellement entre Dieu et l'homme.' His clearest
statements, however, on the role and value of Catholicism in the
theatre are to be found in two letters written to *Le Temps* and *Le Figaro*
in 1914.

In the first of these letters, Claudel suggests that even though they
may appear unreasonable, the demands imposed on man by Christianity
nonetheless fall within his comprehension, though to satisfy them requires
a fearlessness, determination and humility of the kind known only to
athletes. From this struggle for perfection results the tension that ensures
the moral and spiritual health of society; translated into art it provides
dramatic tension: 'le conflit essentiel que le christianisme anime en nous
est le grand ressort dramatique, comme il est la grande ressource de
notre vie morale et sociale'. Moreover since art has a direct influence on
us we will be led in its presence to examine our own position and to
compare our actions with the ideal that Christianity offers. In the second
letter Claudel redefines the same points more clearly still with one important addition which shows that he now has a greater awareness of the

problem basic to religious art and which must also be considered to be a defence of much of his own work.

> Le quatrième avantage enfin est que la Foi soulage et délivre notre nature en lui montrant cette fin dernière à laquelle elle est apte. Par elle tous nos sentiments, toutes nos passions reçoivent enfin leur sens et jouent dans la plénitude de leur vérité. La théorie catholique, en effet, est que l'homme est destiné naturellement au bonheur et qu'aucun des efforts qu'il fait pour atteindre ce but naturel n'est mauvais par lui-même.

Here Claudel is clearly justifying the portrayal of sin and passion in art necessary if dramatic tension is to be maintained, and in doing so is adopting the Augustinian view that even sin has its uses (*Etiam peccata*). This is an argument that reappears most specifically in *Le Soulier de satin* in the guardian Angel's words to Prouhèze: 'Même le péché! Le péché aussi sert.'

Jacques Guicharnaud's view that each of Claudel's plays is a 'parable meant to illustrate concretely a lesson in advance' has, in all probability, been prompted by such theories as those set out above. To some extent, however, his definition is misleading, for it denies much of the complexity of Claudel's work and also his very keen sense of the theatre; though as far as his early plays in particular are concerned there is some truth in it, as Claudel himself readily admitted. In his *Mémoires improvisés* he recalls that it was in 1909 that he began to judge his theatrical writings more critically, viewing them with the eyes of an outsider and – more importantly – of a producer. His inspiration remained the same, but his means of expression began to be modified and sharpened. Already his experience was extensive: *Tête d'Or, La Ville* and *La Jeune Fille Violaine* had each appeared in two versions, so had *Le Repos du septième jour* and the first versions of *L'Echange* and *Partage de midi*, all of them becoming known by an increasingly large reading public. Copeau, who in 1905 had argued that the French stage had only been saved by the works of foreign playwrights, could now be found admitting that Claudel was 'énorme [. . .] par sa suggestion', even though his work had yet to be performed. Copeau's words were indeed prophetic, for there was little in *La Ville* and even in *Tête d'Or* to suggest the complexity of *Le Soulier de satin* or the adventurous experimentation that we find in such later pieces as *Le Livre de Christophe Colomb* or *Le Jet de pierre*. Claudel's decision in 1909 to view his work more objectively was perhaps his most important, since it led him into the initial stages of his search for a 'drame total', a vision of a theatrical experience of Wagnerian scale and complexity in which meaning and form would come together and interdepend totally on one another. Once embarked on, this course proved to be one of the most significant theatrical developments in France during the twentieth century, if not at any time. Production became as important for Claudel as initial creation, a fact that goes much of the way to explain the different versions in which the text of so many of his plays appear. He maintained that alterations and modifications made at the final stage level were all an integral part of the creative process, and that only in performance could his work be seen to have assumed its full significance. 'C'est vraiment passionnant de travailler un geste, un ensemble, une attitude et de voir tout cela s'animer et prendre figure', he wrote to Gide in 1912. He developed no single theory, but instead a number of basic requirements constantly variable to suit his tastes and aims. The austerity of some of the settings for *L'Annonce faite à Marie*, the baroque splendour of *Le Soulier de satin*, and the cinema screen in *Le Livre de Christophe Colomb*, each have a specific function within the context of the particular play concerned, and would be out of place elsewhere.

Unlike many of his contemporary dramatists, Claudel seemed reluctant to define his plays by any of the traditional labels. We find that the first version alone of *L'Annonce faite à Marie* is called a 'mystère'; *Protée* is a 'drame satyrique', and *La Lune à la recherche d'elle-même* an 'extravaganza radiophonique'; but in general the title is free of further description. In discussing his work in Prefaces or elsewhere, however, he uses the word 'drame' almost without exception, though he seems by this to have no more in mind than a basic notion of conflict and action. In the 1948 Preface to *Partage de midi*, for example, he is explicit, and is so in terms that recall the two public statements on the Catholic theatre which we have already noted. 'La chair, selon que nous en avons reçu avertissement, désire contre l'esprit, et l'esprit désire contre la chair,' and four years later in the Preface to the second version of *L'Echange* we read: 'Ce drame [. . .] nous montre un de ces conflits où les amants, malgré une attraction réciproque, née précisément de la contrariété, sont séparés par des intérêts divergents.' The immediate danger as far as theatrical representation is concerned is either for this conflict to become intellectualised and turn into the 'interminables discussions' to which Claudel objected in Racine's work, or for it to produce two-dimensional characters whose function is no more than to act as spokesmen for opposing views. In *Le Repos du septième jour*, *L'Otage* and *Le Père humilié* Claudel himself is at fault. In the first of these plays the discussion about hell between the Devil and the Angel is a totally non-dramatic, non-theatrical presentation of one of the play's issues. In the second we rarely find more than two people on stage at once, even if their debates are more central to the

action than those in the earlier play, while in *Le Père humilié* the only
two worthwhile scenes are those between Orian and Pensée (Act II,
Scene i, and Act III, Scene ii), the rest of the play being very largely an
arid discussion of Claudel's conception of eternal love and of the role of
the church in the modern world. Fortunately such examples are for the
most part limited to his early works. In his *Conversation sur Jean Racine*
he also argues the case for action, even of a violent kind : 'ce public dans
la salle [. . .] a besoin de temps en temps d'un coup de rouge, d'un coup
de dent, d'un coup de fouet' and examples are readily found – violence
in *La Ville*, suggested rape in *L'Annonce faite à Marie*, murder in *L'Otage*,
human degradation in *Le Soulier de satin*. But while such violence as this
features with some regularity in his work, it has a minor role only,
subordinate to (though an integral part of) the theory of the *drame total*,
of which Claudel provides the first outline as early as 1897 in *Connaissance de l'Est*, in the poem 'Théâtre'.

The main point to emerge from 'Théâtre' is not only the complete
integration on the stage of gesture, discourse and music, but the involvement of the audience to the point where it too has a responsive role to
play. Its disbelief is suspended : 'Comme les acteurs sont cachés dans leur
robe, c'est ainsi, comme s'il se passait dans son sein même, que le drame
s'agite sous l'étoffe vivante de la foule.' The description here clearly
presages some of the techniques that appear in *Le Soulier de satin*, which
Claudel was to begin to write more than twenty years later. During this
time he absorbed and adapted to his own use the ideas and features of
other playwrights and artists wherever he found them. It was in Brazil,
for example, that he came across Nijinsky's work in ballet, the influence
of which can be seen in the dance sequences of many of his later plays.
In the Orient various forms of the Japanese theatre impressed him deeply,
the Noh and the Kabuki for the precision and beauty of the actors'
movements, and the Bunraku in which puppets enact a story that is being
read out, thereby giving the performance an unreal, oneiric quality that
Claudel creates in *Le Livre de Christophe Colomb*. It was in Japan, too,
that he began to appreciate fully the extent to which music could be used
as an integral part of a production, serving either as an emotive background to the action, or as an element in its own right. The rhetorical
qualities of language also served the same purpose, and Claudel's deep
concern in later years for the manner in which his words were read, his
insistence on the value of consonants rather than vowels, and his very
precise instructions to his actors on general points of delivery, all stem
from these early years, however idiosyncratic and peculiarly French they
may seem to foreign audiences. Similarly, some of his ideas about actual
stage sets came to him only after he had seen those constructed by the

Russian designer Salzmann at Hellerau, where *L'Annonce faite à Marie* was performed in 1913:

> Pas d'accessoires, pas de peintures, pas de cartonnages. Aucune recherche du pittoresque. Tout est subordonné à l'interprétation dramatique. La scène n'a pour but que de fournir d'avance à l'action son armature et la construction organique de plans et d'élévations suivant lesquelles elle doit se développer.

Here too was a perfect illustration of the theory which Claudel was to develop, that stage props should be considered as 'acteurs permanents' adaptable to meet various requirements – table/altar for example – but remaining both materially necessary and symbolically important.

However passionately interested Claudel may have been in such technical aspects of the theatre as these, they could only be worthwhile if they ultimately provided the means for expressing his ideas adequately. As early as 1894 he asked Pottecher if it were possible to have 'un théâtre de pensée? et si l'on peut maintenir le public devant un tel spectacle, de quelle efficacité peut-il être sur lui?' The rest of his career as a dramatist, or at least until the completion of *Le Soulier de satin*, was largely taken up with his search for this style of play in which form and content fuse together and fully complement one another.

Claudel's dramatic works divide most readily into three categories. The early plays written before the first version of *Partage de midi* (1905) are, as we might suspect, closely related to his private life. Hence, in *Tête d'Or*, Simon Agnel's struggle for power and his refusal to submit is, as Claudel has admitted in his *Mémoires improvisés*, a direct reflection of his own struggle against the faith that was already calling him. Similarly the elements of conquest and destruction that feature in this play and in *La Ville* may be seen to be an allegorical transcription of the need Claudel felt at this time in his life to break away from the 'monde congestionné, étouffant' of his family and Paris. His actual escape, of course, came in the form of his being appointed to the position of vice-consul in America, but in many ways the change brought him little relief. America was, he recalls, 'certainement peu agréable' and we have only to read the bitter indictment of life there with its superficiality and concern for material fortune in *L'Echange* or Anne Vercors's words in the second version of *La Jeune Fille Violaine* to understand how Claudel felt. For a man to whom the reality of religious faith had only recently been revealed American society seemed shallow: 'Tout est fait à la mécanique, la garniture du corps et celle de l'esprit'. An inevitable consequence of this close relationship between his private life and his work was that much of the former often came through undigested and unperformable in spite of attempts to allegorise it, and for this reason alone considerable revision became essential.

The second – and most successful – part of his career as a playwright, from *Partage de midi* until *Le Soulier de satin*, of which he wrote the first version between 1919 and 1924, was, as is generally known, set in motion by a single event. In 1900, only weeks after he had been on the verge of entering religious orders, he had a passionate love affair with a married woman on board the *Ernest-Simons* on which he was sailing to take up a new post in China. The conflict which these extreme situations, experienced in such a short space of time, created in his mind was to fire this whole period of his writing, and was not to be resolved in dramatic terms for fifteen years. It is a subject to which Claudel frequently returned in later life; in *Mémoires improvisés* he remarks; 'Ce qui s'était passé dans *Partage de midi*, je suis arrivé à le comprendre, et *le Soulier de satin* dans sa dimension n'était qu'une espéce d'explication de ce qui s'était passé dans deux cœurs humains.' Even so it was not until 1949 that Claudel could be persuaded to allow *Partage de midi* to be publicly performed. His old doubts of conscience lingered on, in spite of his having admitted to Gide in 1909 that it was 'La seule pièce qui pourrait peut-être être actuellement jouée . . .' In 1948 Jean-Louis Barrault finally won the day and the play was revised for performance in the following year, but just how important the play had been for Claudel, particularly in view of his opinions on the role of literature in the world, can be judged from his correspondence with his producer at this time :

> La pièce que vous m'avez, sans doute providentiellement, imposée a pris sur moi une importance énorme. Il ne s'est guère passé de jour que je n'aie médité sur elle. [. . .] Il s'agit de toute ma vie dont j'ai été amené à essayer de comprendre le sens. Il s'agit de beaucoup plus que de littérature.

Given its unique source of inspiration, and Claudel's deep uncertainty as to the solution of the problem, *Partage de midi* is undoubtedly one of his most complex and rewarding plays, and one in which, as we shall see, the ideas are given an extra dimension by their setting. The same notion of conflict, however, was also responsible during these years for Claudel's historical trilogy. Accused by some of taking liberties with history, Claudel defended himself, in a letter to *Le Figaro* in 1934, with the argument that historical reality was only a springboard; it was his right as an artist to embellish history in order to give it a new and particular meaning, and in *Le Soulier de satin* so grand is his scheme that similar liberties tend to be overlooked.

If, as I have already suggested, we understand no more by 'drame' than conflict, then *Le Soulier de satin* may be said to mark the end of this type of play in Claudel's work. In its own right it is, to be sure, much more than a final resolution of the problem which motivated his work from *Partage de midi* onwards, but in that his subsequent plays are, in the main, exercises in theatrical techniques – though this is by no means to deny their importance in the development of his ideas – such a view would seem to be justified. In 1940, in answer to an enquiry organised by *Le Figaro* on the general state of the theatre and of the arts in France, Claudel showed himself to be totally in favour of experimentation, and in doing so summed up and justified his own achievement during the previous fifteen years, even though he modestly made no reference to it:

> L'argent de l'Etat serait beaucoup mieux employé à encourager les chercheurs, les pionniers d'un art nouveau, plutôt qu'à perpétuer ces cimetières que sont les théâtres subventionnés. Quand on repasse, mon âge me le permet, l'histoire artistique de ces cinquante dernières années, on trouve que le rôle de ces sinistres établissements n'a guère été que celui d'un frigidaire.

Most of Claudel's work during these years was commissioned, three pieces – *Le Festin de la sagesse, Jeanne d'Arc au bûcher* and *L'Histoire de Tobie et de Sara* – by the Russian dancer and mime artist Ida Rubinstein. All of these, together with the others written at this time, and of which *Le Livre de Christophe Colomb* is the most successful, reveal the influence of the Japanese theatre and of music. In *Christophe Colomb*, however, the techniques of the Noh theatre are expanded by Claudel's use, in place of a conventional back cloth, of the cinema screen which serves as 'une espèce d'affiche et de projection de pensée'. Thus as the hero reads about Marco Polo's adventures, the screen provides the audience with a visual image of them; when he says goodbye to his family, it records the same event but in a different setting from the one on the stage, thereby intensifying the scene's emotional impact. While it may be argued that Claudel is here shaping a relatively modern artistic form for his particular purpose, we should also remember that it is a technique that is directly presaged in the shadow scene of *Le Soulier de satin*. It may be evidence to underline Claudel's capacity for assimilation and adaptation, but it should not obscure his own inventiveness and the continuity that is characteristic of his work both in terms of ideas and of techniques. For this reason it is perhaps a little unjust to divide Claudel's work into these three sections, for there are quite clearly a number of continuing features which establish its homogeneous nature. It is arguable, for example, that the same spirit of adventure motivates both Simon d'Agnel in *Tête d'Or* and Christophe Colomb; similarly the important heraldic gesture of allegiance with which *Partage de midi* closes is also to be found in *L'Otage* at Sygne's death, at the end of *L'Annonce faite à Marie*, and in its most complete form in *Le Jet de pierre*. The use of a prologue, to outline the events of the drama for us in advance, is a technique which appears in *L'Annonce faite à Marie* and in *Le Soulier de satin*. A further reason for not allowing ourselves to accept this division too readily is Claudel's own ever-growing awareness of the theatrical possibilities of his work and the revisions that this inspired.

As Jacques Madaule has pointed out in his introduction to the Pléiade edition of Claudel's plays, revision was most importantly the reflection of Claudel's growing awareness and understanding of the debate that existed in his own mind between the claims of divine and mortal love. It is not the intention of this chapter, however, to trace this ideological development other than in its effect on theatrical representation, nor is there space to examine these revisions to any extent. Some, such as that of *Le Soulier de satin* or of the early plays with their 'pareilles extravagances' were self-evidently necessary, though on its first stage performance *Le Soulier de satin* still lasted for five hours, of which the first *journée* occupied two and a half, and few individual scenes more than ten minutes. An example which serves our purpose more usefully is that of *La Jeune Fille Violaine*, in its two versions, and the subsequent *L'Annonce faite à Marie*.

Even a superficial reading of the two versions of *La Jeune Fille Violaine* will immediately reveal a number of material changes. Claudel has substantially reduced the number of secondary characters – the children and beggars for example – leaving the dialogue to be dominated by the protagonists alone, thereby centring our attention on them more firmly. This, in addition to the recasting of the opening scene with the introduction in the second version of Pierre de Craon, ensures that the play is more tightly constructed and that its theme is more clearly defined. Even so it remains basically something to be read rather than seen. Very little of *La Jeune Fille Violaine* is visually exciting, and what symbolism there is tends to be used rather sketchily, such as the tree/cross suggestion in Act II of the first version, or too apparent – Anne Vercors's (God's) departure from Combernon, for example, or the wind/holy spirit association in the miracle scene. That Claudel was aware of the play's imperfections and of its unsuitability for theatrical representation is clear from a letter which he wrote to Jacques Rivière in 1909:

Hélas! hélas! quel déchet! Ces vieilles choses font l'effet de friperies dans une armoire oubliée qui ont encore vaguement gardé la forme de votre corps. [...] Je vais tâcher de rendre la pièce scénique grâce à une idée qui m'est venue, en refondant complètement le personnage

de Pierre de Craon et en supprimant les divagations architecturales
de la fin.

He set about rewriting it and in 1912 *L'Annonce faite à Marie* became the first of his plays to be performed. Once again we find that there
has been more attention to detail; the action now takes place at the end of
the Middle Ages and not at some unspecified date between the Renaissance and the present day, while the timing of events is slightly rear-
ranged so that the miracle occurs on Christmas Day, thereby increasing
its significance and, incidentally, recalling Claudel's own conversion of
1886. Another more subtle pruning of material can be seen in the treatment of the role of Mara (Bibiane in the earlier version). In the first play
it is her actions which cause Violaine to decide not to marry Jacques and
to become a beggar. In the second version the opening scene between
Violaine and Pierre de Craon already tells us that the former is going to
renounce human love. In other words, Violaine is already committed
before the break with Jacques actually occurs, and her sister's role is in
consequence far less central. In *L'Annonce faite à Marie* Violaine is no
longer sought by others generally as a worker of miracles, but by Mara
alone, who is obliged to join her in recognition of God's will even if she
continues to blaspheme him. In this way, Mara's role can be seen to
become increasingly isolated over the years, but it is in no way reduced
in importance; not only does her withdrawal throw Violaine's role into
sharper relief, but in her supplication to her to bring her child back to
life she is intended to be representative of society as a whole, brought to
the point where it must understand that it can never be self-sufficient. In
reducing the action of the play to its barest essentials Claudel has sharpened and underlined his theme.

The revision of this particular play extended over a period of eighteen
years if, that is, we exclude as being of far less significance than those
which had gone before, a further variation of Act IV for stage performance to be found in the 1938 version. This search by Claudel for the
most suitable dramatic expression for his ideas also manifests itself in
other ways. It has, for example, resulted in his use of images and themes
whose intensity and effectiveness vary as they are adapted to suit the
particular tone and setting of individual plays. In a body of work that is
so rich in symbol, there are inevitably occasions when Claudel's technique
breaks down, but beyond his very early plays examples are relatively
rare, and in general seem to belong to the realm of implied social and
political comment that is essentially apart from his main concerns. Hence
in *Le Père humilié* the costumes worn by the Prince and Lady U, which
are meant to symbolise Rome old and new, do not add any significant

dimension to the play, even though they are also to be related to the religious views expressed later by the Pope and Frère Mineur. Similarly the character of the Jew Ali Habenichts in *Le Pain dur* or Anne Vercors's words on America (which Claudel cut from his revision of *La Jeune Fille Violaine*) offer little that is directly relevant to the action. Elsewhere, however, individual incidents stand out as underlining Claudel's general intention: Violaine's burial in her wedding garments, symbolising not only the marriage that should have been hers with Jacques, but also her eternal bond with God and the way in which suffering and self-denial in this life bring joy and fruition after death; the approaching eclipse of the sun throughout the second act of *Partage de midi* which parallels the accelerating disintegration of Ysé's marriage and her movement into adultery; and Sygne's nervous tic in Act II of *L'Otage* which perpetuates her refusal through the rest of the play. His characters' names too are often (though by no means always) significant, some more obviously so than others – Habenichts, for example, whose material greed contrasts with his spiritual paucity, Sygne (*cygne*) who combines purity and the capacity for self-sacrifice, or Marthe whose humility recalls that of her namesake in the Bible. Less evident perhaps are Mara, which in Hebrew means bitter, or even Violaine with its suggested undertone of rape (*violer*) and violence. Claudel's use of this technique is undoubtedly irregular, but there is no question that it can be, and is on occasions, effective.

More noticeable still, however, is the way in which certain symbols reappear throughout Claudel's work as a whole with the regularity of a motif. Not surprisingly the most common of these is the cross, which in its widest significance is the symbol of suffering that leads ultimately to reward and salvation. This idea, which is basic to all key relationships in Claudel's plays, is perhaps more clearly expressed by Prouhèze in *Le Soulier de satin*:

> Je sais qu'il [Rodrigue] ne m'épousera que sur la croix et nos âmes l'une à l'autre dans la mort et dans la nuit hors de tout motif humain! Si je ne puis être son paradis, du moins je puis être sa croix.

The cross also symbolises unity and strength of faith. In *L'Otage* Sygne's restoration of the crucifix signifies the role that faith has in her life, in *Le Pain dur* the same crucifix is destroyed, and Louis's selling the pieces of metal to the Jew Habenichts indicates that faith has become meaningless and the spirit of Sygne dead. By its very shape, of course, the cross denotes a striving upwards towards God, and as such it forms one of the two basic structural forces in Claudel's plays. This 'direction verticale' as Claudel called it (and we should note that the movement of stretching upwards is a ritual gesture of Noh drama) is contrasted to and hence in conflict with a horizontal movement of separation. This also appears in a number of different forms. It may be a physical (*Le Soulier de satin*) or a temporal separation (trilogy); a material barrier like the *espalier* in *L'Announce faite à Marie*, the casket of flowers containing Orian's heart in *Le Père humilié*, or a castle wall in *Le Soulier de satin*; a person (Pierre de Craon in *L'Annonce faite à Marie*), or simply a veil such as the one worn by the Princess in *Tête d'Or* or by Prouhèze. Whatever the form, it is basic to the idea of conflict which results from the fruitless attempts to overcome the barrier. The horizontal movements of attempted union on earth must be converted into or transcended by the vertical movement of the striving for union with God.

Within this overall structural pattern other images and motifs recur with varying degrees of frequency. Fire (as Michael Wood has shown) can either be the consuming fire of hell as in *Le Repos du septième jour* and associated with the ashes thrown into Violaine's eyes in *La Jeune Fille Violaine* and her dead leprous flesh in *L'Annonce faite à Marie*, or it can be a pure flame, an inextinguishable response to God. Children, sometimes unborn, underline the indissolubility of marriage and symbolise hope for the future. Moreover, the manner in which the colour of Mara's child's eyes changes to that of Violaine's after she has brought it back to life is picked up years later in *Le Soulier de satin*, where Prouhèze's daughter is the child of the *spiritual* union between herself and Rodrigue. In many cases such use of symbolism is supported by a careful structuring of the plays themselves. It is not uncommon to find an echo of much neo-classical drama in the way in which the action is shared basically between four people, rather, as Claudel said himself, like a game of whist. In *L'Echange*, *Protée* and *Le Pain dur*, for example, we have on the one side sensuality, represented by an old man and his mistress, and on the other the innocence and promise inherent in a much younger couple. Each of these 'games' develops in the same way, with the older couple attempting to possess the younger one, and with the young man either accepting the new situation or surrendering to the attack. In *L'Echange* it is particularly successful. Claudel's intention is that we should contrast Marthe with the others as an idealist in opposition to those obsessed by materialism, but there is more to it than this. This strange group of people act out their own private drama as though it were a play within a play. Perhaps this was in Claudel's mind when he wrote to Jacques Copeau in 1913: 'Je voudrais que Marthe seule eût l'air d'une femme vraie entre trois marionnettes sinistres aux gestes raides et aux visages *impassibles* (il faudrait presque des masques)'. Certainly there is more than a hint of Marivaux in this play where characters become caricatures of themselves and, by extension, of society as a whole, while the careful limits of time and space that Claudel has chosen to impose also underline the essentially artificial nature of the life to which Marthe is introduced. Another play in which the overall structure is of significance for the movement of the drama is *Partage de midi* (which also contains a group of four). In this play the sense of confinement and isolation is made more acute with succeeding scenes – the ship, the cemetery, and finally the small room. Moreover, within this overall pattern, and strengthening the sense of enclosure, we find the omega symbol [Ω] repeated in the shape of the tomb or the arm-chair, which on the point of death eventually holds Ysé and Mesa together like a nuptial throne. It is often argued with some justification that the conflict between emotional necessity and theological design in this play is not fully worked out, and that (to use Bernard Howell's words) it is both enigmatic and ambiguous. Certainly there are a number of intriguing matters: the eternal circle (alpha-omega), the close links throughout between life and death, and the very shape of the omega character which, with the water surrounding the boat in Act I and the small dark room in Act III, hints strongly at the image of a womb, with all that this implies. My concern here, however, is not to estimate whether or not Claudel should present us with a neat solution, but to ascertain the extent to which his theatrical skill matches the problem portrayed. If, therefore, we ultimately leave *Partage de midi* with its conflict still unresolved, this is precisely because the play is a faithful representation of Claudel's own state of mind at that time.

In 1939 Barrault selected *Tête d'Or*, *Partage de midi* and *Le Soulier de satin* as *la sève*, *l'épreuve* and *la synthèse* of Claudel's work, a summary with which few would disagree, particularly if those pieces written after *Le Soulier de satin* are considered to be largely explorations of the limits of theatrical production. By its synthetic quality this play is indeed the finest example of Claudel's *drame total*. Historically and geographically its scale is immense; so too is the vision of the world and of the vocation of mankind that Claudel offers us. Initially unplayable, it says much for Claudel's skill that he could reduce it to more manageable proportions and yet retain its original complexity, for it is as though only a production of this size would allow Claudel to include all those theatrical values in which he so sincerely believed. Tragedy, burlesque, ballet, music, mime, and a chorus in the figure of the Jesuit father, are all to be found. The involvement of the audience, the illusion of going behind the scenes, the use of the stage to represent past and present, distance and proximity at once, visual symbols like the thorn hedge through which Prouhèze struggles in the Première Journée, or the *ombre double* which reveals Claudel's meaning to us, and even the appearance of such supernatural figures as Prouhèze's guardian Angel, all have their place. *Le Soulier de satin* is indeed a piece of creation with Claudel as God. Theologically his interpretation of the Augustinian view of sin may be an oversimplified one, but within the context of the play it must be accepted on its own terms. In his *Mémoires improvisés* Claudel remarks that 'une œuvre d'art, formant un monde à part, qui n'est pas du tout le monde de la théologie ou de l'apologétique, a simplement pour objet la délectation du spectateur'. Such a statement as this must be read in the context of the very particular views that Claudel held on the nature of drama, and to which attention has already been drawn. For him, we recall, Christian life itself is a drama; it is a state of continuous struggle between those eternal values that can only be experienced through a relationship with God, and the transitory pleasures of this world.

In spite of his obvious concern for the moral effect of literature, in his later years Claudel, like Mauriac, disclaimed any suggestion of *deliberate* didactic intention in his work: 'Je n'ai jamais écrit dans un but de démontrer quelque chose, ou de montrer la vérité, j'ai écrit simplement pour donner satisfaction à un ensemble dont les spectateurs pourront tirer tout ce qu'ils voudront et, ce que j'espère, un avantage spirituel.' On this opinions will always differ, but as I have tried to show, it is an argument that takes us beyond the limits of his theatre into the realm of ideas. Claudel's sense of the theatre and mastery of its techniques are undoubted. We do not have to share his particular brand of Catholicism to appreciate the role of Prouhèze's guardian Angel nor the miraculous rebirth of Mara's child, since they stem naturally from and are part of the drama that has gone before. Like the spectators in *Le Soulier de satin* we too must enter and accept the world that Claudel creates for us, with its demands and values. However enigmatic they may at first appear, the last words on Claudel's theatre deserve to be his own: 'Pour entrer dans mon drame, il n'y a précisément aucun besoin d'être chrétien, il y a besoin simplement, si je peux dire, d'être claudélien.'

Select Bibliography

CLAUDEL, PAUL
   Théâtre   Paris, Gallimard (Bibliothèque de la Pléiade), 1956, 2 vols. (Vol. II, revised in 1965, contains a number of prefaces, documents, etc., some of which were hitherto unpublished)
   Œuvre poétique   Paris, Gallimard (Bibliothèque de la Pléiade), 1957
   Œuvres en prose   Paris, Gallimard (Bibliothèque de la Pléiade), 1965
   Mémoires improvisés   Paris, Gallimard, 1954
   Mes idées sur le théâtre   Paris, Gallimard, 1956

Cahiers Paul Claudel   Paris, Gallimard, 1959 etc. Vol. V (1964) contains Claudel's correspondence with Lugné-Poe, and vol. VI (1966) that with Copeau, Dullin and Jouvet.

Cahiers de la Compagnie Madeleine Renaud – Jean-Louis Barrault Vol. XII (1956), 'Connaissance de Paul Claudel'.

BEAUMONT, ERNEST   *The Theme of Beatrice in the Plays of Claudel*   London, Rockliff, 1954

FOWLIE, WALLACE   *Claudel*   Cambridge, Bowes and Bowes, 1957

GRIFFITHS, RICHARD, ed.   *Claudel, a Reappraisal*   London, Rapp and Whiting, 1968

LESORT, PAUL-ANDRÉ   *Paul Claudel par lui-même*   Paris, Editions du Seuil, 1963

MADAULE, JACQUES   *Le Drame de Claudel*   Paris, Desclée de Brouwer, 1964

3

GIRAUDOUX   *Henri J. G. Godin*

Jean Giraudoux began his career as a dramatist at the age of forty-six. In his youth he had received, as a brilliant scholar at the Ecole Normale Supérieure, the highest form of education available in France; he had served with distinction both in France and in the Middle East in the 1914–18 war; he had paid several visits to the United States of America and Canada, and he was a member of the French Diplomatic Service. He had written some ten books consisting of memoirs and novels and, although they had not met with great success, they had established him as a gifted writer with abundant imagination and a dazzling style.

That he should turn to writing for the stage in the mid-1920's comes as something of a surprise. For a spontaneous and prolific writer as he was to impose upon himself the constraints of the dramatic genre presupposes a necessity of a very urgent kind. A combination of circumstances undoubtedly influenced his decision. If we are to judge him by the behaviour of certain of his characters, we may asssume that, around 1924, he experienced that moment of 'illumination' in which an individual suddenly discovers his true vocation. At the same time he saw himself outstripped by men like Gide, Valéry and Curtius who had already gained high reputations for taking up the post-war cause of internationalism and Franco-German rapprochement through the medium of articles and lectures. Because of the 'préciosité' of his style, the influential *Revue de Genève* kept him at bay until 1925. His *Siegfried et le Limousin* (1922), in which he had attempted to pave the way for a new *entente*, had a limited circulation and made little impact. He thus felt compelled to seek in the theatre a larger and more attentive audience for his views. As a specialist in German history and literature, he thought it his special duty to expose the myth of a permanent Franco–German enmity and to advocate the closest interchange of cultural activities, lest Germany might turn eastwards. Already he had adapted a scene from his novel *Siegfried et le Limousin* for the Charles Andler *Miscellany* (1924), and this was the obvious starting point for a full-length play. Thus *Siegfried* came into being; with the invaluable collaboration of Louis Jouvet, it was presented at the Comédie des Champs-Elysées on May 3, 1928.

Siegfried is really a Frenchman, Jacques Forestier, who was found on the battlefield in the early days of the 1914–18 war, unconscious and unidentifiable. He has been re-educated in Germany, given a new personality, and now he has become an eminent German statesman and leader. He is eventually tracked down by Geneviève, his former fiancée, who is employed to teach him French. She succeeds in proving to him his real identity and he is faced with the choice of remaining in Germany as a popular and honoured Chancellor or of returning to France to live a simple provincial life and pick up the threads of his past. He decides on the latter course, convinced that he has something to contribute to the 'science nouvelle' of bringing France and Germany closer together.

The play was on the whole well received and showed that there existed in France a climate of public opinion favourably disposed towards an understanding with Germany. But some critics were outraged by the presence of German officers in uniform on the French stage, and it was clear that influential voices would still be heard perpetuating the spirit of hate. Giraudoux's words, however, made a deep impression and many were conscious of their prophetic ring. It is true that a second war had to be fought and thirty years had to pass before General de Gaulle was able to achieve the reconciliation which Giraudoux, and before him Ernest Renan, had dreamt of (see my Introduction to *La Guerre de Troie n'aura pas lieu*, University of London Press, 1958), but the purpose of the play is seen today to have been fulfilled.

No less prophetic is the presence of General de Fontgeloy, the descendant of the first Huguenot to be driven out of France by the Revocation of the Edict of Nantes on October 18, 1685. For him the choice has long been made: France is unworthy of his allegiance; like numerous colleagues, he is the sworn enemy of that country and his hope is to be one day stationed as a member of an army of occupation in the former family manor at Fontgeloy in Touraine. Giraudoux was well aware of the harm caused to France by Louis XIV's disastrous Decree and rightly suspected that all its consequences had not been worked out. Huguenot descendants Von Huttier and Von François had been outstanding commanders in the 1914–18 war; in 1940, Admiral Arnauld de la Périère took over the port of Brest and General Galland was chief of Hitler's Luftwaffe in Western France. We might add the name of Von Salomon, whose book *Les Réprouvés* caused a sensation in France and may be considered as prophetic of Nazi lust for action and murder. Giraudoux envisages here the problem of peaceful co-existence between people of different religions, nationalities or ideologies and the dangers inherent in all dogmatic attitudes.

It is already obvious that, with Giraudoux, no subject is ever presented in its absolute simplicity. For him, the pattern of truth is complexity, but he does not always respect the fact that 'complexity is structurally incompatible with the pattern of our understanding, so that truth has inevitably to be lopped into conciseness before it is digestible' (Rupert Crawshay-Williams, *The Comforts of Unreason*, 1947, p. 45). His plays matter as much by their implications as by their apparent content. This is all the more evident if we compare *Siegfried* to Jean Anouilh's *Le Voyageur sans bagage* (1936), the best stage version of the ex-soldier who has lost his memory. It is infinitely more *entertaining* than Giraudoux's play, and full of theatrical devices which are quite unfamiliar to him; but it lacks the depth of *Siegfried*. For instance, it contains no expression such as 'créé sans matière première'. Giraudoux, in his first effort as a playwright, reveals some highly personal views on life and the world. It is good, he believes, to be born 'sans bagages': it confers a superiority which one's contemporaries will envy; it enables you to show your 'trait distinctif' (André Gide, *Le Prométhée mal enchaîné*, 1899, p. 50), to réaliser [votre] dissemblance' (Gide, *Le Retour de l'enfant prodigue*, in *Morceaux choisis*, p. 270), and to feel free from the unflattering thought that your life is due to the 'épanchements peu sacrés d'un couple bourgeois' (*Siegfried*, p. 12). But what Giraudoux really expresses is his longing for man to be self-made. He would prefer men without past, without ancestors, without predetermining links. He likes every human being to be original and unique, for he believes in *aseity*.

Siegfried is also meant to prove how easy it is for the human mind to absorb, even as an adult, any language, any culture, any political system which happens to be imposed upon it. Masses of men can thus be swayed to accept any creed and be made to fight for it. This terrifying realisation was to be elaborated later in *La Guerre de Troie n'aura pas lieu* (1935). In *Siegfried* Giraudoux expressed one of the greatest needs of mankind: the faculty of self-evaluation and with it the courage to renew, if necessary, one's whole attitude to life, whatever denials and reversals this might entail.

In this play Giraudoux was presenting his obsessional theme: the duality which faces every individual in life and the attitude to be adopted towards it. Practically insensitive to the body and soul dualism, he was nevertheless deeply conscious of the essential diplopia in every thoughtful man. Monocular vision is the proprium of the majority and, to Giraudoux, a deplorable infirmity. He is fascinated by his own power of double vision and is thus driven to the artistic form in which the dialogue dominates. At first his discussions were based on contemporary contingencies, but gradually he passed to the more stylised philosophical dialogue and tended to neglect dramatic action altogether.

The duality of the 'France and Germany' theme was admirably brought out in *Siegfried* and it was further to be developed as a 'War and Peace' dialogue in *La Guerre de Troie n'aura pas lieu*, when circumstances demanded it. But while a period of relative calm lasted, Giraudoux's attention could be turned to another of his preoccupations as an unprejudiced observer: the 'Heaven and Earth' controversy. He decided to stage a confrontation between representatives of each side. It was natural and undoubtedly instinctive that he should choose the most famous of all 'doubles': Amphitryon.

Giraudoux never gave a completely positive view on the subject of the existence of gods or God, but the problem baffled him in the sense that a considerable section of humanity firmly believed in an after-life and a divine presence. The gods and God appear episodically in many of his plays. In the still euphoric climate of the post-war years, he decided to treat the theme in the style of comedy, while at the same time stimulating serious thoughts. Thus *Amphitryon 38* was born on November 8, 1929.

It is a highly amusing and titillating play. Indeed, it had to be slightly bowdlerised for its English presentation. It thrives on ambiguity, but one fact is certain: Alcmene has been tricked into believing that it was her husband who had unexpectedly returned from the front and spent a night with her, while actually it was Jupiter. The birth of Hercules is thus assured and the subsequent imbroglio is entirely superfluous and farcical. What does matter, however, is Alcmene's verbal encounter with Jupiter. The two are well matched, being equally endowed with their creator's brilliant intelligence and verve. Neither has an obvious advantage: each is in some way incomplete. Jupiter has a nostalgia for the Earth – 'la planète où il est le plus doux d'atterrir et de séjourner' (p. 126), says Mercury – and Alcmene a nostalgia for Heaven: she has spent her youth making 'signs' to the gods. Each has an aspiration towards an ideal; it is in fact a 'magnetic' attraction to some inexplicable otherness. Perhaps 'aimantation' is the secret of the universe: gods are attracted to women; women attract precious stones, beautiful flowers, husbands' hands, but are themselves attracted by the mystery of the Beyond and long for the divine embrace. Earth has turned out very different from what the gods thought they had created: having plunged it into the transforming insubstantiality of Time, they have seen their creation creating itself anew every minute. The Earth has found its own enchantment, and the gods are merely responsible for throwing humanity into a terrible muddle of stupors and illusions in which it has to struggle along as best it can. The gods blackmail us with threats to our happiness and health, interfere with our private lives and never do what we most fervently expect of them : heal and punish.

Alcmene deems it wise not to accept Jupiter's offer : she refuses to be a star – the night air is bad for her complexion; she refuses immortality – that would be betraying humanity; she has no natural desire for eternity : death must be imagined sweet, constant, smooth as the full tide. Alcmene will not shrink from her fate : she opts for solidarity with her planet. She also refuses adultery with a god (though she has committed it unwittingly), and stands for the harmonious and unassailable unity of the married human couple. But she is a generous creature : she does offer friendship to Jupiter. She would rather keep him in her thoughts than *believe* in him, since belief is an inherited habit, a product of the will, whereas thought comes from the heart. Giraudoux would not approve of a wife who shared her love between a husband and a god. He also makes it clear to what kind of woman his preference goes: Alcmene is an 'acceptatrice'; she needs no conversion to life.

Giraudoux's position as a humanist seemed to have been plainly stated, even though he showed willingness to concede a measure of sympathy for those who clung to a belief in the 'extra-human'. In *Judith* (November 4, 1931), his attitude appears at first to harden; in the person of Holofernes he makes a powerful attack against the gods and, indeed, against the God of the Jews who is here specifically the target. God is represented as weak, needing men's love to preserve his divinity. God, says Holofernes, pollute the universe with their vices and foul smells. The world is like a barrack-room full of gods. Fortunately he alone knows a few places in the world to which they have not gained access: his tent is one of them. He invites Judith, who has been sent to kill him, to join him there and enjoy the bliss of a corner of Eden before the Fall, where even insects are untainted with original sin: 'Je t'offre pour une nuit cette villa sur un océan évanté et pur' (p. 278). Here men can be men and escape from this 'âge de dieux'. He himself can be 'un homme enfin de ce monde, du monde'. Holofernes is God's worst enemy and he wonders what Judith is doing among the Jews: how beautiful would be her day if she were freed from terrors and prayers, free from the thought of Hell, of mortal sin, of angels and demons: 'Songe à l'homme innocent' (p. 278). Heaven is a dreadful sucker of energies; without it, men could be happy. Happiness causes God to flee. How much more beautiful a woman can be when stripped of her God! Judith does not disagree, but she is shrewd enough to know that such ideal conditions cannot last and that Jehovah soon returns. She agrees to share the joy that Holofernes offers her for a brief while, then she kills him in order that he may not awaken from his beautiful dream : 'la vue d'un corps endormi peut-elle appeler autre chose que le meurtre

comme suprême tendresse!' (p. 298). As she sees Holofernes asleep, enjoy-
ing the bliss of innocence and satisfaction, she is overcome with an infinite
pity for him and spares him a return to reality and the awful routine of
yet another of life's dreary mornings. She cannot understand why more
women do not do the same for their men: how can they be so cruel as to
let them face another day's toil in this implacable world?

With this extraordinary twist to the apocryphal story, Giraudoux is
now faced with the difficulty of dealing with a girl of twenty who has
killed for love and not to carry out God's command. She is accused of
adultery towards God. In a most unconvincing third act, Giraudoux in
an apparently repentant mood, turns a drunken guard into a spokesman
for God who brainwashes Judith into believing that her night with Holofernes was watched by God and his servants and that not one of her acts
was purely voluntary. The confounded Judith is a sorry spectacle and
God's strange ways can hardly be enhanced in the minds of the spectators.
To be told that God may take a thousand years to turn sacrilege and lust
into holiness is of little comfort to man in his short span of life. More
deceit seems added to an already deceitful power and man's absolute help-
lessness in the face of such arbitrary behaviour can inspire only revolt.
But Giraudoux is committed to his double vision and tries hard, for the
sake of balance, to argue the case for God. He is so clumsy at it, however,
that his penchant for humanism becomes all the more obvious. The
trouble with the play is that once the splendid Holofernes has disappeared
from the stage interest flags, and Judith, who should now take over the
heroic role and sacrifice herself to the Jews to defend the truth of her
human love, is mercilessly shorn of her once defiant personality and reduced to grovel in as abject a manner as Sartre's Electre in Les Mouches.

Such anticlimax is not welcome in the theatre and was not to be expected after Alcmene's earthy attitude in Amphitryon 38. The play was
a virtual failure, a fact which saddened Giraudoux for the rest of his days.
Presented in Christopher Fry's English translation at Her Majesty's
Theatre in June 1962, the impact was no greater. The Times dramatic
critic saw in it 'a dated and brittle essay on the sex war, spiced with tired
romanticism'. Holofernes is, however, an unforgettable creation. His
message is conveyed in no uncertain terms, but what is disturbing is the
ambiguity of the latter part of the play. Are we to understand that
women cannot dispense with supernatural assistance, and is their lot
always to submit to it? Perhaps man has the wrong kind of partner for
his Promethean adventure: Gide's Alissa and Antigone succumbed to
the mystical temptation. The separation of the sexes is a theme germin-
ating in the mind of Giraudoux.

After the failure of Judith, Giraudoux must have felt that the tragic vein should be abandoned at least for a time. A return to the highly successful manner of *Amphitryon 38* seemed essential to regain the approval of a hostile public. Serious subjects could well be treated in an apparently facetious manner and still retain their deeper meaning. What could be more serious in life than the temptation of Death? Once again Giraudoux takes up a duality theme, 'Life and Death', and, in *Intermezzo* (February 27, 1933), offers the choice to one of his most charming heroines, Isabelle, a young school-teacher, always accompanied in her natural history lessons round the countryside by a bevy of delightful little girls who worship her and support her unorthodox teaching. She is one of those privileged creatures whose intuition is so subtle that she can interpret the hidden meaning of things. She is 'simple' and 'nette', equally at home in the world of reality and in the supra-human world, one of whose denizens manifests himself to her as a 'ghost'. Being a virgin she has the added gift of seeing the world through cleansed doors of perception. Truth, she knows, cannot be reduced to a single dimension: there is around us a fullness which we do not appreciate. Education, especially as understood by the Inspector, has killed the elementary in us. We have lost the power of believing in the abnormal and we are insensitive to 'signs' and portents. We should never refuse the beckoning of the Beyond.

The important thing is always to be 'in tune' with the cosmos, as the Chemist (a kind of wise onlooker like Jaques) reminds us. He describes himself as an 'Ensemblier', a man with a total vision of the universe, but even he has to carry his tuning forks in his pockets to ensure that he remains in harmony with his environment. He believes that 'une note juste' gives us the greatest feeling of security in this uncertain world.

Isabelle very nearly opts for the Romantic lure of Death and the strange companionship of the 'ghost', who is vulnerable to the bullets of those who do not believe in him, but once 'dead' immediately rises again apparently unscathed! Isabelle falls into a cataleptic state from which her earthbound friends energetically recall her by making loud human noises: 'Il ne s'agit pas de la ramener à elle, mais de la ramener à nous' (p. 93). This picture of human solidarity is comically presented but deeply moving. Whatever may be the composition of human groupings – here mostly people with monocular vision: positivists, Freudians, anti-Freudians, free-thinkers – they generate a collective warmth which is essentially human. Isabelle revives and decides to share the not unpoetic life offered her by the Controller of Weights and Measures.

This is a strange play, absolutely typical of Giraudoux's art and ideas, and most important for the proper understanding of his theatre. He reaffirms here his humanism and suggests ways in which, as Gide was to write in his *Nouvelles Nourritures* (1935): 'la vie peut être plus belle que ne la consentent les hommes'. Let us try to enjoy our presence on this planet, not necessarily seeking happiness, for God, says Giraudoux, has only provided *compensations*: fishing, love, dotage; but enriching our lives by cultivating our sensitivity to the sur-reality which surrounds us and access to which is not beyond anybody's reach. There is magic in the Unseen and we have everything to gain by not refusing 'toutes autres invites que celles de ce monde' (p. 51).

Intermezzo was an interlude, one of those moments which Giraudoux loved so much when Time stands still, as in Holofernes's tent, and man can take a calm survey of his situation and fate. But the post-war euphoria was now at an end and it had become clear to Giraudoux that since 1930 France and her allies had entered a pre-war phase of heart-searching and anxiety. Once more the Franco-German theme had to be debated symbolically in public and with it the everlasting subject of War. At this time the League of Nations had lost most of its prestige, two of its members, Italy and Abyssinia, were at war, and France herself felt betrayed by Britain's unilateral naval treaty with Germany. The glide down to the abyss had begun.

Giraudoux's wish was to present the case for and against war on a high philosophical level, and his exposition is remarkably similar to that of Renan in *Le Prêtre de Nemi* (1885). Basically, both used an idea expressed by Pierre Charron, a follower of Montaigne:

> Let us call to minde that the greatest alterations of the world, the most generale and fearfule agitations of States and Empires, armies, battels, murthers have risen from light, ridiculous and vain causes, witness the wars of *Troy* and *Greece*, of *Silla* and *Marius*, *Cesar* and *Pompey*, *Augustus* and *Antony*. The Poets signifie as much, when they set all *Greece* and *Asia* on fire for an Apple. The first occasions and motives arise of nothing, afterwards they grow and increase: a testimony of the vanity and folly of man. (Charron, *Of Wisdome*, 1651, I, xxxvi. Quoted by Jacques Chabaud, *Simone Weil*, 1964, p. 155)

It was, indeed, the 'vanity and folly' of men which caused Giraudoux such deep sorrow as he calmly observed the world. *La Guerre de Troie n'aura pas lieu* (November 21, 1935) is a powerful condemnation of narrow-minded nationalism, of the stupid arrogance of self-righteousness, or, in a theological sense, of triumphalism. Giraudoux opposes here, as in a musical composition, two sets of characters: the warmongers and the 'pacifists'. They carry on a running logomachy which is prophetic of those interminable 'negotiations' which are held today while fierce wars rage.

Giraudoux is a master of the antithetic dialogue. The characters he sets in opposition rarely understand one another or deliberately misinterpret each other's statements. They all seem to express themselves in a different key, each seeing an aspect of the problem invisible to the other. Cassandra and Andromache fail to communicate; Hector understands neither Helen nor Ulysses. Giraudoux contrives his dialogue in such a way that the 'normal', rational and apparently sane person always appears at a disadvantage when confronted by a more glamorous, more brilliantly intellectual opponent, though on closer analysis, the latter's words, while inspiring some kind of awe, make very little sense.

It is not so much failure to communicate as refusal to communicate which brings about situations that lead to war. Conflict within the same camp – that of the Trojans – is a bad enough omen: Hector leads those who believe in Peace and Justice as the highest of all values, and who rate the preservation of human life as the only worthy aim of men. Against these are arrayed the 'fantoches', those who have only monocular vision and who support values that are accessory and contingent. Men fall headlong into conflict for failing on most occasions to recognise the essential. Thus concepts such as Beauty, Love, Woman, War, Heroism, Patriotism, Destiny, Gods, are given the status of absolutes and deemed worth fighting for by those who know they will not have to fight, while true values, according to the human scale, such as Peace, Justice, Reason, Reality, Logic, enjoy little credit among the majority of mediocre men and women. But such is the ever-present feeling of insecurity in the world that man prefers the irrational to the rational, fantasy to fact and superstition to common sense.

Hector, who is undoubtedly Giraudoux's favourite hero and the nearest incarnation of himself, goes out to destroy the illusions according to which men live. He has himself experienced many, but he has had the privilege of 'illumination' on the battlefield. Until then, making war had been part of his life and he felt that strange excitement which war gives to the real soldier. But, all of a sudden, as he was about to kill, he became aware of the discordant 'note' which warned him that he was not being true to himself. From that moment on, he began to hate war and determined to stave it off even at the cost of the most humiliating insults. He almost succeeds, but by a wicked trick of Fate becomes himself responsible for starting the war. The symbolic gates of War which he had hoped to close for ever are now seen to open slowly once more.

Whatever concessions Giraudoux may have made to the frivolous taste of the day, and despite a bawdy episode and some coarse language, this play is the most moving in his theatre. He was no sentimentalist by nature and some of his characters are the hardest and most unrelenting ever created, but in *La Guerre de Troie n'aura pas lieu* he shows his deep feelings for the couple Hector/Andromache and their perfect unity in love. We are touched by the tragic vision of Helen who sees, in the future, Hector lying dead, and his wife and son weeping over his body. We share Andromache's ardour when she begs Helen to love Paris in the true human sense so that their mutual affection might be worth defending.

The message of the play was clear to all, and it could be stated in the words of Euripides, whose *Helen* was acted 2,347 years earlier and in some respects was imitated by Giraudoux: 'You are mad to seek virtue in war'. Indeed, the manner in which Giraudoux treated the theme of the Trojan war so impressed Simone Weil that she elaborated it with her usual persuasive vehemence in a series of articles in the Spring of 1937 under the title: 'Ne recommençons pas la guerre de Troie' ('The Power of Words', *Selected Essays*, 1962). No more telling confirmation of Giraudoux's attacks on 'nationalism', 'patriotism' and 'fatality' could possibly have been written. The play had struck the right note and, between them, Giraudoux and Simone Weil completely discredited the traditional causes of war.

It should be noted that Giraudoux took care, *in extremis*, not to antagonise his audience by some horror spectacle beyond the Gates of War as they opened. Brilliantly outlined against the cyclorama are Helen and young Troilus kissing passionately. The spectators go home with a smile: eroticism was, after all, one of Giraudoux's *compensations*.

Love-making is certainly the principal occupation of the people of Otahiti, in Giraudoux's *Supplément au voyage de Cook*, a curtain-raiser to *La Guerre de Troie n'aura pas lieu* (November 21, 1935). Nature provides them with all the necessities of life without requiring any work from them in exchange. They live entirely according to their instincts and attach no moral sanctions to their behaviour. When Captain Cook's expedition arrives off the island, in 1769, an advance party is sent ashore, led by Mr Banks, a Presbyterian sidesman from Birmingham who is duly shocked when Chief Outourou offers him a choice of his wife, daughter or young aunt as company for the night. It would not be 'convenable' for him to accept, as he believes and teaches that 'tout ce qui est corporel est méprisable' (p. 123). He sees little hope for the islanders until the fifteen ministers whom he has urgently summoned from England arrive.

This is a scathing satire on Puritanism and repressive Christian morality. In two admirable temptation scenes, both Mr Banks and Mrs Banks are forced to admit that, while observing the strictest continence towards one another, they have the power to conjure up in their imaginations the most lustful encounters with ideal partners. Mrs Banks, in typical Giralducian terminology, goes as far as to say: 'A la présence de Mr Banks, tout superbe qu'il est, je préfère même l'absence de Mr Banks' (p. 154). Outourou shrewdly understands the implications of that remark and is shocked at the thought that some men and women deliberately create their own obstructions to the perfect union of the human couple which, in the eyes of the Otahitians, is the supreme good of life: 'Oh, Mrs Banks!' he says, 'ce n'est pas la question des couples qui compte en ce bas monde, mais celle des couples heureux!' (p. 150).

Otahiti is another oasis in Giraudoux's universe, a stopping place where man-made inhibitions do not apply, where the words 'honte' and 'repentir' are unknown, where the purpose of life is to make humanity beautiful. He expresses his nostalgia for an innocent, sinless world and deplores the notion of a Fall.

In his next play, *Electre* (May 13, 1937) 'cette combinaison de Sophocle, de vous et de Jouvet' (Simone Weil to Giraudoux), he was to portray a character longing for absolute purity.

Electra has in her very name a curious ambiguity: she has the brilliance and purity of light, but she is also *a lektra*, bedless, unmated, virgin in mind and body. She has found herself fatherless, unloved by her mother and suspicious of the circumstances in which her father died. She awaits the return of her brother on whom she can count for protection and affection. The Regent is determined to marry her off to the gardener, since he considers her a dangerous creature capable of making 'signs' to the gods and unleashing their indiscriminate wrath.

It is evident that Giraudoux expects us to be familiar with his previous plays, for his plan is successively to explain his ideas in greater depth. As single units, his plays are difficult because we have to learn his language and give due weight to certain 'mots-clefs', or privileged words. He wants his theatre to form a coherent corpus of views in a steadily unfolding pattern. Thus the rather obscure notion of 'Destiny' exposed in *La Guerre de Troie n'aura pas lieu* is clarified in *Electre*. Helen has handed over to Electra the role of being 'une de ces rares créatures que le destin met en circulation pour son usage personnel', and whose function is to stir the gods into a disastrous interference in human affairs. Aegisthus, who has learnt Hector's lesson, tries to condemn Electra to a life of oblivion in order to ensure that the gods, those blind boxers, will not be shaken out of their lethargy and go rampaging murderously around. This curious, primitive and absurd conception of mankind shrinking itself away into insignificance to avoid being seen by malevolent forces and fearing betrayal at the hands of certain 'elected' creatures, is really a parody of the ancient notion of Fate. Through it Giraudoux succeeds, up to a point, in inspiring a certain uneasiness in his audience, but he knows perfectly well that it is unconvincing. So he deftly drops the rather tiresome discussions on Destiny and the gods by endowing Electra with an iron will to pursue her vengeance once she has realised that her mother and Aegisthus were the perpetrators of her father's murder. She takes over from the so-called 'extra-human' forces on an essentially human level and shows that will commands destiny.

We understand better also, for having seen Hector suddenly discovering his true vocation as a man of peace, how Electra becomes Electra the avenger. Giraudoux has now found a suitable expression for this moment of 'illumination' in which we are given the revelation of our archetype: he calls it 'se déclarer', and he gives the Beggar a long monologue to demonstrate how all creatures in the world 'se déclarent'. Electra's example is, in fact, so contagious, that all the characters around her are transformed as if by magic into their authentic selves. The scales drop from their eyes: dissimulation, hypocrisy and pretence are thrown by the board and all appear in their true colours. The debate rises therefore to a higher level and Aegisthus, now finding in himself the stuff of a king, proves a worthy adversary for the intransigent Electra. The dialogue reaches the greatest philosophical heights, and Giraudoux revels in opposing pragmatic and teleological views.

With the threat of war becoming each day more insistent, Giraudoux may have wished to harden his countrymen's feelings and reawaken in them a dwindling sense of Justice and Truth. With Electra he turns away from his gentle heroines, the 'acceptatrices', and presents a type who normally attracts little sympathy: the 'revendicatrice'. Electra is an 'acharnée', a 'femme à histoires', 'la ménagère de la vérité'. She seems convinced of an immanent finality in the universe and to her Justice and Truth must transcend such puny contingencies as the destruction of a nation and the suffering of thousands of innocent victims. She spurs on a rather reluctant Orestes to kill their mother Clytemnestra and Aegisthus. Thus murder breeds murder, but in Electra's eyes this is just retribution, and in the fullness of time her example will bear witness to the cause of righteousness.

To some, Electra could appear as a pathological case whose obsessional chastity has been sublimated into a superhuman ideal of purity for which she claims universal allegiance. More specifically, perhaps, she is the symbol of eternally unsatisfied womanhood. Men know what they mean by 'happiness' and are content to accept compensations; women care only for the absolute. And thus the gap between the sexes widens again.

Electre was found difficult both in its original production and when it received the official consecration of admission to the repertoire of the

Comédie Française in 1959. The second act, especially, is in parts considered tedious and there is always the danger of turning the dialogues
into shouting contests. It is always helpful to consider *Electre* in relation to
Anouilh's *Antigone*, when the former is seen clearly to gain in depth. But
Anouilh's heroine is infinitely more moving in her pointless sacrifice
than Electre. Not having a sense of 'mission' towards humanity and
thereby a moral obligation, Antigone is not a 'revendicatrice' but a pure
and lovable 'renonciatrice'.

Two light and fanciful curtain-raisers follow *Electre*: *L'Impromptu
de Paris* (December 3, 1937) and *Cantique des cantiques* (October 12,
1938). The former is modelled on Molière's *L'Impromptu de Versailles*
and the actors are just themselves discussing on the stage the principles
of their craft. Giraudoux, now a well-established playwright, uses this
device to codify and defend his views on what the theatre has to offer to
the public. It is an acted *Préface de Cromwell*. The purpose of the play
is to 'dire leur vérité aux gens' – in other words, shake people out of their
comfortable concepts and propose ethical revaluations which may not
always be palatable. The audience must be considered as generally obtuse
and need not be expected to 'understand'. But it must be made to 'feel'
with its senses and its imagination: intellectual reaction is superfluous.
Jouvet re-echoed these ideas in his article 'A propos de la mise en scène
de la "Folle de Chaillot" ' (*La France Libre*, XI, March 15, 1946). All that
matters is 'style'; good writing will create the enchantment and hypnotise
the spectator with the dazzle of multiple hues. The theatre is, in fact,
the privileged place so often wished for by Giraudoux – 'un lieu de
lumière', 'de beau langage'. Life can be better understood after seeing a
good, well-written play. Style smoothes the soul ruffled by the week's
toil; the theatre is a tranquilliser. Public affairs are exhausting and the
State should understand that a nation will only have a great real life if it
has also a powerful irrational life. The play is also an excuse for attacking
those critics who had misunderstood *Judith* and *Electre*. It is a most useful
clarification of Giraudoux's ideas and theatrical aims.

Cantique des cantiques, taken in part from *Eglantine* (1927), is a
charming bitter-sweet reflection on advancing age in a man. In the
context of Giraudoux's theatre, it is one of his most typical plays, teeming
with his favourite ideas and mannerisms. The characters are differentiated
in status only and all possess their creator's verbal virtuosity. The privileged place this time is the 'terrasse' of a fashionable Parisian café to
which the 'President' goes when he needs 'une heure supra-terrestre . . .
un balcon de sérénité . . . une terrasse d'euphorie'. Yet on this podium
a sad and moving episode will take place: the President's charming girl-
friend has come to say goodbye, she is marrying an insignificant young

man. The simple theme of King Solomon and the Shulamite is presented in Giraudoux's inimitable style, and despite nonsensical conversations, the antics of Gypsies and the display of glittering jewellery, the emotional content of the fable is admirably transmitted. Giraudoux has reversed the tiresome attitude of Molière in *L'Ecole des femmes* and has given the President outstanding qualities of intellect and manners which make him worthy of being loved for himself. But age is against him and Giraudoux finds here another incompatibility between the sexes which saddens him intensely. Florence is genuinely sorry to leave him – she cannot 'see' her young man, Jérôme, very well – but she cannot escape her biological destiny. When the age for love has passed, man must turn to other 'compensations'. Fortunately for the President, the Republic is in danger: he flies to its rescue. This is a real collector's piece: Giraudoux is at his best in this delightful lyrical episode.

He was to remain in this wistful mood with *Ondine* (April 27, 1939). The theme, taken from the German story by Frédéric de la Motte Fouqué, is the well-known one of the water-sprite or mermaid who takes the risk of entering by marriage into the society of men. 'Ne va pas chez les hommes!' cries the King of the Mermen. But Ondine has made up her mind and accepts the pact with her people: if Hans, the knight errant, is unfaithful to her, then he will have to die. Giraudoux has found here an admirable device to express judgements on humanity through a creature who belongs to another realm. Ondine certainly finds some aspects of life on dry land attractive: men can be very handsome; their language, especially, is quite remarkable: for each object they see, each action they perform, there is a name. They persuade themselves that they are in the right element by clever nomenclature. They play 'games', and ride creatures called 'horses', but they are so wrapped up in their occupations that they have lost all curiosity for what is beyond their ordinary life. Their worst defect is having 'memory': Ondine finds it hard to think that since the past cannot be obliterated it must act as a determinism on our future. Balzac had realised that too: 'Oublier est le grand secret des existences fortes et créatrices . . .' (*César Birotteau*). As an elemental creature, Ondine possesses the gift of wiping out the past from her mind and when finally she returns to her people, her unsuccessful human adventure leaves only a strange and inexplicable pattern of habits and learned responses. 'Le souvenir est une invention de malheur', thought Gide (*L'Immoraliste*, p. 244). All mermaids in folklore eventually return to their waters after a spell on Earth: they symbolise man's longing for his lost domain (see my article 'Mélusine et la philologie', in *Revue du Bas-Poitou*, March–April 1964), or as J. C. Powys would say, his nostalgia for his Ichthyosaurus days (*In Defence of Sensuality*, 1930). Giraudoux does not despise man, but tries hard to make him aware of his deficiencies and suggests ways of enhancing life. *Ondine* is another lesson in humanism.

It was an outstanding success and ran for many months even after the outbreak of war. Giraudoux, after a brief spell in the Government, retired to Cusset and became passionately interested in the cinema. He produced *La Duchesse de Langeais* in 1942. In the meantime the Jouvet company had gone to Rio de Janeiro where they staged a short play which Jouvet had been sent from Switzerland by Giraudoux. It was called *L'Apollon de Marsac* (June 16, 1942). This is a very light-hearted short play with little substance, but it is extremely interesting for the student of Giraudoux as it contains all his tricks and especially his characteristic verbal jugglery. As usual, all his characters share his volubility and are indistinguishable in the power of their eloquence. As in *Ondine*, they indulge in endless enumerations of disparate objects. Giraudoux's glossolalia attains here an unprecedented exuberance. He is a master of the 'surenchère', or extension of an already adequately expressed idea. The effect is, to say the least, overpowering. The play has, nevertheless, a certain charm. It deals with the comfortable concept of Beauty. A young woman in search of a job meets a gentleman from Marsac, later called Bellac (Giraudoux's birthplace) who advises her to say to all the men she meets: 'Comme vous êtes beau!' This works admirably and brings about an unexpected harmony among the company directors. Women who try to interfere and proclaim a contrary assertion are rejected and dismissed. Their realistic vision spoils the lives of men who prefer gentle and unsophisticated young girls uttering flattering remarks. Again we see the male sex satisfied with a modicum of illusion. When performed in London in 1957, the *Times* critic wrote: 'The little fantasy has a tired wartime ring' (May 15), and Gabriel Marcel thought it 'la virtuosité presque réduite à ellemême'.

How Giraudoux could pass from *L'Apollon de Bellac* to his most sombre play on the great problem of the relationship between the sexes, *Sodome et Gomorrhe* (October 11, 1943), still remains to be explained. He seems suddenly to have lost his faith in the unity of the married couple of which he had given such glowing examples in *Amphitryon 38* and *La Guerre de Troie n'aura pas lieu*. A personal experience might be involved. Now man and woman are on trial, each being the prosecutor of the other. The debate has ceased to be academic, for it takes place in the sight of God whose Angel and Archangel are either present or within hailing distance. Unless a truly happy married couple is found and identified under the beam of the heavenly beacon, the Cities of the Plain will be destroyed and, with them, mankind.

The two spokesmen for the Divinity explain the purpose of Creation: man and woman were created one (as in the myth of the androgyne) and were then severed one from the other, each being granted freedom of action. It was assumed by the Creator that this freedom was a pure formality and that the attraction of one sex for the other would result in the happy reunion of all pairs. But there has been a 'malfaçon': men have abused their gift of individuality and so have women. The chasm between them has deepened with their increasing self-pride, and God's original idyllic vision of the blissful couple has been shattered – 'A quoi bon un duo?' God's ultimate threat – amounting to blackmail – has also failed, and his only solution is to destroy the species. At the end of the play men and women stand in their segregated groups awaiting their doom, as Alfred de Vigny had predicted in *La Colère de Samson*.

Giraudoux expresses no new ideas in this play but seems to gather up from his various writings all the criticisms of men by women and of women by men and turn them into insults which his protagonists, Lia and Jean, hurl at each other. His misogyny, already evident in *Electre*, now reaches its climax. Lia is another 'revendicatrice', utterly contemptuous of man whom she cannot 'see', longing only for transcendence to escape from the musty smell of the human condition. She turns to the Angel on whom she tries all her charms, but in vain. Jean is made at first to submit to the lashes of her tongue, but when he has the chance to counter-attack, he is equally ruthless. Man on his own would have been a sufficient and excellent creation. Woman might have been acceptable if she had been merely a near duplicate of himself, but by her frantic assertiveness, her fury of domination, her statuesque frigidity, she has driven him into solitude or sodomy. The root of the misunderstanding is that we never see ourselves as we are but have the unfortunate faculty of casting a sharp and penetrating eye on others. Objective knowledge wrecks relationships.

This play is a philosophical and metaphysical dialogue without plot, action or peripety. It is bathed in an atmosphere of gloom and foreboding from the start, for, as in the case of *La Guerre de Troie n'aura pas lieu*, the fate of the Cities of the Plain is already known. But there is no relief from the tragic intensity of the debate. It commands respectful attention solely by its profound human accents and by its often sublime expression. With Edwige Feuillère in the exhausting role of Lia, Giraudoux had ensured the success of the original presentation.

His last two plays were to be staged after his death (January 31, 1944). The first of these, probably written during the dark days of the black market in 1943, was *La Folle de Chaillot* (December 19, 1945). This is a curious and sinister pantomime. Unscrupulous speculators are planning to prospect for oil in the Parisian sub-soil. Companies have been set up and drilling operations are about to begin. The madwoman of Chaillot invites all the company directors to the cellar in which she lives and from which they can go down a secret passage to the oil well. This is in fact a disused sewer from which all escape is impossible. Once they are all inside, she closes the secret door and it must be assumed that all will be asphyxiated. She and her friends rejoice that the wicked men and women have been disposed of. The city becomes a happier place and the madwoman will be able to turn her attention once more to stray cats and dogs which are more interesting than men.

This is a highly entertaining satire and fantasy, full of farcical dialogue, grotesque characters and crazy incidents in the grand Giraudoux manner. A new device creeps into the first act: most of the characters involved recite their potted life-story. Each autobiography is full of the eccentricities expected of Giraudoux, who seems to have found his comic genius once more. The scene is set, typically, outside the Café Francis, Place de l'Alma, where confusion is constantly caused by flower-sellers, street-singers and even an expert juggler.

On the more serious side, we find Giraudoux, the humanist, still hunting down sections of humanity which compromise the possibility of general happiness. Men of goodwill are exhorted to be less tolerant of parasites, and to act against them instead of bemoaning their presence. Men who turn themselves into beasts should be destroyed: 'La mort d'un vaurien n'est rien.' There are sly swipes at freemasons and the much maligned 'Two Hundred Families'. But it is good to see Giraudoux featuring again, though briefly, the love of a young couple. Love will endure if it is seized without hesitation at the right moment. Having now ceased to torture his mind with the idea of Fate, having reduced the gods and God to the level of empty myths unworthy of our intellectual consideration, Giraudoux sees a way to human happiness as possible, since it is the sole concern of man.

His last play, *Pour Lucrèce*, was not staged until November 4, 1953. Jouvet was dead, but in the capable hands of Madeleine Renaud, Jean-Louis Barrault and Edwige Feuillère the play was an outstanding success. Giraudoux has here fallen again into one of his sombre and pessimistic moods. It is interesting to note that he goes further than before in exploring the faculty of 'vision' in a woman. In *Pour Lucrèce* he founds the tragedy on Lucile's ability to 'see' in others a moral flaw. 'Sur chaque être débauché, je vois une bête' (p. 231). Toads, newts and worms appear to her to issue from the mouth, nose, ears and eyes of the 'impure', and in their presence she remains silent. The consequences of this hypervision are grave, for the town of Aix-en-Provence was, until the arrival of Lucile and her husband, M. Blanchard, the Public Prosecutor, a haven of love and unrestricted pleasures. When all was permissiveness, there was no sense of guilt, but now that Virtue stalks the streets, vice is revealed and evil enters the city: 'Tu redonnes à la ville le péché originel', says Eugénie to Lucile (p. 231). Paola, who feels particularly guilty under Lucile's gaze, accuses her of betraying her sex, 'la maffia des femmes'. Husbands become suspicious and 'pretend' to be indignant, since, as we already know, they only mimic their sentiments. Paola and her friend Marcellus, who has been branded by the Prosecutor as the embodiment of vice, are determined to wreak vengeance on 'Lucile the chaste'. She is drugged, taken to the house of a procuress, and everything is so arranged that, on waking, Lucile will be convinced that she has been raped by Marcellus. No one, in fact, except the woman Barbette, will have been near the house; but the hoax has its desired effect. Lucile's power of visual detection fails her where she is herself concerned and she believes she has been defiled. 'Sa grande spécialité en ce bas monde', says Paola ironically, 'Mme Blanchard l'a reniée elle-même. Elle n'est plus la pureté, puisqu'elle n'a rien deviné à sa pureté' (p. 307). Eventually her eyes are opened by Barbette, but by that time Marcellus has been killed in a duel by Paola's husband, and the Prosecutor shows nothing but hate and disgust towards his wife who now 'sees' him as he is, totally lacking in love and sympathy. Appalled by 'la bêtise des hommes, la grossièreté des hommes, la méchanceté des hommes' (p. 316), Lucile takes poison and dies. Giraudoux gives Barbette the task of expressing over Lucile's body his obvious sympathy for his heroine. Barbette becomes the philosopher of the piece and movingly recognises Lucile's purity and saintliness: 'La pureté n'est pas de ce monde, mais tous les dix ans, il y a sa lueur, son éclair' (p. 315).

Giraudoux owes his inspiration to Shakespeare's *Rape of Lucrece*, though he has greatly modified the details and it is no longer 'the story of sweet chastity's decay'. But he has retained the idea of 'holy-thoughted Lucrece', of 'this earthly saint', and he has written the tragedy of innocence without resorting to the edifying devices of hagiographers. The message of *Pour Lucrèce* is the Biblical one: 'anoint thine eyes with eyesalve, that thou mayest see' (Rev. iii, 18). Imperfect vision is our greatest infirmity and the prime cause of dissension among human beings. The whole of Giraudoux's theatre confirms this view: it is really an illustration of Blake's belief that 'If the doors of perception were cleansed, everything would appear to man as it is, infinite' (*The Marriage of Heaven and Hell*). Just before Lucile dies, she, too, sees the world as it should be seen and exclaims: 'Le monde est pur, Paola, le monde est en beauté et lumière!' (p. 314). Giraudoux had long been seeking for the kind of heroine who could command admiration and respect for her sense of purity and innocence without appearing sanctimonious or, like Electre, arrogant. At the end of his life, he found Lucile, the woman of his dreams.

It must now be plain that Giraudoux is his own best commentator: the full appreciation of any of his plays depends on a knowledge of all the others. This is perhaps the main obstacle to their survival in the theatre. The comedies and the more spectacular plays, if elaborately staged, will no doubt retain their appeal, but it is already clear that the others have had their day even on radio and television. Since 1957, when Robert Kemp declared 'Giraudoux en péril' (*Le Monde Hebdomadaire*, February 26 – March 6), productions have been on the wane; but, on the other hand, academic interest in Giraudoux has been thriving. Giraudoux's theatre is essentially literary and intellectual. Its appeal is in direct proportion to the degree of culture of those who listen to it or read it. It is, in fact, so rich that no limit can be set to the studies it may inspire. It may well be that, through these studies, it will, after a time, emerge once more, for in a world of changing values, ideas and attitudes which were not previously appreciated (such as, for instance, his Fourierism) will again become popular subjects of discussion. The artistic content of Giraudoux's plays is such that they can afford to wait; they have enough substance to satisfy many generations to come, as Jouvet, the man most closely involved in them, well knew: 'Les pièces changent de thème et de ton périodiquement, comme les serpents changent de peau . . . La pièce de théâtre est inépuisable. Un chef-d'œuvre est sans fin' (*La France Libre*, art. cit., pp. 348, 352).

Select Bibliography

GIRAUDOUX, JEAN   *Théâtre*   Paris, Bernard Grasset, 1958, 4 vols.

ALBÉRÈS, R. M.   *Esthétique et morale chez Jean Giraudoux*   Paris, Nizet, 1957

INSKIP, DONALD   *Jean Giraudoux: the Making of a Dramatist*   London, Oxford University Press, 1958

LESAGE, LAURENT   *Jean Giraudoux, His Life and Works*   University Park, Pennsylvania State University Press, 1959

VAN DE LOUW, GILBERT   *La Tragédie grecque dans le théâtre de Giraudoux*   Université de Nancy, 1967

4

MONTHERLANT   *H. T. Mason*

Whereas Anouilh's theatre abounds in technical ingenuity and Claudel's in dazzling display, each one revealing the hand of an obvious craftsman, Montherlant as playwright is almost entirely innocent of such devices. 'Pur', 'sobre', 'dépouillé': these are the words that appear most readily in criticism of his plays. In stagecraft as in language, his theatre is transparent, an artful concealment of art. Nor is Montherlant much given to discussion of theatrical technique. His *Carnets* are largely devoid of references to the theatre; when they occur they are generally in the line of the whole collection, *moraliste* and psychological rather than truly dramatic. The 'Notes de théâtre' and the various commentaries on individual plays are similarly scanty in clues about method and approach. If Montherlant discussed on occasion with the producer the detailed technical matters of performance, those discussions have not yet been made public. We gather that he insisted upon a realistic approach to detail in *Le Maître de Santiago*: the chevaliers should enter with snow on their boots, and he would have liked the actress playing Mariana to shiver with the cold (*Théâtre*, p. 381); but this does not take us very far into his craft. At best he provides, on rare occasions, an example of how his language becomes more select and forceful, like this from *Celles qu'on prend dans ses bras*:

> un homme entre dans une chambre où se trouve une femme qu'il aime, qu'il n'a jamais vue pleurer, et qui pleure. De premier jet, j'écris: 'Qu'y a-t-il? Mon Dieu! C'est vous que je vois pleurer!' Je biffe et j'écris: 'Qu'y a-t-il? Mon Dieu! C'est vous qui pleurez!' Je biffe et j'écris: 'Qu'y a-t-il? Mon Dieu! Je vous vois pleurer!' ('Notes de théâtre', *Théâtre*, p. 1096).

But such comments are exceptional. The reason is evident. Montherlant's plays are deliberately and resolutely psychological. As he told a BBC interviewer in 1962, his plays are not political, didactic, ideological or lyrical; they aim to show 'avec autant d'acuité que possible, les cheminements d'âmes humaines' (*Va jouer avec cette poussière*, p. 77). Hence all is subordinated to that one sole end. 'Une pièce de théâtre ne m'intéresse que si l'action extérieure, réduite à sa plus grande simplicité, n'y est qu'un prétexte à l'exploration de l'homme' (*Théâtre*, p. 1101). Or again:

> Quand je lis Shakespeare ou Racine, je ne me demande jamais si c'est ou non 'du théâtre'. J'y vais chercher une connaissance plus profonde des mouvements de l'âme humaine, des situations pathétiques, et de ces mots 'qui portent à leur cime une lueur étrange' (Hugo) (*Théâtre*, pp. 1103–4).

By 'théâtre', as he explains elsewhere, he means the well-constructed play, the ingenious but sterile plot, full of external actions: *péripéties, coups de théâtre*, even *quiproquos*. Instead, as we see from these comments, what counts is interior action: psychological portraiture, enhanced by careful attention to situation and language. Not only is the well-made play rejected; implicit in this order of priorities is a refusal also of *avant-garde* theatre, where situation and language become objects in their own right.

Even the *mise en scène* is soberly restrained to fit this end. Not for Montherlant the affirmations of Artaud, that the staging is the essentially theatrical part of theatre, much more so than the play as it is written and spoken. The decor is often reduced to anonymity, as in *Fils de personne*, or in *La Ville dont le prince est un enfant*, where the simplicity of the set in Act I serves only to stress the Abbé de Pradts's 'indifférence totale aux choses extérieures' (*Théâtre*, p. 853). Montherlant prides himself upon writing, for example in *Fils de personne*, 'une pièce qui n'existât que par son action intérieure' (*Théâtre*, p. 269). But in plays more dense in texture, such as *Port-Royal*, *Le Maître de Santiago*, *Le Cardinal d'Espagne*, or *La Reine morte*, a more deliberate use of the stage is to be observed. To take but one of these, in *Port-Royal* the decor is once again extremely simple, but a most effective use is made of light and darkness. At the beginning the August sun is pouring on to the stage through the open window. The convent is brutally open to the impact of the outside world, as the first words, spoken by the father of one of the nuns, makes immediately clear. The sun menaces, like the enemy outside; and the two are dramatically linked by the partial reopening of the shutters when the Archbishop arrives (*Théâtre*, p. 1036). The Archbishop brings with him not only the unwanted light of the mundane world, but colour too, gay and striking golds, reds and blacks; nonetheless, the effect is grotesque. The ecclesiastic dignitaries are as discordant on the aesthetic plane as on the religious:

'ils semblent une assemblée de magnifiques et un peu monstrueux insectes' (Théâtre, p. 1037); this alarming splash of colour is heightened yet
further when the forces of the law arrive a little later: 'insectes corus-
cants et effrayants – d'énormes insectes de la forêt vierge' (Théâtre, p.
1044). Amid surroundings of such pure austerity as Port-Royal, the
intrusion is presented by an effective artistic contrast. A similarly striking
contrast in colour tones occurs at the end, when the twelve 'Sœurs de la
nuit', clothed entirely in black, replace the dozen nuns of Port-Royal,
white-robed, who have been banished. A moment before, Sœur Angélique has departed into her own private hell of night, darkness and doubt;
the new Sisters are a visible symbol that, for a while at least, darker
elements have triumphed.

In between the two periods in the play when light falls upon the
stage, the shutters are drawn, by Sœur Angélique, for whom the long,
hot days of August convey a sense of imprisonment and abandonment by
God; they remind her of 'le char de feu quand il rasa la terre entre Elisée
et Elie' (Théâtre, p. 1028). Not only for Port-Royal in general, but for her
spiritual health, 'la menace monte avec le soleil' (Théâtre, p. 1026). To
shut out the light is to shut out, at least partly, her own anguish; she
thanks God for the night, and the serenity of the stars (Théâtre, p. 1027).
But Montherlant's use of light and darkness is not so simple as this.
Sœur Angélique fears the darkness too, for it represents increasingly for
her the way her loss of faith is developing apace, as she imagines herself
drawing closer to 'ces Portes des Ténèbres dont Dieu parla à Job' (Théâtre,
p. 1032). Only the starlit sky gives any relief to her in her doubts. Port-
Royal is a triumph dramatically of blacks and whites, enhanced by the
'coloured insects' in their absurd and ultimately irrelevant attire.

Similarly discreet, and similarly effective, is the playwright's use of
sound, especially sounds off-stage. The nuns of Port-Royal recite the office
of nones, commemorating the mystery of Christ's death, as they await
the arrival of the foreign 'Sœurs de la nuit' at the play's end. The final
act of La Guerre civile is played against an almost constant background of
vultures and crows, leaving us in no doubt that Pompée's cause is hopeless. In Le Cardinal d'Espagne the herald of death and desolation is a
barking dog throughout the final minutes; his is the last voice heard in
the play. Often these outside sounds function on two levels. The vultures
in La Guerre civile not only utter their ominous cries, at one stage near
the end, as Pompée's despair mounts, they hide the sun and (somewhat
improbably) cut off the light. More skilful because less far-fetched is the
way Cisneros's growing impotence as he nears death is linked to the dog
barking outside. Twice he tries to get someone to silence the dog; but this
man, who formerly held such authority in all Spain, cannot now find

anyone to obey his most modest command. Perhaps the most imaginative use of off-stage sounds occurs, however, in *La Ville dont le prince est un enfant*. As the Supérieur discusses with the Abbé de Pradts the spiritual crisis generated in the school by the expulsion of Sevrais, the school choir begins rehearsing in the room adjacent. Not only are we forcibly reminded of the school going about its daily activities in the midst of the crisis; not only do the purity of their voices and the sacred music they sing serve to emphasise the purity of the love between Sevrais and Souplier and the elevated spiritual atmosphere of the school; it also gives rise to a crucial development in the plot. Suddenly de Pradts realises, with the insight born of his love, even obsession, for Souplier, that the latter is missing from the choir. This is the cue for the Supérieur to tell him the catastrophic news that Souplier too has been expelled. It is a brilliant stroke on Montherlant's part to indicate thereby what de Pradts's love means to him: almost too improbable to command belief, it stays just within the bounds of credibility, for one feels that a man of extraordinary sensitivity and perception would be attuned to the voice of his beloved pupil to just this degree.

Equally impressive in Montherlant's theatre is the *absence* of sound. Consider, for instance, the elaborate tableau of apotheosis and betrayal at the end of *La Reine morte*, of which the author is rightly proud:

> Au delà encore du silence, il y a la solitude terminale, entre l'abandon et la trahison... Quand le page, quand le mauvais petit ange marche finalement, sur la pointe des pieds, dans la direction du troupeau, après un dernier regard à ce qu'il trahit et abandonne, nous sommes à la pointe extrême de ce qui est pour moi l'émotion, – bien au delà des cloches, de l'agenouillement et de la prière. (*Théâtre*, pp. 1101–2)

In the first two acts of *Le Maître de Santiago* 'quelques sonneries discrètes de cloche, mais sans en abuser', are heard; but even this muted accompaniment is stilled in the final act (*Théâtre*, p. 597), as the play mounts to its climax of mystic ecstasy. Compare the way Claudel handles a similar technical problem in *L'Annonce faite à Marie*; he even brings in a heavenly choir before the end! Montherlant's way, by contrast, is ever restrained. Psychology and interior action are the *raison d'être* of his drama; visual and auditory effects may help on occasion, but one must always beware of melodramatic abuse.

The same discretion marks the use of leitmotifs. Montherlant will have nothing of such an obvious device as making a character repeat a particular line: 'c'est le mystère en carton-pâte' (*Essais*, p. 1003). Such recurrent themes as he devises are more general. We have seen the use of light and darkness in *Port-Royal*, both as theme and as visual theatre.

Similarly, *La Reine morte* turns around the same contrast on both levels. 'La cour est un lieu de ténèbres', says Ferrante to Inès. 'Vous y auriez été une petite lumière' (*Théâtre*, p. 156). For him the faces around compose a collective face 'aux yeux d'ombre' (p. 182); as things abandon him, he is reminded of 'ces cierges qu'on éteint un à un, à intervalles réguliers, le jeudi saint, à l'office de la nuit'. His desperate attempt to illuminate the scene as he dies serves only to heighten the effect for Inès, the 'petite lumière', who returns, dead but in glory. The chiaroscuro is nowhere better indicated than in the analogy between Ferrante and the fireflies he loves: 'elles lui ressemblent: alternativement obscures et lumineuses, lumineuses et obscures' (*Théâtre*, p. 209). Such a fitful flickering vividly sums up 'ce nœud épouvantable de contradictions' (p. 234) that is Ferrante's character. This analysis could be taken much further, as it could be in *Le Maître de Santiago*; indeed, one must wonder whether Montherlant has not unduly exploited this particular theme in his theatre.

Water is another recurrent image. Inès is generally associated with water at its most fresh and natural. Her love is like the waterfall: 'elle ne lutte pas, elle suit sa pente' (*Théâtre*, p. 199); the water from the fountain sustains her: 'cette eau si fraîche, mon seul soutien de toute la journée' (*Théâtre*, p. 188); Ferrante sees her eyes looking up at the starlit sky 'comme des lacs tranquilles' (p. 232); her unborn baby moves within her 'comme une barque sur une eau calme' (p. 188); her love affair with Pedro has been played out in Inès's garden, 'assis au bord de la vasque, avec le jet d'eau qui envoyait parfois sur nous des gouttelettes', so that she has made of Pedro too 'cette vasque qui continuellement déborde, sans cesse remplie' (p. 152). Only when she thinks of the threatening future does the image become sombre: 'cette sensation d'une pluie noire sans cesse prête à tomber'. By contrast, it is the shallowness of Pedro's character which is emphasised when Ferrante contemptuously refers to him: 'le Prince est une eau peu profonde' (*Théâtre*, p. 158). As for Ferrante, he too is defined in terms of water, and in one of the finest images in the play: 'vouloir définir le Roi, c'est vouloir sculpter une statue avec l'eau de la mer' (p. 190). The water image has its place in *Le Maître de Santiago* also. An early clue to the deep affinity between Alvaro and Mariana is supplied by her when she enthusiastically supports his decision to serve water rather than wine to the Chevaliers. It is so pure: 'elle me brûle. On dirait que je mange du feu' (*Théâtre*, p. 599); just as that other symbol of purity, the Order of Santiago, 'ne brûle plus vraiment que dans le cœur de votre père' (p. 598), as Mariana's companion tells her. For Montherlant, such thirst is a sign of nobility; it is found again in Malatesta. The dramatist cites an Arab proverb à propos of both: 'Le lion et le rossignol sont toujours altérés' (pp. 551, 600).

It is characteristic of Montherlant that the imagery he employs is usually taken from nature, and is general rather than specific. *La Reine morte* is full of such poetic allusions. Inès's eyelash is reminiscent of a swallow's feather (*Théâtre*, p. 200); but L'Infante's cries have more desolate overtones of 'l'oiseau malurus, à la tombée du soir' (p. 221). Ferrante is like 'un lion tombé dans une trappe' (p. 211), and L'Infante tells Inès twice that kings have lions in their hearts (pp. 192, 221). Egas, on the other hand, is naught but 'une de ces mauvaises flammes qu'on voit se promener sur les étangs pourris' (p. 176). And so on. The allusions are deliberately universal, in keeping with the generally classical style that the dramatist aims at, particularly in his costume tragedies.

Such language is evidently noble, even rhetorical, and consciously stylised. Montherlant, characteristically unfashionable in the contemporary theatre, does not hesitate to aim at the sublime. Consider the following sentence, beautifully constructed, the period reaching out to ample length before the dying fall – a phrase which connotes Ferrante's world-weariness quite as much as it denotes it: 'Je me suis écoulé comme le vent du désert, qui d'abord chasse des lames de sable pareilles à une charge de cavaliers, et qui enfin se dilue et s'épuise; il n'en reste rien' (*Théâtre*, p. 212). Such a self-conscious artist clearly walks a delicate path in our iconoclastic age; the dividing-line from pomposity is narrow. When Caton says: 'le Meurtre et le Suicide, qui se promènent sans cesse parmi nous, et quelquefois, au passage, nous serrent doucement le bout des doigts' (*La Guerre civile*, p. 106), the hollowness of the personalisations seems patent to at least one reader's ear. It is not surprising that the difficulty grows with Montherlant's modern dramas. In *Celles qu'on prend dans ses bras* the analysis of Ravier's obsessive love for Christine is often subtle and moving, but unfortunately it is spoiled because the characters talk so much of the time like Renaissance heroes and ancient kings rather than ordinary people. One's patience is tried when Ravier, apparently a successful *roué*, tries to win over the young Christine in such terms as these: 'j'ai beau avoir pâti assez de vous avoir parlé à cœur si ouvert, rien ne m'empêchera jamais de continuer à le faire' (*Théâtre*, p. 770). If Montherlant avoids 'théâtre', in the bad sense, he is not always so successful with 'littérature'. From time to time he complains that a remark intended to be taken seriously has provoked laughter in the audience (e.g., *Essais*, p. 1316); the reader may be inclined to answer, a little uncharitably: 'The proof of the pudding...'

Montherlant's theatre is technically not without serious faults, therefore, to the extent that some would not name his as classical or neo-classical but simply as pseudo-classical. The present writer does not share this harsh view, but he sees that some evidence for it is forthcoming.

The handling of the plot is generally one of Montherlant's strongest qualities, so much so that for plays as spare in style as *La Ville dont le prince est un enfant* he is not unworthy to be mentioned, as he often has been, in the same breath as Racine. Whether or not, as Sevrais avers, 'Le théâtre classique n'est bien que dans la litote' (*Théâtre*, p. 885), throughout this play, Montherlant uses litotes well, evoking sympathy for the victims of sacrifice by understating the expression of it. Here economy is paramount; but even in less well-ordered plays it is rare to find repetitiveness of theme or superfluous scenes. Montherlant is particularly good at establishing unity of time. In *Port-Royal* he deliberately runs together into one incident two days in history at an interval of five days apart (*Théâtre*, p. 983); but more impressive than this technical detail is the way he infuses his play with a sense of tragic crisis from the opening words. Perhaps the outstanding aspect of *La Guerre civile* lies precisely in the moment of time chosen: Pompey, not at the moment of defeat, but in triumph, a brilliant paradox, for in the hour of triumph Pompey's later downfall is fully explained, and Caesar absent could hardly have been surpassed as a terrifying figure by Caesar actually on the stage. As for unity of place, Montherlant's *penchant* for closed worlds admirably suits his theatre: a school, a royal court, a convent, an army in exile, a family isolated, all these allow for greater focus and concentration. But there is one curious weakness in the handling of plot: the exposition. The author seems indifferent, and the results are often mechanical. *Le Maître de Santiago* starts out most effectively, demonstrating that with Montherlant the exposition can even be a strong point. But in *La Guerre civile* Acilius badly recapitulates recent history with a centurion who knows it all anyway (pp. 19–21), Ravier has to remind Christine of her own circumstances when she is already fully conversant with them (*Celles qu'on prend dans ses bras*, in *Théâtre*, p. 769), and a similarly improbable scene serves to fill in the past in *Fils de personne* (*Théâtre*, pp. 283–6). The machine, once warmed up, functions admirably; but it is sometimes slow in starting.

Before leaving the matter of technique, it is perhaps worth noting that Montherlant does not always obey his own injunctions about false theatricality. Occasionally he too gives way to *coups de théâtre* artificially invoked. *Malatesta*, in many respects one of his most interesting plays, is flawed by the denouement. Just when Malatesta's confrontation with Porcellio seems likely to attain to some tragic self-revelation, the author takes the melodramatic way out; instead of triumphing over his master by force of argument, Porcellio, in the best traditions of Renaissance cunning and villainy, poisons his wine, unnoticed by the latter but in plain view of the audience. (It is interesting to note that this is the only important detail where Montherlant diverges from the purely historical account of Malatesta's life, cf. *Théâtre*, p. 433.) The ending of *Don Juan* is melodrama pushed to the grotesque, and must have contributed to its failure when first produced in 1958; the death mask which the hero puts on sticks to his face and cannot be separated from it. Was Montherlant borrowing too mechanically from the mime of Marcel Marceau? But *Don Juan* represented a particular problem for Montherlant, because here, unlike in most of his plays, he tried to combine farce and tragedy. Montherlant is not especially gifted as a comic writer, and his humour, on the rare occasions when he attempts it, tends to be heavy-handed; but in *Don Juan* one faces the extra difficulty of not knowing whether to take the hero as a comic or a tragic figure. The author has maintained that the reasons for its unpopularity lie with the French audiences, who are steeped in the 'dogme des "genres tranchés"' (*Don Juan*, p. 181). It is an unconvincing excuse; dramatists like Giraudoux and Anouilh had long established the popularity of 'impure' tragedy. Perhaps Montherlant's real talent lies in the exploitation of a more traditional vein of tragic drama.

Montherlant's view of theatre is a surprisingly conservative one, if we are to take seriously a note written in 1948. In this he wondered whether the aesthetic of the novel was not the same as that of the theatre, 'quand ceux-ci sont d'une certaine qualité' (*Théâtre*, p. 373); the rest of the note suggests that the kind of theatre he is considering is the sort which he himself composes. He goes on to claim that the play can attain the same degree of psychological analysis as the novel, and he seems to feel that such theatre is merely the novel stripped down to its essentials. This is not the place to discuss the merits of this view; indeed one might argue that Montherlant has proved his case on grounds of psychological analysis alone. What seems astonishing, however, is the scant consideration shown for any other aspects of theatrical technique. As we have seen, Montherlant is a talented playwright in terms of staging, although there are curious omissions. When he falls from grace, is it because he does not take specifically theatrical considerations sufficiently into account? *Celles qu'on prend dans ses bras* seems a good example of a play which might well have been more successful as a psychological novel. It would make for an instructive exercise to look at Montherlant's most recent novel, *Les Garçons*, and to carry out a comparative study of it alongside *La Ville dont le prince est un enfant*, whose basic plot it repeats.

It is time, however, to consider Montherlant's success in psychological analysis, since here is where he makes his main claim to greatness. His tragic theatre is based on character, not situation: 'Le tragique dans mon théâtre est bien moins un tragique de situations qu'un tragique provenant de ce qu'un être contient en lui-même' (*La Guerre civile*, p. 186).

Such being the case, what kind of character? There is a strong family likeness among Montherlant's heroes, and the likeness can be identified, on his own admission, with elements in his personal make-up. By this one naturally does not mean that Montherlant is representing himself directly in people like Alvaro or Ferrante, an assertion all too often made in superficial criticism of his work, and one against which he has had constantly to battle. It would be more accurate to say that these characters represent tendencies or inclinations already found within himself. At the simplest level, he has transcribed phrases already used by himself in conversation. Cisneros in *Le Cardinal d'Espagne*, suffering an apparently fatal attack, asserts: 'On meurt comme on est, et on meurt comme on le veut', and goes on: 'Tout à l'heure, n'est-ce pas? j'ai crié: "Ah! c'est horrible"', to which, upon Cardona's affirmative reply, he adds: 'Vous ne direz à personne que j'ai crié cela' (*Le Cardinal d'Espagne*, p. 194). Montherlant in similar circumstances had uttered the same words (*Va jouer avec cette poussière*, p. 43). But the resemblances go deeper than this. The dramatist gives us a fascinating account of how, in the middle of the night after reading Guevara's play *Reinar*, the characters gradually became part of his own life and experience, to be given back to the world in *La Reine morte*:

> L'infante devenait malade d'orgueil, parce que je fus ainsi en certaines périodes de ma jeunesse. Le roi, dont le caractère est à peine esquissé chez Guevara, prenait forme, pétri de moments de moi . . . Chacune de ces créatures devenait tour à tour le porte-parole d'un de mes moi . . . Bref, *la Reine morte* rentrait dans la règle qui gouverne toutes mes œuvres . . . qu'elles ne sont jamais, l'une ou l'autre, que des fragments de [mes] mémoires. (*Théâtre*, p. 238)

Certain of these characteristics are particularly evident. Much has been made, not least by Montherlant himself, of his capacity for portraying the incoherence and contradictoriness within the individual personality. When asked by a BBC interviewer in 1962 what he considered the essential trait in his character, he replied: 'En ce qui concerne les sentiments, je trouve la diversité et la mobilité de ma nature' (*Va jouer avec cette poussière*, p. 77). From this springs the elusiveness of so many of his protagonists. In both *Fils de personne* and *Demain il fera jour*, the parents' attitudes towards Gillou keep shifting. The phrase 'Bien meilleur et bien pire', as applied by Ferrante to himself, sums his own fickleness up succinctly. A similar phrase is used of Don Juan: 'l'homme le pire et le meilleur du monde' (*Don Juan*, p. 106); indeed, Montherlant speaks of Don Juan in almost the exact terms he was to apply to himself some years later on the BBC: 'Le trait essentiel de son tempérament, c'est la mobilité'

(*Don Juan*, p. 178). Like Don Juan, Malatesta can swear sincere love to a woman in one scene, and in almost the next shrug it off completely, with equal sincerity. Such evanescence poses considerable problems for the artist, as Gide had seen many years before in *Les Caves du Vatican*: how do you retain any notion of unity if man is merely a bundle of unpredictable attitudes? Montherlant restates the difficulty in writing about *La Reine morte*: 'Le théâtre est fondé sur la cohérence des caractères, et la vie est fondée sur leur incohérence' (*Théâtre*, p. 254). He seems to resolve it by developing a notion of Destiny, which he describes, for instance, as the fourth character alongside the three who appear in *Fils de personne*: 'une fatalité absolue les relie et les entraîne dans leur destin' (*Théâtre*, p. 371). This vague statement is not very helpful, but it would seem that by Destiny Montherlant has in mind some regularly recurring pattern of personal characteristics when faced with new and changed circumstances. Ferrante does not know when he begins his all-important dialogue with Inès (Act III, Scene vi), that at the end of it he will have resolved on her death; but for the audience, his attitude towards her naive optimism in life and especially towards her revelation that she is pregnant are quite consistent with the scepticism and world-weariness shown earlier.

Scepticism and world-weariness occur frequently among Montherlant's heroes; once again the inspiration may be found in his own outlook: 'Un sentiment très fort, obsédant, de l'inanité, de l'inutilité et de l'absurdité de presque tout m'a dominé depuis ma jeunesse' (*Théâtre*, p. 690). It is, he says, the attitude described in Ecclesiastes: *Vanitas vanitatum*; the attitude of those 'qui sont morts au siècle, ou qui aspirent à l'être'. Alvaro, the nuns of Port-Royal, Cisneros, Jeanne of Castille, Pope Paul II, Caton, Georges Carrion all experience it. So many of Montherlant's people are 'fatigués'. A soliloquy by Caton may serve as a paradigm:

> Il [Pompée] est fatigué de lui-même; moi, je suis fatigué de me dévouer . . . Fatigué de me sentir capable de mourir pour un homme . . . Fatigué de me sentir capable de mourir pour une cause . . . Je suis fatigué du courage. Je suis fatigué de prévoir et de prédire, fatigué de ne m'être trompé jamais, fatigué du manque d'espérance ou plutôt de la mauvaise espérance, fatigué de la contradiction . . . (*La Guerre civile*, pp. 109–10)

The temptation, then, to withdraw from the world is ever-present – most of these characters, indeed, already have withdrawn, in whole or in part. Cisneros is torn between the temptation to renounce all and the temptation of keeping power; divided as he is, he finds himself constantly defeated in argument by Jeanne, whose scorn and horror of the world are absolute. Like Sœur Angélique in *Port-Royal*, she is attracted by night: 'Les ténèbres me plaisent; avec la fin du jour je suis mieux' (*Le Cardinal d'Espagne*, p. 113); but unlike Angélique, she has come to terms with it, has welcomed with open arms the chance of total solitude. Jeanne's renunciation has reached the point of madness and become an obsession. Even so, her single-minded contempt for the derisive advantages of living in the world is compelling, and Cisneros is shaken by it: 'elle m'a fait entendre la voix de la vérité sortant de la bouche de la folie' (*Le Cardinal d'Espagne*, p. 159). She enjoys the knowledge for which, one feels, so many of Montherlant's heroes are groping, the knowledge that self-realisation lies in isolation. Ferrante, Caton, Carrion, Pope Paul, Cisneros, Angélique, Don Juan are unable or unwilling to accept it. Perhaps the success of *Le Maître de Santiago* has much to do with the fact that Alvaro eventually achieves this insight, albeit at untold cost to his daughter.

It would be wrong to suggest that Montherlant has been tempted uniquely by this particular desire, has been a man unwillingly prolonging his stay in the world when he would really be better off in a private cell. One needs only to read his *Essais* and *Carnets* to realise the extent to which he has been in and part of society. Nonetheless, the attractions of retirement go hand in hand with a side of Montherlant frequently overlooked, and which characteristically emerges in his theatre. Too often his plays have been branded as 'théâtre de la grandeur', despite his own protestations to the contrary; the formula suggests stoic mastery of passions, heroic self-control. What it overlooks completely is the sensitivity, almost pathological on occasion, to which many of these heroes are prone. In *Fils de personne*, Georges's treatment of Gillou may be callous and blind, it nevertheless is the action of a man whose love for his son, subjected to disillusionment, has broken his heart (*Théâtre*, p. 283). The same disappointed parental love is one of the many elements in Ferrante's dispiritedness. If Pompée fails, it is largely because of a nervous deficiency which renders him incapable of striking a decisive blow at his enemy. Sometimes the physical manifestations of this sensibility are remarkable. Alvaro suffers a brusque transference from exaltation to depression when he sees how alone he is even among his own fellow-chevaliers (*Théâtre*, p. 618). Montherlant compares it to Pascal's fainting fit in similar circumstances; but he points out that he did not know of the incident when he was writing this scene – the insight is apparently a subjective one. Cisneros suffers near the end of *Le Cardinal d'Espagne* an attack that might be entirely explicable in terms of his extreme age and fatigue; but it is noticeable that it comes when Cardona tempts him to destroy all the result of his political work, a temptation all the more diabolical because it appeals so strongly to one side of Cisneros's nature. However, perhaps the best example of emotivity in the whole of Montherlant's drama is Malatesta: moved to tears by the Pope whom he had come to kill (*Théâtre*, p. 471), given to abrupt changes of mood ranging from wild fervour to profound dejection, he has, as his wife tells the Pope, 'nerfs de femme' (p. 502). When he decides to go and kill the Pope, he is so fired by the idea that he actually suffers a fever (p. 458). These are representations of Montherlant, the 'grand sensible', who recounts the following incident:

> J'écrivais l'acte I [de *Malatesta*] à Grasse, à l'hôtel Muraour, l'hiver 1943–1944. Le Maître d'hôtel qui me sert me dit une parole impolie. Je quitte la salle sur-le-champ, monte dans ma chambre, me jette sur mon lit, où je me mets à trembler convulsivement, parcouru de frissons (j'étends sur moi mon manteau), et en vérité tressautant sur le lit ... (p. 555)

The emotional reactions, and even the words used, find their way, he says, into Act I of *Malatesta*.

With this sensitivity goes a curious feeling of vulnerability which is very special to Montherlant, an almost primitive fear of losing a precious part of one's identity to another, a sense that at certain moments one is completely defenceless. When Pope Paul gives Malatesta three months' leave to go home, he is immediately assailed by doubts: 'Il y a comme une vague qui vient de déferler sur moi et qui me plonge dans un fond . . . dans un fond . . . Une extraordinaire tristesse qui soudain m'enfonce et me noie' (*Théâtre*, p. 509). It is as though the virtue has gone out of him, leaving him helpless; his natural suspiciousness increases, and as though to compensate for his sense of desolation, he reduces the leave to two and a half months. Malatesta expresses the same feeling of vulnerability: 'Sais-tu comment j'interprète le mythe de Psyché? L'Amour s'envole, tout est détruit, parce que Psyché a contemplé l'Amour pendant qu'il dormait. Cela veut dire qu'il ne faut jamais toucher à une âme quand elle est découverte et sans défense' (*Théâtre*, p. 528). So does Ferrante: 'il y a toujours quelques heures où un homme fort est si faible, moralement et physiquement . . . qu'en le poussant un peu on le ferait tomber' (*Théâtre*, p. 213). Distrust of oneself, constant wariness about others: these must be necesssary concomitants of such a mentality. Ferrante, in revealing all to Inès, has opened himself utterly to her; as the Infanta had warned her, he would take his revenge on her for being his confidante at his weakest moment. Even when he has killed Inès, he has not repaired the damage to himself; as Montherlant cogently puts it: 'Il meurt d'une émotion, sans doute, mais peut-être aussi parce qu'il a dit ses vérités: *il s'est vidé'* (*Théâtre*, p. 258; my italics). Even love, because it too is a form of commitment, can on occasion represent defeat. Parental love is always vulnerable in this respect, a theme we shall come to presently. So is erotic love. Bruno wonders about this paradox in *Un Incompris*: 'quelle chose étrange que vouloir se faire souffrir, et se créer un malheur dont la seule cause est soi!' (*Théâtre*, p. 418). In the very moment of seduction at the end of *Celles qu'on prend dans ses bras*, a moment which represents the triumph of everything he has schemed for throughout the play, Ravier knows that he is being defeated: 'Tu n'es pas à moi, tu ne me donnes rien, tout est faux dans ce que nous faisons . . .' (*Théâtre*, p. 833). One can think of many instances in Montherlant's plays where love is given freely and happily: Inès to Pedro, Sevrais to Souplier, the nuns to God. Nonetheless, it too can lead to loss of autonomy. One feels behind this particular fear the sensitivity of a man anxious to retain above all his personal freedom. The epigraph to the collection of essays *Textes sous une occupation* could hardly express better the aristocratic desire to avoid being embraced too closely:

> Aussi les hommes de mon espèce parleront-ils de plus en plus une langue incomprise du grand nombre. Leur pensée solitaire monte et ne s'étend pas, comme ce fil de fumée qui s'élève dans le désert, au crépuscule, des feux des nomades: ce fil pur et perdu, mince amarre entre la terre et le ciel. (*Essais*, p. 1377)

The longing to escape earth-bound mediocrity, to aspire to something immaculate, solitary, untouchable – one feels it could be the epigraph to *Le Maître de Santiago*, the end-point of striving for the tortured and blundering, like Ferrante and Cisneros.

Given, then, that there is so much distrust of life, the temptation not simply to withdraw from it but to abolish it altogether and all its works must also be present. We have already seen how Cisneros reacts to Cardona's insidious suggestions that he destroy all traces of his work. In commenting on this, Montherlant reveals how strong the temptation is for him: 'La tentation de détruire tout ce qu'on a construit est une des obsessions de mon œuvre. *Aedificabo et destruam* . . . a été pendant longtemps une des devises de cette œuvre' (*Le Cardinal d'Espagne*, p. 214). Indeed, this is truly 'la "grande tentation"' (p. 261). For the one physical suicide in *Brocéliande*, there are several who drive themselves to death through their obsessions: Cisneros, Don Juan, Pompée, to name no more.

Perhaps it is easy to see why, in view of all this, Montherlant, himself an unbeliever, understands so well certain states of religious faith and exaltation. The problems facing his heroes always involve a judgement on the quality of life. They are essentially moral, subjective problems, what a man owes to his image of himself. However bewildered, the protagonist never loses sight of the possibility that his life might be better, not socially or financially (only the mediocre in Montherlant's theatre ever care about money), but spiritually. Ferrante is lost in contradictions that will turn him into a killer of his son's wife; yet he never ceases to believe in God, or consider himself 'enveloppé de la main divine' (*Théâtre*, p. 230). Montherlant admits that the Georges of *Demain il fera jour* (probably the most unattractive of all his heroes) has become odious – yet not wholly so; even he may be pitied *inter alia* for his 'émotivité' and for the horror he feels at the deed he accomplishes in sacrificing his son (*Théâtre*, p. 748). Even a Pompée demoralised and ready for defeat makes the noble (and as it turns out, frustrated) gesture of letting Acilius go. If these characters fall from grace, they do so with some sense of values still preserved. Montherlant understands the idealist aspirations of the human personality. For Jeanne 'Dieu est le rien' (*Le Cardinal d'Espagne*, p. 131), and likewise for Alvaro in *Le Maître de Santiago*, to use the dramatist's own words, 'Son Dieu est néant plus qu'amour' (*Théâtre*, p. 674). They still, nonetheless, retain a sense of the absolute; in a world of absurdity they do not deliver themselves up to an existentialist ethic based solely on acts. These characters have an element in their make-up that a religious person would not hesitate to call 'soul'; to use a Montherlant expression, they are 'êtres *de valeur*'. If these people are, despite this, overthrown, it is above all because they lack self-knowledge. Ferrante speaks for the others when he wishes to have done with all the terrible anomalies in his personality; but he is more lucid than most in knowing that he does not know himself.

This search for identity is reflected in one element of dramatic structure that has not yet been sufficiently stressed in Montherlant's work; it is the theme of parent and child. Of Montherlant's fifteen published plays, seven (*L'Exil*, *Fils de personne*, *Demain il fera jour*, *Le Maître de Santiago*, *La Reine morte*, *Le Guerre civile*, *Don Juan*) contain an important parental relationship, centring on father and son in all but *Le Maître de Santiago* and Montherlant's early play, *L'Exil*. (Clearly maternal love, as in *L'Exil*, takes less active hold upon his imagination. Marie's affection for Gillou in *Fils de personne* and *Demain il fera jour* is seen as weak and indulgent.) Montherlant allowed himself historical licence in order to involve Pompée's son in the scene at Dyrrachium (*La Guerre civile*, p. 203), and resisted only with some difficulty the temptation to include Caton's son also (pp. 198–201).

These details are already impressive enough; but if one goes further and looks at the quasi-parental relationships as well, then the list is considerably increased. The family link between Cisneros and Cardona in *Le Cardinal d'Espagne* is uncle and nephew, but in essential dramatic respects they form a father–son relationship. This is not the Cardinal's only son, however. He regards the King, for whose coming the whole play is a preparation (it might have been entitled *En attendant le roi*), as his child: 'Je l'ai créé, je suis son père' (p. 168); and because he has created the King, the Cardinal owes him the obligation of everything he has lived for. Not only does Don Juan have a son devoted and grateful because he has taught him 'la connaissance des êtres' (p. 121); his mistress Ana treats him as more of a father than her real father: 'C'est vous qui m'avez rendue femme. Cela est beaucoup plus que m'avoir mise au monde. C'est vous qui m'avez mise au monde' (pp. 159–60). Likewise, Malatesta's love for his young mistress Vannella, 'cette fille chérie' (*Théâtre*, p. 511), has given a new joy to life, just as had the love of his son for Georges: 'J'avais cru que c'était ceci ou cela qui donnait un sens à ma vie: je voyais maintenant que c'était d'aimer' (*Théâtre*, p. 285). (Another instance of the lover–father relationship is supplied by the lieutenant Auligny: 'Il crut découvrir, comme par une révélation, ce qui faisait la singularité de son sentiment pour Ram. C'était qu'il se sentait devant elle ensemble un amant et un père' – *La Rose de sable*, Paris: Gallimard, 1968, p. 344.) Montherlant does not therefore fear to compare family love with sexual love, or indeed to see the common element in all forms of love. As he says in the Postface to *La Ville dont le prince est un enfant*, 'il n'y a qu'un amour' (*Théâtre*, p. 939: one is reminded of the phrase from Lacordaire about human and divine love which Claudel liked quoting: 'il n'y a pas deux amours'). *La Ville* explores another aspect of the matter; the staff at the school are acting *in loco parentis* to the boys. As in *Fils de personne*, says the playwright, 'c'est encore une histoire d'éducation gauchie par la passion' (*Théâtre*, p. 939). As for *La Reine morte*, apart from Inès's unborn child, who plays so important a part in the action, there is a veritable profusion of children, the children of Ferrante: not only Pedro, but the Infanta, Inès and Dino. The Infanta, he says, 'est le fils que j'aurais dû avoir (*Théâtre*, p. 146). With Inès, his daughter-in-law, he confesses himself as might a father to a daughter; she returns the confidence with filial trust, and is betrayed. Dino (whom Montherlant created *ex nihilo*: cf. *Théâtre*, p. 241) brings, like the other pages, the innocence of childhood into the King's life, and reminds him nostalgically of Pedro at the same age (p. 180). In *Port-Royal*, a blood relationship exists between Mère Agnès and Sœur Angélique, her niece, but clearly, in the climactic scene between them, Agnès becomes a spiritual mother to the other in her torment.

In brief, then, we may discern dramatically important links between parent and child in all but four of Montherlant's plays and in all the important ones. Even in two of the others there are significant analogies. Ravier's love for Christine (*Celles qu'on prend dans ses bras*), compounded of tenderness and desire, is a counterpart in frustration to the happy loves of Don Juan for Ana and of Malatesta for Vannella, and she is still, like the other two girls, very young and innocent; Ravier, indeed, compares his love to that of her parents: 'Je l'aime plus que ne l'aiment son père et sa mère ensemble' (*Théâtre*, p. 788). Finally, in *Brocéliande*, the action is inaugurated when the hitherto bourgeois and mediocre M. Persilès, learning that he is descended from Saint Louis, suddenly discovers the potential for greatness within himself: what one might call the parental influence at several removes.

Why this predilection in Montherlant? There are probably a number of reasons, and they can only be touched on here. The first and perhaps most obvious is that for characters isolated from the world in one way or another, the love of a child or parent confers value on living as almost nothing else does. Here is a rare opportunity truly to communicate with another human being. The parent has created the child, and for that fact alone he deserves his child's love, as Alvaro obtains Mariana's: 'Il m'a créée, je l'aime' (*Théâtre*, p. 645); we have already seen a similar gratitude expressed by Ana to Don Juan for making her a woman. Mariana, indeed, in a moment of mystic ecstasy, confuses her father with God and Christ (pp. 651–3). Pompée in his desolation retains at least the loyalty of his son Sextus: 'Mon fidèle petit homme' (*La Guerre civile*, p. 163). The parent may in fact teach 'la connaissance des êtres', as Don Juan does to his son, as Georges attempts to do with Gillou or Ferrante with Pedro.

But alas! the relations of parent and child are strewn with betrayal and sacrifice. 'Dans *la Reine morte* et dans *Fils de personne*, les enfants trahissent les adultes. Dans *la Ville*, les adultes trahissent les enfants' (*Théâtre*, p. 258, note). Even the faithful Alcacer lets his father Don Juan down by thinking of how he will use the latter's money after his death (Act III, Scene iv), while Cardona repays by base treachery his uncle Cisneros's attempt to educate him in the ways of courage. Conversely, Alvaro betrays his daughter by seducing her out of life and into a convent. The sacrifice of child by parent is as common as its counterpart. Montherlant himself notes that, in addition to Alvaro's act, Ferrante sacrifices Pedro (and, we might add, Inès), Georges sacrifices Gillou, and Geneviève in *L'Exil* agrees to sacrifice her son; he observes: 'Le sacrifice d'Abraham est décidément dans mon théâtre une obsession!' (*Théâtre*, p. 660, note). Where there is love, as we have already noticed in Montherlant's drama, there is the risk of betrayal. Hence an important source of dramatic tension.

But there is more than this to the alternation of sacrifice and treason. Just as parents have physically procreated their children, so it is entirely in keeping with Montherlant's theatre that they should wish to engender them morally as well. 'Pour l'homme, ses seuls vrais fils sont spirituels' (*Théâtre*, p. 375). If Georges, Ferrante and Alvaro express in varying degrees the anguished fear of betrayal by their progeny, it is more than the simple disappointment of a father. These children strike at something fundamental in the parent himself. 'Les enfants dégradent', says Alvaro (*Théâtre*, p. 624); 'la famille par le sang est maudite' (p. 633). A family proliferates without reason, unless man uses his higher qualities to make it a true family 'par l'élection et l'esprit'. As Thierry Maulnier pointed out in an interesting study, Inès represents for Ferrante a weakness to which he is in danger of consenting, and Georges abandons Gillou in *Fils de personne* because the latter does not give back to him a satisfactory image of himself (*Théâtre*, p. 362). Just as Ferrante seeks to discover his own identity and in so doing strikes at his children, so are Georges and Alvaro seeking their true self-image in those they have brought into the world. Alvaro's love of God, says Montherlant, is 'l'amour pour l'idée qu'il se fait de soi' (*Théâtre*, p. 674); so is his love of Mariana. In Ferrante, Alvaro and Georges the full ramifications of parental love are revealed.

One further development, however, needs to be noted. In acting thus, these fathers are acting against themselves. Ferrante, in killing Inès, murders his unborn grandson, an apt symbol of the destruction he is practising upon himself, just as Alvaro, by drawing his daughter into the convent, will ensure the end of his family line. They succumb to the 'grande tentation' to destroy their work, Ferrante out of weakness, Alvaro out of principle. Thereby they relate to another great theme in Montherlant – the theme of suicide. Living life fully may also mean losing it (and it will certainly mean great suffering); here is the tragic paradox in these plays. Noble, demanding, occasionally superhuman and even inhuman, such are the aspirations of Montherlant's heroes. Yet they remain, not two-dimensional figures, but individuals who, infused by the author's sensitivity, lay claim to our sympathy. Montherlant points out that his earliest play, *L'Exil*, written when he was only eighteen years old, has a central idea: 'les abstractions ne sont rien, il n'y a que les êtres' (*Théâtre*, p. 11). The same may be said of his whole *œuvre*.

Select Bibliography

MONTHERLANT, HENRY DE
  Théâtre   Paris, Gallimard (Bibliothèque de la Pléiade), 1965
  Essais   Paris, Gallimard (Bibliothèque de la Pléiade), 1963
  Brocéliande   Paris, Gallimard, 1956
  Don Juan   Paris, Gallimard, 1958
  Le Cardinal d'Espagne   Paris, Gallimard, 1960
  La Guerre civile   Paris, Gallimard, 1965

BATCHELOR, JOHN W.   *Existence and Imagination: The Theatre of Henry de Montherlant* St Lucia, University of Queensland Press, 1967
BEER, JEAN DE   *Montherlant, ou l'Homme encombré de Dieu* Paris, Flammarion, 1963
BLANC, ANDRÉ   *Montherlant: Un Pessimisme heureux* Paris, Centurion, 1968
CRUICKSHANK, JOHN   *Montherlant* Edinburgh and London, Oliver and Boyd, 1964
SIPRIOT, PIERRE   *Montherlant par lui-même* Paris, Seuil, 1953

5

ANOUILH   W. D. Howarth

If we take 1952–3, the years of *Les Chaises* and *Godot*, as the division between 'old' and 'new' in the French theatre, two-thirds of Jean Anouilh's work still falls on the far side of the dividing-line. His formative years as a young theatre-goer were spent in the Paris of the late nineteen-twenties, and among the influences he has acknowledged from these years are those of Giraudoux and Pirandello. It is certainly to the 'vieux sorcier sicilien' that he can now be seen to owe the clearest debt, even if from this point of view his earliest plays in the naturalistic manner give the impression of a 'false start'. Unaffected by the surrealism of his youth, he has been equally little influenced by trends in post-war drama. Though the outlook of many of his characters may resemble the despairing nihilism that we associate with the philosophy of the Absurd, the means of expression are totally different. Dialogue and characters, however idiosyncratic, have a traditional, logical coherence, and are rooted in a rationalistic attitude towards the world and man's place in it.

While the intellectual content of his serious theatre is sufficient to earn him the respect of cultured audiences (in spite of the condescending attitude that it has been fashionable to adopt towards him in some quarters), this is a factor which always takes second place to considerations of an aesthetic nature. Unlike a Beckett, whose characters are tormented with metaphysical *Angst*, Anouilh deals with systems of ethical values: he shows us the behaviour of men and women in a social context, not the struggles of Man in the grip of fate. His heroes do not share an identical moral code: the essence of their 'heroism' rather consists in their attempt to be true to an ideal, to defend the integrity of their personality against the corruptions, the compromises and the hypocrisy of the world they live in. The sympathy we are induced to feel for them is akin to the 'admiration' Corneille sought to arouse for his heroes: it does not always go hand in hand with moral approval. It is based on a playwright's intuitive sense of audience reaction, which enables him to enlist our sympathy for a hero animated by an instinctive, amoral urge to stand out defiantly against the values of a society which, by and large, represents that in which we live. Such, at any rate, are the central characters of the early 'pièces noires', with their antithetical division into 'purs' and 'ignobles', doctrinaires and pragmatists. The attitude of the former is governed by an ideal system of values, arbitrary and subjective, intolerant and intransigent, which leads them to reject happiness, hope and even life itself, if these are only to be had by means of compromise. The others, the realists who accept life as it is, are usually sufficiently caricatured for us to see them through the disapproving eyes of the heroes themselves, whose dialectical system we are persuaded to adopt as valid for the duration of the play, however gratuitous it may seem when analysed outside the dramatic context to which it belongs.

The earliest of the series, Frantz of *L'Hermine* (1929 – the date given, unless otherwise indicated, is that of the composition of each play), whose extreme individualism cuts across all conventional moral codes – his 'soif de la pureté' leads him to commit murder – can perhaps by analogy serve as a pointer to the equally individualistic motivation of later heroes whose behaviour is less obviously amoral. On the whole, however, this is one of the least satisfactory of Anouilh's plays. Frantz represents an interesting psychological study, which might have been developed effectively in a novel; but the play does not offer enough scope for the presentation of such a character in depth, and it remains a crude character-sketch rather than a finished portrait. The next two plays, *Jézabel* (1932) and *La Sauvage* (1934), show a considerable advance: especially in *La Sauvage*, character and action are successfully combined, and the psychological motivation in both plays carries more conviction. Paradoxically, both Thérèse (in *La Sauvage*) and Marc (in *Jézabel*) refuse the escape from a life of poverty and hardship, which for Frantz had been the essential condition of his 'purity'; for them, on the contrary, 'le bonheur' must be rejected as demanding too great a sacrifice of their individualism:

> Vous me dégoûtez tous avec votre bonheur! On dirait qu'il n'y a que le bonheur sur la terre. Hé bien, oui, je veux me sauver devant lui. Hé bien, oui, moi, je ne veux pas me laisser prendre par lui toute vivante. Je veux continuer à avoir mal et à souffrir, à crier, moi!

This attitude is to be more typical of Anouilh's heroes – indeed, the opening words of this quotation are spoken by Antigone as well as by Thérèse – but it is just as gratuitous, founded on exactly the same sort of Romantic idealism, as Frantz's. However, within its dramatic context Thérèse's renunciation of the man she loves provides the only possible end to the play. At the point of decision, the pull of her past, the precocious experience, the moral and physical mediocrity represented by her family, prove irresistible. As she suggests, there is even a peace and a serenity to be had when one experiences one's full measure of suffering:

> . . . être enfin arrivé tout au bout de son mal. Vous ne le savez pas, vous autres, mais tout au bout du désespoir, il y a une blanche clairière où l'on est presque heureux . . . Un drôle de bonheur, qui n'a rien de commun avec votre bonheur à vous. Un affreux bonheur. Un sale, un honteux bonheur.

Roméo et Jeannette (1945) provides the last of these 'variations on a theme' in the naturalistic idiom. Jeannette is another of these 'affamés d'absolu' whose purity dictates a dramatic gesture of refusal: 'Je ne veux pas devenir grande. Je ne veux pas apprendre à dire oui. Tout est trop laid.' Unlike Serge Radine, for whom this play shows an 'évolution fâcheuse et régressive . . . le thème même qui a inspiré *La Sauvage*, mais regrettablement déformé et comme rapetissé' (Anouilh, Lenormand, Salacrou, p. 36), I find *Roméo et Jeannette* a positive advance on earlier 'pièces noires'. This is the nearest Anouilh has come to Ibsen's peculiar blend of naturalism and symbolism, in which elements of the realist setting are themselves used to suggest symbolically the menace of impending catastrophe: the incoming tide, a reminder of the elemental forces of nature, serves precisely the same function at the denouement as the millrace in *Rosmersholm*. It is not only the title of the play that suggests a pair of 'star-crossed' lovers: Jeannette's final gesture seems less arbitrary, more inevitable than the renunciation of Thérèse or Marc. We achieve a greater degree of involvement with the character; and since Frédéric goes to his death with her, the ending is aesthetically satisfying at a deeper level than that of a purely naturalistic play. Their death possesses something of the ritual sacrifice, and this very individual adaptation of the Romeo and Juliet myth achieves true poetic quality.

However, by the time *Roméo et Jeannette* was written, Anouilh had already embarked on a parallel series of more imaginative variations on the same theme. *Eurydice* (1941) puts the tragic protagonists of the Orpheus myth into the by now familiar milieu of third-rate itinerant musicians and touring dramatic companies, and the setting alternates between a railway waiting-room and a squalid hotel bedroom. References to the classical myth are discreet but powerfully evocative; there are few more effective 'curtains' in Anouilh's whole theatre than the close of Act I, where the hero and heroine, having fallen in love at first sight, assume, as it were, the identity of their mythological counterparts ('. . . Comment t'appelles-tu? – Orphée. Et toi? – Eurydice').

When Death, in the person of Monsieur Henri, has taken Eurydice away, Orphée's despairing pleas succeed in bringing her back; but he cannot keep to the bargain, and tormented by jealousy and doubt, looks into her eyes and loses her again. Like other heroes, he cannot compromise with life: 'Vivre! vivre! Comme ta mère et son amant, peut-être, avec des attendrissements, des sourires, des indulgences et puis des bons repas, après lesquels on fait l'amour et tout s'arrange. Ah! non. Je t'aime trop pour vivre!' Finally, Monsieur Henri offers him the chance to rejoin Eurydice, and like *Roméo et Jeannette* the play ends with a poetic statement of the view that love can only be preserved untarnished in death. Whatever we may think of this as a comment on real life, it is a valid conclusion from the premises established by the playwright, and Anouilh's version of the myth has dramatic consistency as well as expressing a poignant sense of the vulnerability of Romantic idealism.

One can easily understand why, when *Antigone* was first performed in 1944, the play's dramatic form should have received less attention than its topicality. Antigone herself, another Romantic idealist – 'Moi je suis là pour autre chose que pour comprendre. Je suis là pour vous dire non et pour mourir' – was readily identified with the Resistance, while Créon the realist could easily be seen in contemporary terms as a collaborator. But the very lack of any clear-cut 'message', the fact that it could be – and was – interpreted both as a tribute to the spirit of the Resistance and as an attack on the futility of all opposition to German occupation, is a plain enough indication to us, even if it was not to many of the play's first spectators, that Anouilh was less interested in political allegory than in the aesthetic possibilities of a clash between the same sort of attitudes that he had already portrayed in earlier plays.

More than any other of his plays, *Antigone* raises the question of the possibility of 'tragedy in modern dress'. Anouilh's treatment of the subject would appear, like Sophocles's, to fulfil the Hegelian condition of 'ambiguity' recently reiterated by Camus: '. . . Antigone a raison, mais Créon n'a pas tort'. If other plays reveal something more akin to the black-and-white characterisation of melodrama, here Anouilh has established a fine balance between the emotional sympathy we feel for Antigone in her refusal to obey Créon, and the intellectual assent we give to Créon's defence of the existing order of things. It is true that the debate between the two characters lacks the religious and philosophical dimension that it possesses in Sophocles's play; though no doubt most modern playgoers would be prepared to accept the notions of a purely human tragedy, lacking this metaphysical character. However, even on this score there may be grounds for hesitation with regard to *Antigone*: H. Gignoux perceptively observes that 'ce ne sont pas deux affirmations qui s'affrontent, mais deux négations. De là, un sentiment de gratuité';

and for him the play remains 'un drame psychologique en marge d'une tragédie' (*Jean Anouilh*, pp. 113, 115). Others have objected to the colloquialism of the style and the deliberate anachronisms – references to characters knitting or smoking; mentions of coffee, bloodhounds, or films – as being inconsistent with the dignity of tragedy; however, it can be argued that the author has been successful in making the characters live in twentieth-century terms without vulgarising or cheapening his subject-matter. Perhaps the feature of the play which does stand in the way of our accepting it as a tragedy is the very feature that Anouilh himself uses to point the tragedy: the Prologue-Chorus who introduces and comments on the action. Apt though his definition may be: 'C'est propre, la tragédie. C'est reposant, c'est sûr . . . Dans la tragédie on est tranquille. D'abord, on est entre soi. On est tous innocents en somme. . . Et puis, surtout, c'est reposant, la tragédie, parce qu'on sait qu'il n'y a plus d'espoir, le sale espoir . . .' such a definition surely has no place within a tragedy itself: we become too conscious of the author pulling the strings. And while this no doubt makes for excellent *theatre*: 'Voilà. Ces personnages vont vous jouer l'histoire d'Antigone. Antigone, c'est la petite maigre qui est assise là-bas, et qui ne dit rien. Elle regarde droit devant elle. Elle pense. Elle pense qu'elle va être Antigone tout à l'heure . . .' it is a kind of theatre too contrived and self-conscious to produce the direct emotional impact of tragedy.

Médée (1946) is the slightest of the three plays on classical subjects. It is technically less interesting than *Eurydice* or *Antigone*; and as for style, although Anouilh has been more discreet in his anachronisms, there is an uneasy tension between the prosaic colloquialism of some of the dialogue and the daemonic character of the legendary sorceress and murderer, which comes out so well in the magnificent incantatory invocation to Evil, a soliloquy of great poetic force:

> C'est maintenant, Médée, qu'il faut être toi-même. O mal! Grande bête vivante qui rampe sur moi et me lèche, prends-moi. Je suis à toi cette nuit, je suis ta femme. Pénètre-moi, déchire-moi, gonfle et brûle au milieu de moi. Tu vois, je t'accueille, je t'aide, je m'ouvre . . . Pèse sur moi de ton grand corps velu, serre-moi dans tes grandes mains calleuses, ton souffle rauque sur ma bouche, étouffe-moi. Je vis enfin! Je souffre et je nais. Ce sont mes noces. C'est pour cette nuit d'amour avec toi que j'ai vécu . . .

A striking feature of the play is the shift in sympathy that is for the first time discernible here. Médée is the familiar intransigent idealist; she has sacrificed everything for Jason in the past, and now insists that he shall continue to sacrifice everything for her. Logically, her claim is undeniable, and Jason's desertion of her is indefensible. But Médée's arrogant rejection of all the values of the world around her alienates much of the sympathy we might otherwise feel, and we are more inclined to side with Jason the opportunist, when he says:

> Poursuis ta course. Tourne en rond, déchire-toi, bats-toi, méprise, insulte, tue, refuse tout ce qui n'est pas toi. Moi, je m'arrête. Je me contente. J'accepte ces apparences aussi durement, aussi résolument que je les ai refusées autrefois avec toi. Et s'il faut continuer à se battre, c'est pour elles maintenant que je me battrai, humblement, adossé à ce mur dérisoire, construit de mes mains entre le néant absurde et moi.

Some critics who wrote about Anouilh in the early post-war years saw him as having reached a dead end; they tended to dwell on his repetitive use of similar themes and settings, in a series of plays all exhibiting a misanthropic, nihilistic view of life. However, even without the benefit of hindsight, the 'pièces noires' themselves should have provided clues to future lines of development: particularly a more imaginative attitude towards dramatic technique, suggesting an escape from the restricting formula of the 'well-made play'. The showman-commentator of *Antigone* is the most obvious example, but *Eurydice*, with its dislocated time-sequence, and *Roméo et Jeannette*, with its infusion of poetic atmosphere into prosaic subject-matter, also offer clear pointers. Above all, the 'pièces roses' of the same period show a very different inspiration. The 1942 volume of this name contains three plays: *Le Bal des voleurs* (1932), *Le Rendez-vous de Senlis* (1937) and *Léocadia* (1939); and we may add to these *Le Voyageur sans bagage* (1936) which, although published in the volume *Pièces noires*, is in many ways more typical of the 'pièces roses'.

Were it not for its early date, one might well take *Le Bal des voleurs* as self-parody. The same antithesis underlies the characterisation: while Gustave, the young apprentice pickpocket, is a perfectionist, Peterbono and Hector, his associates, resemble those seedy *bons vivants*, the fathers of Thérèse and Orphée; and the contrast between Juliette and Eva anticipates that between Antigone, the vulnerable idealist, and the more worldly Ismène. But *Le Bal des voleurs* is a 'comédie-ballet'. This is Theatre, interpreted as pure entertainment: an escapist world of fantasy and make-believe, in which respectable financiers act like crooks (and dress up as *apaches*), while professional pickpockets are seen as honest working men (who dress up as 'grands d'Espagne'). The charade is set going and kept in motion by Lady Hurf, the first of a series of amiable, eccentric aristocrats who provide the author with a stage persona in which he can exploit all the tricks and surprises at his command. Throughout, there runs the metaphor of life seen as the acting out of arbitrarily-assigned roles, for which one must constantly dress up and assume disguises; a metaphor which reaches its comic climax in the final ballet-sequence: '. . . un petit pas redoublé qui sert de finale et que les personnages de la pièce, entrés par toutes les portes, dansent en échangeant leurs barbes.'

Le Voyageur sans bagage has the same subject as Giraudoux's Siegfried: an amnesic victim of the Great War who rediscovers his lost identity. But unlike Giraudoux's, a political allegory with far-reaching philosophical implications whose hero lacks conviction on a purely human level, Anouilh's play accommodates the situation to his own characteristic preoccupations. As Gaston progressively realises that he has at last found the family to which he belongs, so the picture he builds up of the young man that he had been, and of the personal relationships he had been involved in, becomes more and more odious, until at last he seizes a chance to invent an imaginary family connection with a young orphan so as to repudiate his real family, and reject the hateful past to which he would again be enslaved. He thus turns his back on reality, in a denouement potentially as 'black' as that of any of the other plays. What saves Le Voyageur sans bagage from being a typical 'pièce noire' is the element of creative fantasy, the approach to personality in Pirandellian terms of reality and pretence. Like Pirandello's Henry IV, Gaston begins by being the centre of a 'performance' stage-managed by others; but like Henry, Gaston too reaches the point where he has to take the performance into his own hands, stepping outside the framework that the Duchess (another of Anouilh's eccentrics) and his real family have arranged for him, and creating his own future. Much more than the extravagant characterisation of the Duchess, or the scenes of pure comedy at the beginning and end of the play, it is this positive twist given to the motif of the 'second chance' which makes of Le Voyageur sans bagage a 'pièce rose' in all but name. At least, this is surely our reaction in the theatre, even if on reflection we realise that the happy ending is achieved only by the most artificial contrivance, and that the underlying view of life is hardly optimistic.

This escapist solution of the problem of the second chance also characterises both Le Rendez-vous de Senlis and Léocadia. In the former play Georges, the hero, himself stage-manages the 'illusionist' escape from reality; tired of the hypocrisy and turpitude of his real life (in which he, his parents, his friend Robert and Robert's wife Barbara – who is Georges's mistress – all live as parasites on his rich wife), he has embarked on an ideal relationship with a young girl, for whose benefit he has created a fictitious family. Now he proposes to introduce Isabelle to his imaginary 'parents', professional actors hired for the purpose. The plan miscarries, and the truth comes out; but Isabelle's youth, courage and optimism give him the strength he needs to renounce his past and make a fresh start. Despite resemblances between Georges and the despairing heroes of the 'pièces noires', the systematic nihilism of these plays is lacking, and *le bonheur* is no longer 'ignoble', but challenging and heroic ('Vous êtes terrible, Isabelle . . . – Je suis le bonheur. Et c'est toujours un peu terrible, le bonheur'). *Le Rendez-vous de Senlis* is the most self-consciously theatrical of all the early plays. The life-as-theatre metaphor is present throughout; for instance, in this passage from the end of the play:

Robert: Vous êtes comédien, je crois, Monsieur?
Philémon: Oui, Monsieur.
Robert: Alors vous allez pouvoir me donner un conseil. Nous avons fini notre scène: comment croyez-vous que nous devons sortir?
Philémon: Mais, Monsieur, une sortie, cela ne s'indique pas comme ça . . . Cela dépend de la situation, du personnage. Quel personnage jouez-vous?
Robert: Les traîtres.

Far from being superficial decoration, the metaphor is essential to Anouilh's conception of the subject, and helps to give the play its full meaning. Whereas Robert and the other parasites are irrevocably wedded to the only part they are capable of playing, Georges manages to escape because he has had the imagination to cast himself in a new role, and the strength of purpose, aided by Isabelle, to make the imaginary become real.

In *Léocadia*, another encounter between fantasy and reality, the fantasy-world is again controlled by one of Anouilh's rich eccentrics, who in order to cure her nephew of a despairing love for a dead actress, has reconstructed in her park the decor of their brief relationship: taxi-driver, ice-cream vendor and *maître d'hôtel* have all been engaged, so that the Prince may indulge in a perpetual re-enacting of his three-day idyll. The Duchess's plan now reaches its climax, as Amanda, a young milliner's assistant who exactly resembles the dead Léocadia, arrives in this world of make-believe, where ultimately her warm, generous nature succeeds in exorcising the ghost of the extravagant, egocentric actress. Despite echoes of *Le Rendez-vous de Senlis*, the obsessive preoccupation with purity and corruption is absent from this play: what Amanda has to overcome in the Prince is really aristocratic world-weariness, not the accumulated burden of a shameful past; and here it is reality, not fantasy, which offers the means of escape. But it would not do to be too solemn about the 'theme' of a play which, like *Le Bal des voleurs* (or the very early sketch *Humulus*), represents a gratuitous exercise of the author's fancy, creating a topsy-turvy world which can only exist in the imagination. And the profound difference which separates Anouilh's highly rational notion of 'nonsense' from that of the surrealists or of the Theatre of the Absurd is well brought out by this fragment of dialogue between Amanda and the *marchand de glaces*:

> – Une glace? Ah! ma pauvre enfant, cela fait deux ans, vous entendez, deux ans, que je n'en fais plus de glaces . . . Je voudrais en faire maintenant que je ne saurais peut-être même plus!
> – C'est bien ce que je pensais . . . Cela me rassure un peu, vous voyez . . . Les choses commencent à prendre un petit air de logique au milieu de leur extravagance. Ce qui m'aurait plutôt paru louche, c'est si vous aviez été vraiment un marchand de glaces, qui vend des vraies glaces, des glaces qui font froid . . .

In 'Absurdist' drama, on the contrary, things never possess that 'petit aid de logique au milieu de leur extravagance'.

Despite a series of rather repetitive variations on a narrow range of similar themes, then, it should have been evident by 1945 that Anouilh had quite outgrown the naturalistic formula of plays like *L'Hermine* or *La Sauvage*. And the plays which followed went further still, and broke away from the rigid polarisation into 'noir' and 'rose'. Most of the plays composing the collections *Pièces brillantes* and *Pièces grinçantes* show a more ambivalent outlook, characterised by mature resignation rather than intransigent *parti pris*. Although 'brillant' and 'grinçant' suggest a development of 'rose' and 'noir' respectively, there is no clear-cut division; what does distinguish the 'pièces brillantes', however, is a striking setting, and a highly stylised attitude towards form and dramatic idiom.

The first two plays of this volume, *L'Invitation au château* (1947) and *Cécile, ou l'Ecole des pères* (1949), continue the manner of the 'pièces roses'. The latter is a one-act pastiche of Marivaux, slight but charming; the former, a sort of amalgam of *Le Bal des voleurs* and *Léocadia*, was one of the big successes of Anouilh's career, both in Paris and (in Christopher Fry's translation, with the title *Ring Round the Moon*) in London. This is a hilarious parody of the well-made play, an extravaganza of disguise, plots and mistaken identity all revolving round the hoary device of identical twins (one good and one bad, both played by the same actor). As Horace, one of the pair, comments: 'Nous sommes en plein dans la plus mauvaise convention théâtrale' – yet everything is done so openly and self-consciously that the audience, as well as the author, delights in the sheer theatricality of it all. Not for Anouilh the motto 'ars celare artem': on the contrary, he draws our attention to the artificiality, as for instance when Horace, unable to join the rest of the characters for the final scene (since his brother Frédéric is already on stage), sends this note: 'Ma tante, pour des raisons que vous comprendrez tous, je ne peux pas me joindre à vous au milieu de l'allégresse générale; je ne l'ai jamais tant regretté...' There are abundant echoes of earlier plays: Isabelle, like her counterpart in *Léocadia*, is hired by Horace to appear at a ball in order to make his brother's fiancée jealous; Frédéric, like the disillusioned Prince of *Léocadia*, is roused from his despairing love, and given courage and self-confidence; and there is a further example of the amiable rich eccentric in Mme Desmermortes, who, although her place as *meneur du jeu* has been taken by Horace, presides like a fairy godmother over the fortunes of Isabelle and Frédéric. Characterisation is minimal: nearly all the roles are caricatures of conventional types, and style and speed are what matter. We are not surprised when Isabelle's mother meets a girlhood friend in Mme Desmermortes's companion, and the two converse in bad alexandrines – any more than by the incredible complications of plot that Horace keeps inventing, or the stylised attitudes of anger, jealousy or despair with which most of the characters express their cliché-like emotions.

The mood of the other two plays in this collection, for all their 'brilliance', is much blacker. *La Répétition, ou l'Amour puni* (1950) presents a savage *reprise* of the 'second chance' motif. 'Tigre', the Count, is a wealthy aristocrat who has carried the art of living to an extreme of self-conscious refinement; he is an aesthete, for whom 'C'est très joli la vie, mais cela n'a pas de forme. L'art a pour objet de lui en donner une et de faire par tous les artifices possibles, plus vrai que le vrai.' For the first time, 'real' life itself is given a meaning by his love for the young *ingénue* Lucile: '... tu découvres que vivre c'était au fond beaucoup plus simple, beaucoup plus grave – et bien meilleur que tu ne le pensais.' He is willing to sacrifice everything in order to begin again; but he is robbed of this chance, and Lucile's innocence and trust are brutally shattered, when at the Countess's instigation she is seduced by a cynical libertine, who persuades her that the Count has tired of the make-believe and asked him to take her off his hands.

The life-as-theatre image is given one of its most explicit, and most striking, embodiments, in the form not so much of a 'play within a play' as the term is generally understood, as of a sort of 'contrapuntal' arrangement, with continual cross-reference between the rehearsals of Marivaux's *La Double Inconstance*, for which the Count is preparing the other characters, and the equally mannered existence of these twentieth-century aristocrats: an existence which is just as foreign to Lucile, brought in from the outside to play Sylvia, as is the life at the Prince's court for the heroine in Marivaux's play. There is not an exact correspondence between the two situations, and the plots diverge widely; but the one illuminates the other most effectively, as the attraction of Sylvia's naive grace and charm for the Prince is seen to mirror Lucile's for the Count. As the Count himself comments:

> Sylvia et Arlequin s'aiment sincèrement. Le Prince désire Sylvia, peut-être l'aime-t-il aussi? Pourquoi toujours refuser aux princes le droit d'aimer aussi fort, aussi simplement qu'Arlequin? Tous les personnages de sa cour vont se conjurer pour détruire l'amour d'Arlequin et de Sylvia ... C'est proprement l'histoire élégante et gracieuse d'un crime.

Whether *La Double Inconstance* can really be called 'l'histoire d'un crime' is highly debatable; but it is a description which fits *La Répétition* perfectly. And that it remains 'l'histoire *élégante et gracieuse* d'un crime' is due to the handling of the life-as-theatre metaphor: the parallel with Marivaux's play not only serves to disguise the fierce egoism, the 'crime' of the Countess and her associates, by focussing on the mask of urbane good manners and marivaudage, but also reminds us that in their 'real' life these people are only acting out preordained roles. Tigre has chosen to play a certain part, and must act it out to the end according to the conventions; unlike the hero of *Le Rendez-vous de Senlis*, he is not allowed to change roles. He is cruelly punished by his wife – not for infidelity, for that is entirely consistent with their accepted roles, and indeed she has the Count's current 'official' mistress as her ally – but for wanting to step outside his part, and to break the rules of the game.

The subtitle of *La Répétition* could equally well be applied to *Colombe* (1950), another play in which genuine love of the ideal romantic kind is worsted in an encounter with the realities of life. Here, however, the character in whom love is 'punished' or defeated is not an experienced man of the world, seeking to make a fresh start: Julien is one of Anouilh's intransigent young heroes, reacting with puritanical revulsion against the hypocrisy and corruption they see around them, in this case the artificial and shallow life of the theatre, as represented by his mother, Madame Alexandra, a 'monstre sacré' round whom revolve as satellites other actors, her director, a playwright, and her other son. Julien has preserved his independence – 'J'ai refait un monde à moi où tout est plus difficile et plus pur' – but he cannot impose this view of things on his young wife Colombe, who succumbs to the friendliness, the excitement and the meretricious glamour of his mother's world. *Colombe* carries further the development in characterisation that we have noted in *Médée*: Julien is too self-righteous, too rigid and inhuman, to be fully sympathetic, while the wayward, amoral Colombe is a warm-hearted, attractive personality. It is as if the roles of earlier protagonists were reversed: whereas Antigone had had the emotional sympathy of the audience and Créon our intellectual approval, now all Julien earns is our intellectual approval, and it is Colombe who has our sympathy in the fuller sense. Despite the pessimism resulting from this, there is no longer the same polarisation into black and white.

Not only is this a play 'about the theatre': theatricality is everywhere present, and once again theatre is a metaphorical representation of life. Characters see themselves, or are seen by Julien, as 'comparses', 'pantins', 'un confident de tragédie'; and more important still, in a crucial scene at the climax of the play, Julien himself is coached by La Surette, his mother's secretary, in his own new role, that of 'le cocu': 'C'est pas si simple, monsieur Julien, c'est un vrai rôle, tout en nuances, le cocu. Il y a tout un rituel, tout une danse . . . C'est tout un métier à s'entrer dans la peau . . .' The last act contains a highly theatrical structural feature: a 'flashback' to the first meeting of the couple; this is the first play, except for *Eurydice*, in which the time-sequence has thus been dislocated (though such devices become more frequent in later plays), and far from being the capricious product of a playwright's fancy, it is prompted by a sure sense of dramatic effect. The immediate purpose was no doubt to give an enigmatic answer to Julien's anguished question: which is the real Colombe? But into the bargain the closing moments, in which the boy and girl acting out their scene of love at first sight, rush off hand in hand into the future, acquire a remarkable poignancy from our knowledge of what life will do to this love.

As the General says at the beginning of *Ardèle* (1948), the first of the 'pièces grinçantes': 'Il y a l'amour, bien sûr. Et puis il y a la vie, son ennemie'. The play points the contrast between one example of ideal love as yet untarnished by the world, and a series of illustrations of what passes for love in practice. The ideal is represented by the General's unmarried sister Ardèle, a hunchback, who late in life has fallen in love with another hunchback. A council has been called in order to find means of preventing her from bringing ridicule and disgrace to the family name, and we see the deceits and falsehoods, practised by all the other members of this apparently normal family. Formally, *Ardèle* resembles one of Shaw's discussion-plays like *Getting Married*; there is no development of character or of plot, and the discussion is brought to an arbitrary conclusion by two revolver-shots offstage, as the hunchbacked couple shoot themselves in despair. The curtain descends on the General's young son and a small cousin playing at love-making, their mimicry providing a grotesque parody of the passion, the jealousy and the lust of the grownups. Despite the sombre tone of some scenes, and the sensational denouement, the overall mood remains one of comedy – albeit comedy of a rather black kind. For one thing, a sophisticated comedy *à trois* between the General's other sister, the Countess, and her husband and lover – dressed identically, behaving identically and no doubt, says the author in a stage-direction, belonging to the same club ! – occupies a considerable place; there is a good deal of autonomous verbal *comique* of a lighthearted character; and above all, the heroine's remoteness and singularity prevent the audience from feeling any involvement with her: not only is she a hunchback in love with another hunchback, but she never even appears; she remains shut in her room, and communication with her is only possible through a locked door. Our emotions are not engaged, and our response remains detached and intellectual.

La Valse des toréadors (1951) also presents a remarkable mixture of tones, though it remains for the most part in a lighter key. The setting is virtually the same: the France of 'la belle époque', with the same retired general, General Saint-Pé, as the central character. He is another victim of unattainable ideals, but the way in which the theme of the 'second chance' is treated here is highly comic. In addition to his relationship with his wife, whose love for him has turned her into a neurotic invalid, and a series of promiscuous affairs, the General has for seventeen years cherished a romantic love for a girl he had met at a cavalry ball; but when the moment comes for him to make a fresh start with Ghislaine, she throws him over in favour of Gaston, his young secretary. Ghislaine herself, the General's two daughters and Gaston are pure caricatures; the action makes frequent use of the most mechanical comic processes; and the 'denouement by revelation', in which Gaston turns out to be the General's natural son, is pure farce. Altogether, the play would be no more than a parody of Anouilh's more serious theatre, were it not for a much more sombre fourth act entirely devoted to a dialogue between the General and his wife, a searching examination of the marriage relationship which is more reminiscent of Strindberg than of the author's own 'pièces roses', and which ends with the General provoking her husband into nearly strangling her. It is the greater depth given to his situation by this act, and the humanity of the character which emerges in his philosophical discussion with the Doctor in Act V, which make Anouilh's portrait of the General much more than a two-dimensional farcical stereotype.

We laugh at him, but with a large measure of sympathy; and in spite of the farcical situations it contains, *La Valse des toréadors* is noteworthy for the author's very understanding treatment of characteristic human frailty.

L'*Hurluberlu* (1958) is the third play of what might be called a trilogy; though it does not form part of the volume *Pièces grinçantes*, it has more in common with *Ardèle* and *La Valse des toréadors* than either of the remaining plays of this collection. Setting and characters are similar, though the time has moved forward more or less to the present day. The portrait of a retired general writing his memoirs and plotting a political coup is not without a mild satirical appeal, even if the treatment is again predominantly farcical: the General is 'l'Hurluberlu', an amiable incompetent, who has never got further than the title of his volume of memoirs, and whose conspiracy is an open secret. If the comic processes, and the attitude towards character, in *Ardèle* and *La Valse des toréadors* had occasionally put us in mind of Molière, the reference here is unmistakable: the subtitle, *Le Réactionnaire amoureux*, is an explicit reminder of the subtitle of *Le Misanthrope*; there is something too of Arnolphe in the portrait of the General as the jealous husband of a much younger wife; while the 'visionnaire' Tante Bise, who thinks that all men are in love with her, is a copy of Molière's Bélise. The General and Aglaé are surrounded with caricatures, and the plot consists of a series of largely episodic scenes of farce; but the central relationship is handled in a charitable and humane manner, and Anouilh has resisted the temptation to rewrite *Le Misanthrope* by showing an intransigent Julien outwitted and outmanoeuvred by a more sophisticated version of Colombe. His conclusion, it is true, is enigmatic; the General is addressing his young son, as the curtain is about to go up on the performance of a play they have all been rehearsing:

Toto: Oh! je sais! J'ai déjà été au guignol.
Le Général: Eh bien, tu verras en grandissant, Toto, que dans la vie même quand ça a l'air d'être sérieux, ce n'est tout de même que de guignol. Et qu'on joue toujours la même pièce.
Toto: Alors on ne doit plus jamais rire?
Le Général: Si. L'homme a cela de charmant, Toto. Il rit quand même.

And as the 'real' curtain begins to fall, the curtain of the 'petit théâtre' on stage opens to reveal 'Aglaé ... dans les bras d'un jeune homme masqué qui l'embrasse'. Jacques Guicharnaud comments on this scene as follows: '... at the end of *Hurluberlu* the hero, after both his conspiracy to save France and his marriage have failed, has no other solution but to act in

an amateur theatrical...' (*Modern French Theatre*, p. 129) – but I think
that Vandromme's interpretation is more perceptive, more in keeping
with the mellower and kindlier view that this play offers us of the essential human relationship:

> Une ombre plane encore sur Aglaé. Les femmes ne cesseront pas
> jusqu'au bout d'être des occasions de périls. Mais ... ce n'est plus la
> guerre que soutient contre elles Jean Anouilh; c'est la paix qu'il
> leur offre ... Jean Anouilh a bouclé la boucle. Il a réconcilié l'amour
> et la vie dans l'amour de la vie – loin des impératifs catégoriques,
> contre la Sauvage et sa devise de tout ou rien. (*Jean Anouilh, un
> auteur et ses personnages*, p. 132)

While the theme and setting of *Ornifle* (1955) differ from those of
the 'trilogy', Anouilh again here pays tribute to Molière (as he was to
do most directly of all in his biographical homage *La Petite Molière*, of
1959). *Ornifle* is his *Dom Juan*. Like *Eurydice*, it is a restatement of a myth
in modern terms, with enough reference to the original to provide, at
times, a strong feeling of a secondary level of illusion: these are twentieth-
century characters acting out the roles assigned to them in a centuries-old
legend. The metaphor of the theatricality of life is present throughout,
and it is perhaps clearer than in any play so far that the important thing
for the spectator, as well as for the author, is the effects of pleasure and
surprise to be gained from the dramatic confrontation of attitudes, rather
than our identification with this or that attitude represented by the
characters. *Ornifle* does in fact show more clearly than most plays, too,
Anouilh's emancipation from the rigidity of his early dialectic. Fabrice,
Ornifle's illegitimate son, who arrives out of the blue, full of ideals, intend-
ing to avenge his mother's honour by shooting his father, is cast in the
mould of Julien, but he is very much a caricature; and the same is true of
Mlle Supo, the other 'pure' character in the play: a virginal secretary whose
warnings of the vengeance that Heaven has in store for her employer
remind us of Sganarelle's warnings to Don Juan. The focus of interest has
now passed to Ornifle himself, a libertine who embodies the egoism,
hypocrisy and materialism always associated with Anouilh's 'ignobles'.
His single-minded pursuit of pleasure raises these attributes in him to
almost heroic proportions; but more important than what he stands for is
the quality of showmanship, the brilliant way in which he manipulates
the other characters and makes them fit in with the role he wants to play.
This quality is already present in Molière's Don Juan, and that may well
be what attracted Anouilh to the subject; but whereas it is difficult not to
feel some moral disapproval for Molière's hero (and equally difficult not
to believe that this was Molière's purpose in writing the play), the pure

theatricality of *Ornifle* makes it much easier for us to suspend our moral judgement and to applaud the consummately succcessful showman.

The same period also produced another kind of play, very different in subject-matter and style. Adding *Pauvre Bitos* (1956) to the plays which form the volume *Pièces costumées*, we have a group of four plays based on historical subjects; though this is history treated in a most theatrical way, and 'pièce costumée' is a very apt label indeed for this kind of drama.

In *L'Alouette* (1952), the treatment of history is straightforward enough as regards the selection of historical material; but Anouilh is obviously less interested in Joan as a character, or in fifteenth-century history, than in the sort of attitude that Joan could be made to represent. When Jeanne cries out to Cauchon: 'Cognez dur, c'est votre droit. Moi, mon droit est de continuer à croire et à vous dire non . . .' she is first and foremost an embodiment of the uncompromising idealism she shares with other Anouilh heroines, and only in second place a dramatic representation of the historical figure of Joan. Moreover, from a structural point of view *L'Alouette* is put together so as to present a carefully-edited, 'second-hand' view of the historical events, not a straightforward dramatic representation of those events in the order in which they happened. The play opens as follows:

> . . . *En entrant, les personnages décrochent leurs casques ou certains de leurs accessoires qui avaient été laissés sur scène à la fin de la précédente représentation, ils s'installent sur les bancs dont ils rectifient l'ordonnance . . .*
>
> Warwick: Nous sommes tous là? Bon. Alors le procès, tout de suite. Plus vite elle sera jugée et brûlée, mieux cela sera. Pour tout le monde.
>
> Cauchon: Mais Monseigneur, il y a toute l'histoire à jouer, Domrémy, les Voix, Vaucouleurs, Chinon, le Sacre . . .
>
> Warwick: Mascarades! Cela, c'est l'histoire pour les enfants. La belle armure blanche, l'étendard, la tendre et dure vierge guerrière, c'est comme cela qu'on lui fera ses statues, plus tard, pour les nécessités d'une autre politique. Il n'est même pas exclu que nous lui en élevions une à Londres . . .

– so that we look at Joan's story retrospectively, from the vantage-point of the future glory of the canonised saint. Similarly, at the end of the play, at the very moment when Jeanne is about to be burnt, the pile of faggots is dismantled so that the Coronation, which had been omitted, can be played after all; as Charles says: 'La vraie fin de l'histoire de Jeanne est joyeuse, Jeanne d'Arc, c'est une histoire qui finit bien.' This makes for a first-class spectacle, judged as pure theatre, but it has a superficial sort of brilliance. These are not dramatisations of the historical characters, or indeed dramatic 'characters' in the conventional sense at all; they are too obviously actors putting on a performance.

This is less true of *Becket* (1958), though here too Anouilh dislocates the time-sequence and arranges the events in a 'significant' order: the play opens and closes with scenes showing Henry's penance at Becket's tomb. All the action within this framework is therefore presented as a flashback; and once again, it is not the straightforward dramatisation of events that we see, but an edited version: we are shown how the worldly courtier becomes Archbishop and martyr, but his martyrdom is the premise from which we start, not the consequence of a complex pattern of cause and effect. The result – and no doubt the intention – is akin to what we have been taught to call, in Brechtian terms, 'alienation': intellectual detachment is substituted for the emotional impact of tragedy. But whereas in practice, whatever Brecht's theoretical views on the *Verfremdungs-effekt*, a play like *Galileo* leaves us with the powerful impression of an individual caught up in the complex processes of history, *Becket* once more shows Anouilh's complete disregard for the properly historical character of his subject. The programme-note to the London production in 1961:

> ... All this I read one day in Augustin Thierry's *Norman Conquest of England*, which I had bought solely for its handsome green binding ... In the relationship between these two men ... I already had my play. I hope the English will forgive me, not only for a few satirical digs which I couldn't resist, but also for never bothering to find out what Henry II, or even Becket, was really like. I created the King I wanted, and the ambiguous Becket I needed

conveys, despite its flippant tone, a profound truth about Anouilh the dramatist. If a playwright cannot use historical material without distorting the facts, says Christopher Fry in the Foreword to his play *Curtmantle*, 'let him invent his characters, let him go to Ruritania for his history'. In the strictest sense, Anouilh *has* 'invented' his characters, and *Becket* is not a historical play. It is a confrontation of attitudes, and the purpose of the confrontation is primarily an aesthetic one. *Becket* is more 'cinematic' than any of Anouilh's plays so far: it is extremely ambitious in the range of effects it tries to convey visually on stage; structurally, it resembles a film-script in its quick succession of short scenes (the 'fading' of the assassination into the final scene of the King's penance is a particularly good example of the cinema's influence); and perhaps above all, the episodic structure leaves more to the director as regards the establishing of coherent and consistent characters than is the case with more conventional forms of dramatic writing.

La Foire d'empoigne (1961) is an utter travesty of the historical subject it portrays. Napoleon is seen as an actor, purely and simply, returning from Elba in order to 'se faire une sortie. Il l'avait ratée la première fois'. It is no longer a case of the theatre being a metaphorical representation of life. History has now become theatre, and the only concern of kings and emperors is to play to the gallery: 'Mon petit ami, nous ne sommes pas au théâtre. Ou plutôt, si, nous y sommes . . . Mais pas dans la tragédie, dans le mélo, comme au boulevard du Temple. Moi, je suis un acteur de drame historique.' Entertaining though it may be, *La Foire d'empoigne* remains a superficial charade, which offers little in the way of valid comment either on the Napoleonic legend itself, or on the 'politique de composition' of 1945 to which we are evidently meant to relate it.

All three of these 'pièces costumées' are flawed by the author's antihistorical approach. The characters are at best twentieth-century characters assuming a medieval, or a nineteenth-century, disguise; and whereas it can be aesthetically satisfying, and moving, for characters who are obviously our contemporaries to identify themselves with figures from the great myths of antiquity – witness *Eurydice* – such an obvious impersonation of figures from history is nearly always unsatisfactory except at the level of the charade. Anouilh's most successful 'historical' play, *Pauvre Bitos*, succeeds on the other hand precisely because it is more openly theatrical, and makes no bones about showing us the events and characters of the Revolution from an avowedly twentieth-century point of view. The *dîner de têtes* organised by Maxime, one of Anouilh's master-showmen, is neither more nor less than a charade – though a charade with a sinister purpose, the humiliation of one of the players. The characters in the 'outer' play remain twentieth-century types, making themselves up, rehearsing, and playing their eighteenth-century parts under Maxime's direction; and while the picture of the Revolution that we are given in the middle act may be a gross over-simplification from the historian's standpoint, at least, presented as it is on a secondary plane of illusion, as a dream-sequence taking place in the mind of the unconscious Bitos, we are able to accept it on its own terms as a subjective commentary: it does not ask to be taken 'literally' as an objective dramatic representation of the historical events themselves. Similarly, when the third act returns us to the present day, the 'play within a play' that we have just witnessed continues to affect our reaction to the contemporary issues in a way that the indirect allusions of, say, *La Foire d'empoigne* quite fail to do. In other words, the structure of *Pauvre Bitos* is an example of simile, not metaphor; but far from losing anything by being too explicit, the comparison between framework and inner play enables Anouilh to speak with more sincerity and conviction than anywhere else in his theatre so far.

The tragedy of the 'épuration', the vindictive reprisals against collaborators which followed the Liberation, is a subject on which Anouilh, by no means a writer who wears his heart on his sleeve, has written eloquently elsewhere; and the two pieces on Robert Brasillach reproduced by Vandromme (*Jean Anouilh*, pp. 175–81) are proof, if proof were needed, that *Pauvre Bitos* is a play with a message. Not in the sense that it preaches a particular ideology, or defends a given political system: the 'message' of *Pauvre Bitos* is one of simple humanity. Pierre Fresnay, remarking on the political controversy aroused by the play, underlines this: 'On a écrit que c'est une pièce politique: c'est une pièce contre la politique, quelle qu'elle soit. On a dit que c'est une pièce de haine: c'est une pièce contre la haine' (*Paris Presse-L'Intransigeant*, October 19, 1956). Anouilh's own Louis XVIII was to philosophise: 'Oublier cette foire d'empoigne où nous avons tous vécu, rentrer chez lui se marier. ., avoir des enfants . . . Autrefois c'était ça, une vie d'homme. Avant que les Français se soient mis à faire de la politique et à prendre théâtralement la vie . . .' But the form of the later play, its flippant attitude to characterisation, with the same actor playing both Napoleon and Louis XVIII, makes it an inappropriate and ineffective vehicle for the message it is meant to carry. *Pauvre Bitos* expresses the same humane outlook: does it do so more successfully?

Despite its technical brilliance, the play suffers from the lack of a sympathetic protagonist. Bitos himself is the pure, uncompromising idealist; but the series Orphée–Julien–Fabrice–Bitos represents a progression from heroic idealism towards inhuman rigidity. Alone of these characters Bitos is unloving and unloved; and although he is a victim of odious persecution, we feel little sympathy for him. His persecutors are equally unsympathetic, and it is only among the minor characters that we meet positive examples of real humanity to set against the inhumanity that Anouilh is lampooning. Admittedly one of these is shown in the final scene, as the gentle Victoire saves Bitos from himself; perhaps this is sufficient to redeem the author from a charge of complete misanthropy, but certainly the savagely critical picture of man as a political animal outweighs any constructive presentation of a more humane alternative.

Having traced the evolution of Anouilh's characteristic manner through to the nineteen-sixties; having seen, as it were, Romantic idealism à la Musset give way in turn to sophisticated *marivaudage* and then to the mellow humanism of a Molière, we now arrive at a period for which the 'pièces costumées' have already prepared us, in which the paramount influence is without a doubt that of Pirandello. *La Grotte* (1960) could be called Anouilh's own *Six Characters*; as in Pirandello's play, we see the author in the throes of composition, with the characters taking shape and, at the decisive moment, assuming an autonomous existence. The nominal 'plot' of the play is that of a detective-story – but plot is of minimal importance: what matters is the relationship between the dramatist and his characters, the various possible ways of presenting 'character' and 'action' in a play. The Commissaire, expressing a policeman's liking for a plain, unvarnished version of the truth, may be said to stand for a type of dramatist in the naturalistic tradition, with a penchant for the logical manner of the 'well-made play'. The Author, however, knows that character is too subtle and complex to be reduced to the black-and-white terms of a police dossier: all we have to go on is a series of enigmatic actions, gestures, remarks, silences; and instead of clear-cut relationships of cause and effect that can be traced by inductive reasoning, the human personality, as seen by others, consists of a collection of independent and often contradictory facets. This is, of course, a direction in which Anouilh's own treatment of character had long been tending in practice, and the relationship between the creative writer and the world of his creation is presented in *La Grotte* both imaginatively and with great originality (in spite of the obviously Pirandellian starting-point). At the end of the play, for instance, when the Author steps inside the framework of his own imaginary universe and takes the place of the absent Count in order to console the latter's dying ex-mistress, the scene has a surprisingly moving quality. Anouilh has found a way of endowing what could easily have been presented as a sordid 'roman policier' with humanity and compassion, and this is an excellent example of the way in which the devices of 'alienation' can produce the result, as Robert Bolt has said, of 'reculer pour mieux sauter': the dramatic portrayal of this relationship between a playwright and his character creates, not destroys, sympathetic involvement on the audience's part.

On the other hand in *Le Boulanger, la boulangère et le petit mitron* (1968), a real *tour de force* in terms of theatrical imagination, the effect does seem to be to evoke an intellectual rather than an emotional response. This play presents the highly sophisticated interplay of various levels of illusion. The primary level – what we conventionally accept as 'reality' in the theatre – is constantly interrupted by sequences representing the day-dreams of three characters: husband and wife, who have reached a critical point in their marriage, and their son Toto, the victim of their continual quarrels. While Elodie in her imaginary world becomes a fashionable society hostess with a *maître d'hôtel* and a titled lover, and Adolphe creates a fantasy-life in which he can turn the tables on his overbearing employer and display the social and sexual prowess of the ideal man of the world, Toto's imagination is busy interpreting his history homework in the light of the domestic situation, and he longs for some catastrophe which will bring his parents together, like the final months of imprisonment of Louis XVI and Marie Antoinette after the abortive flight to Varennes. The second act builds up to a climax with a scene of savage recrimination between husband and wife, reminiscent of Act IV of *La Valse des toréadors*, and the play closes with Toto's nightmare in which his parents are massacred by Red Indians and he is rescued by an old flame of Elodie's.

In spite of one or two comic passages, the overall mood of *Le Boulanger* is very dark: a recent reviewer, B. Poirot-Delpech, comments that here Anouilh has achieved 'le double record d'illusion technique et de désillusion morale' (*Le Monde*, October 10, 1969). The technical virtuosity is plain for all to see: the author makes freer use of cinematic effects here than in any other of his plays, with a rapid succession of short 'sequences' rather than finished scenes, cutting and fading very much in the manner of the *scénariste*; though the construction of the play, with each act leading up to a fantasy based on Toto's reaction to the situation, reveals a sure sense of dramatic form. Although the disjointed, episodic structure would be quite inappropriate to the establishment of 'rounded' characters in the naturalistic manner, Anouilh is not concerned here to produce portraits of individualised characters with a complete *état civil*. Rather, Adolphe and Elodie are Everyman and his wife; and as a modern morality play, this is more grimly far-reaching in its view of human relationships than any of the plays in the *Ardèle–Valse des toréadors–Hurluberlu* trilogy, where relative precision of setting, and greater depth of characterisation, to some extent limit the general application of the author's pessimistic outlook. It is not a misanthropic outlook, by any means: neither Adolphe nor Elodie are presented unsympathetically; but however charitable the later Anouilh has become towards the shortcomings of ordinary men and women, *Le Boulanger* offers an uncompromisingly pessimistic view of marriage as a workable institution.

Cher Antoine (1969) is the most subtle of all Anouilh's Pirandellian exercises, but perhaps the subtlety misfires. This time it is not the characters of an author's imagination who get out of hand and assume an autonomous existence; on the contrary, it is the author who is unable to accept the 'real' characters of his own life as authentic personalities, forever turning them into products of his imagination; as one of the women he had loved says: 'Au fond, le malheur d'Antoine, c'est qu'il n'arrivait à croire que ce qu'il imaginait . . .' On Antoine's death, his widow, ex-wife, former mistresses and friends have gathered for the reading of his will. As their attitudes towards him are revealed, we learn in a flashback that three years before, on leaving Paris for a remote Bavarian castle, he had written a play (with the same title, *Cher Antoine*) in which the same characters were shown coming together after his death. A second flashback shows him rehearsing for a performance of this play shortly before his death, and we see professional actors impersonating his relatives and friends, both according to the script of his play and impromptu; it is no doubt significant that the script of the 'play within a play' is word for word the same as that of the 'real' confrontation at the beginning of Act I, and that it is only the actress hired to play the part who can succeed in conveying to Antoine the 'real' feelings of the young girl with whom he has spent his last three years. But in dramatic terms, all this does not quite seem to work: more seems to be lost than gained by the double flashback, and although the underlying theme is treated in a thought-provoking way, the structure is too capricious. Again, the spectator is offered intellectual challenge, not emotional experience.

The latest play is *Les Poissons rouges* (1970), which treats in the manner of *Le Boulanger* various other aspects of the life of Antoine de Saint-Flour. In addition to the familiar pattern of marital and domestic relationships, the most striking feature of the play is the love–hate relationship between Antoine and La Surette, a 'fils du peuple', which reproduces that between Becket and the King, transposed into a more comic key. The comedy has its dark side, however: despite his fame and success as a playwright, the hero feels persecuted by the spite and malice of his wife, family and friends. This is a play full of reminiscences of Anouilh's past theatre: proper names, quotations, allusions, opinions, prejudices. *Pauvre Bitos* is particularly heavily drawn on, as well as *La Répétition* and *L'Hurluberlu: Les Poissons rouges* is the point of convergence of so many favourite themes and motifs that it gives a strong impression of being a 'confessional' play about Anouilh's own career.

If Anouilh's increasingly narcissistic preoccupation with the interplay between reality and the world of the imagination is responsible for certain shortcomings in these latest plays, it is also the source of the considerable fascination that such plays offer as the culmination of the dramatist's whole work so far. We must beware of considering any play as representing a fixed, final attitude on the part of a dramatist who no doubt still has it in him to surprise the theatre-going public by his versatility; but it is difficult not to believe that the author may be very largely identified both with the dramatist-figure of *La Grotte* and with Antoine de Saint-Flour. Indeed, this retiring playwright, who has seldom given an interview, seems to have declared himself more clearly here than anywhere else. In his early theatre, although one was always conscious of the author's presence in the wings, as it were, manipulating the characters like so many puppets, he succeeded in keeping the creatures of his imagination at a certain distance; and an Ornifle, a Bitos, a Becket had a detached, objective existence. Now his characters seem to have become a part of his world, and he a part of theirs. He, Jean Anouilh, is the Author who confesses at the beginning of *La Grotte*: 'Ce qu'on va jouer ce soir, c'est une pièce que je n'ai jamais pu écrire'; and he too, like Antoine de Saint-Flour, has become the prisoner of his own imaginary world, living in a new intimacy with his created characters, who possess – if we are to believe Antoine – a reality more real than that of the world itself. This is the dilemma in which the Anouilh of the nineteen-seventies finds himself; it will be interesting to see what new direction he takes to escape from it.

Select Bibliography

ANOUILH, JEAN
    Pièces noires   Paris, La Table Ronde, 1958
    Pièces roses   Paris, La Table Ronde, 1958
    Nouvelles Pièces noires   Paris, La Table Ronde, 1963
    Pièces brillantes   Paris, La Table Ronde, 1960
    Pièces grinçantes   Paris, La Table Ronde, 1961
    Pièces costumées   Paris, La Table Ronde, 1962
    (Separate plays not yet included in the standard edition):
    L'Hurluberlu   Paris, La Table Ronde, 1959
    La Grotte   Paris, La Table Ronde, 1961
    Le Boulanger, la boulangère et le petit mitron   Paris, La Table Ronde, 1969
    Cher Antoine   Paris, La Table Ronde, 1969
    Les Poissons rouges   Paris, La Table Ronde, 1970
    (Plays published in periodicals):
    Y avait un prisonnier   In *La Petite Illustration*, May, 1935
    Episode de la vie d'un auteur   In *Cahiers Renaud-Barrault*, no. 26, 1959
    Le Songe du critique   In L'Avant-Scène, no. 143, 1959
    La Petite Molière   In L'Avant-Scène, no. 210, 1961
    L'Orchestre   In L'Avant-Scène, no. 276, 1962

GIGNOUX, HUBERT   *Jean Anouilh* Paris, Editions du Temps Présent, 1946
HARVEY, JOHN   *Anouilh: A Study in Theatrics* New Haven, Yale University Press, 1964

JOLIVET, PHILIPPE   *Le Théâtre de Jean Anouilh*   Paris, Michel Brient, 1963

LUPPÉ, ROBERT DE   *Jean Anouilh*   Paris, Editions Universitaires, 1959

MARSH, EDWARD OWEN   *Jean Anouilh, Poet of Pierrot and Pantaloon*   London, Allen, 1953

PRONKO, LEONARD CABELL   *The World of Jean Anouilh*   Berkeley and Los Angeles, University of California Press, 1961

RADINE, SERGE   *Anouilh, Lenormand, Salacrou: trois dramaturges à la recherche de leur vérité*   Geneva, Editions des Trois Collines, 1951

THODY, PHILIP   *Anouilh*   Edinburgh and London, Oliver and Boyd, 1968

VANDROMME, POL   *Jean Anouilh, un auteur et ses personnages*   Paris, La Table Ronde, 1965

6

SARTRE   *Philip Thody*

The well-known remark by which Sartre gave critics so useful a basis for any approach to his novels – 'une technique romanesque renvoie toujours à la métaphysique du romancier; la tâche du critique est de dégager celle-ci avant d'apprécier celle-là' (*Situations* I, p. 71) – is one that appears at first sight rather difficult to apply with much consistency to his plays. Almost without exception, they follow well-established literary *genres*, and show little of the desire to experiment with new techniques that characterised *Le Sursis* or some of the short stories in *Le Mur*. For while the second volume of *Les Chemins de la Liberté* contained an enterprising attempt to use the 'simultanéisme' of Dos Passos to express both the historical atmosphere of the Munich crisis and the disorder of a world in which there is neither God nor omniscient narrator to provide order or harmony, none of Sartre's plays shows a similar attempt to inaugurate a new style of theatrical writing or to disturb his audience by an unusual way of presenting human experience. In its use of classical myth, *Les Mouches* added little to a convention already well-established by Cocteau and Giraudoux, while in 1944 so many critics (such as J.-M. Renaltour in *L'Œuvre*, June 3, Armory in *Les Nouveaux Temps*, June 6, and the reviewer in *Défense de la France* for September 22) noted the resemblance between *Huis clos* and Sutton Vane's *Outward Bound*, that it is difficult to believe that this now rather dated play was not at least the starting point for Sartre's portrayal of hell. And even if Sartre had undergone no Anglo-Saxon influence in this respect, it is not exactly original to base a play on the eternal triangle. Readers of Faulkner or Richard Wright have little difficulty in recognising Sartre's debt in the creation of *La Putain respectueuse*, and the scene contrasting the golden-hearted but simple-minded whore with the hypocritical representative of conventional middle-class values goes back to the purest traditions of the Victorian melodrama.

It is equally noticeable, as one moves from Sartre's early plays to his more ambitious attempts to treat politics and philosophy on the stage, that his work still continues to follow already existing dramatic models. In *Les Mains sales*, Hugo tells his story in something under three hours, and the play consequently observes, albeit indirectly, at least one of the three unities; the basic plot recalls the situation in Shakespeare's *Hamlet*, where the hero is held back from committing a murder by his habit of reflection and analysis; its similarity to a detective story is underlined by the bombs, revolvers and machine-guns that are essential to its action and atmosphere; while the portrait of Hugo himself is in a long tradition of adolescent rebels unable to break convincingly with their bourgeois and idealistic pasts. *Le Diable et le Bon Dieu*, with its peasants, priests, soldiers and bankers, is in direct descent from the Romantic drama envisaged by Victor Hugo in the *Préface de Cromwell*; *Kean* is openly modelled on Dumas's original play; and certain scenes in *Nekrassov* could equally well have been written by the Marcel Aymé of *La Tête des autres*. And as Dominique Fernande pointed out in *La Nouvelle Nouvelle Revue Française* (November, 1959), at the time of its first production, *Les Séquestrés d'Altona* has all the ingredients of a classic nineteenth-century melodrama – heavy father, incestuous sister, mad brother, dull brother, adulterous sister-in-law – and its detailed stage directions give as much importance to decor as any production at Antoine's *Théâtre Libre*. It may be merely coincidence that the one play by Sartre which has not proved a long-standing favourite with theatre audiences and directors, *Morts sans sépulture*, should also be the one in which he made a serious attempt to break with an established theatrical convention. Interest in the dramatic possibilities of the Resistance movement waned rapidly after 1946, so that no director has so far been tempted to repeat the famous torture scene which caused so much disagreement when the play was first performed. Nevertheless, it may well be that this attempt to defy the classical convention of all violent action taking place in the wings contributed heavily to the relative lack of success of *Morts sans sépulture*, certainly the least accomplished as well as the least popular of Sartre's plays.

The fact that Sartre is not, on a technical level, anything like as audacious an innovator as he is in the realm of ideas, adds to the impression which he gives, when compared to Beckett, Ionesco, Genet, Arrabal or Peter Weiss, of still belonging to the nineteenth century. Like Shaw or Ibsen, he presents his public with a series of problems and ideas that are rationally formulated and which depend for their appreciation more on the spectator's intellect than his imagination. Unlike *La Cantatrice chauve*, *En attendant Godot*, *Les Nègres* or the *Marat/Sade*, *Les Mouches* and *Les Mains sales* are immediately comprehensible, and do little to extend the range of the average theatre-goer's aesthetic or imaginative experience. Sartre's theatre attracts and retains his middle-class audience by continuing to rely upon the belief that anecdotes are meaningful and important, that what people say is a reliable guide to what they are and what they think, and that the creation of character is still an important part of the playwright's function. It may well be, of course, that this adherence to convention reflects a deliberate choice on Sartre's part. If one is presenting a series of new and challenging ideas, it is perhaps unwise to introduce the added complication of unusual techniques, and few of their admirers would contend that the social or philosophical content of Beckett's or Ionesco's plays was anything but fairly rudimentary. It is only in the case of playwrights like Sartre that ideas matter more than technique, and that it is legitimate to move fairly quickly from the manner of saying to the thing said.

Yet it would be a mistake to assume, because Sartre's plays are written in accordance with certain well-tried formulae, that it is only the speeches and openly expressed attitudes of the characters which deserve analysis. What distinguishes Sartre from an Augier or a Brieux, and lifts his plays far above the level normally attained by even the most efficient *pièce à thèse*, is the fact that his ideas are never presented as static entities. In his best work, in *Les Mouches, Les Mains sales* and *Les Séquestrés d'Altona*, and to a lesser extent in *Le Diable et le Bon Dieu* and *Kean*, he is not presenting solutions but offering challenges; and there is, from one play to another, a constant interplay of ideas and situations which reinforces the view that his books can be understood only dialectically, as a series of dynamic confrontations between problems that themselves evolve each time they are formulated. My aim in this chapter is to consider some of the recurring patterns and problems in Sartre's theatre and use them to establish a relationship between a number of his plays and the political circumstances under which they were written.

I shall, in so doing, naturally be concerned with Sartre as a committed dramatist who takes up certain fairly well-defined attitudes on specific issues. But I shall be equally or more concerned with how the recurring patterns in his plays suggest an interpretation of political events which he is not openly putting forward. I recognise, of course, that I am influenced in arriving at some of these interpretations by my own political opinions. Unlike Francis Jeanson or R. D. Laing, I do not regard Sartre's work as a kind of triumphant progression towards a coherently left-wing philosophy of political action. I think of his theatre, in particular, as a debate on the possibility of effective political action in the France of his day, and one that is therefore concerned, to a considerable extent, with his own attitude towards the Communist Party. But it is not, for me, a debate that reaches the kind of conclusion which a reader sympathetic to Communism would want to welcome. And, because Sartre himself would obviously like to be more sympathetic to the Communist Party than he actually is, the conclusion which I draw from the recurring patterns in his plays is not one which I think he put there deliberately. I shall be arguing, in short, that the different patterns in Sartre's plays reflect his changing hopes and sometimes unacknowledged fears about the direction which left-wing politics have taken since 1945; and that it is consequently impossible, when analysing his plays, to introduce any rigid separation between technique and ideology. His basic, traditionalist technique of placing issues and events squarely before the spectator reflects his fundamentally rational approach to human experience as well as an optimistic presupposition that political problems can be solved if people take the right action at the right time. But the apparently unconscious recurring patterns are equally important indications that he is not so convinced as might appear, from his professed Marxism, that historical events are rational and predictable.

If one excepts *Huis clos, La Putain respectueuse* and *Morts sans sépulture*, all Sartre's plays describe the adventures of a hero whose final exit, taking place at the very end of the last act, is either a clear assertion of triumph or an open admission of defeat. Thus, in *Les Mouches*, Oreste leaves Argos with the conviction that by asserting his own freedom and liberating his fellow countrymen, he has done his duty and committed a necessary and justifiable act. In *Le Diable et le Bon Dieu*, Goetz concludes his 'adventure with the absolute' by the recognition that 'il y a cette guerre à faire et je la ferai', while at the end of *Nekrassov* the confidence-trickster Valera is clearly about to give up his purely individualistic and amoral attitude in order to accompany Véronique in her organised political struggle against capitalist society. In rather similar vein, Kean abandons his attempt to be treated as an equal by the aristocratic society of eighteenth-century England and openly accepts his ambiguous position as an actor. At the same time, he attains a more authentic relationship with Anna Damby than he has ever achieved with any of his previous mistresses, and this solution to his personal problems offers a close parallel to Valera's alliance with Véronique. There are, it is true, very important differences between these apparently similar endings. Oreste does not commit himself to the destinies of Argos to anything like the same extent that Goetz becomes involved in the peasants' war. He assumes that it is possible to bring liberty to people by acting once and for all time on their behalf, and has no recognition of the continual, day-to-day, communal struggle which the creation of a socialist society is said to involve. It is also difficult to make a sustained comparison between the Goetz whose first act on assuming responsibility for the peasant army is to kill a rebellious soldier, and the Kean who will, after all, continue to earn his living as an actor in exactly the same way as before, in spite of the humiliating experiences which he has undergone. Yet these differences become far less important when *Les Mouches, Le Diable et le Bon Dieu, Kean* and *Nekrassov* are looked at in comparison with *Les Mains sales* and *Les Séquestrés d'Altona*, for what is significant about these two latter plays is that there is no possible solution for any of the problems discussed. Hugo Barine and Frantz von Gerlach suffer for nothing, and are so defeated by what they themselves have done that they end the play by killing themselves. Before discussing the political reasons which might explain the fundamental differences between the two sets of plays – those in which the hero overcomes certain problems and is able to go off to new adventures, and those in which he is defeated by events and commits suicide – it would be as well to make a more detailed analysis of what actually happens in *Les Mouches, Les Mains sales, Le Diable et le Bon Dieu* and *Les Séquestrés d'Altona*.

These four plays are all alike in that the central action committed by the hero is what most modern legal systems would call a crime of violence. It is also, moreover, a deed which is emotionally repugnant to an important aspect of the hero's personality. Oreste kills not only Aigisthos, the usurper, but also his own mother, Clytemnestra. Hugo shoots Hoederer, a man of whom he has become extremely fond and who has almost replaced the biological father he had rejected before the play began. Goetz kills a peasant soldier, one of the very class to whom he intends to devote the whole of his life, while Frantz von Gerlach, who had earlier risked his own life to save a Polish Rabbi, ends up by torturing the Russian partisans whose struggle against the German army is at least partly directed at protecting other Jews. Each of these heroes acts, in this particular instance, freely and consciously. Oreste kills Aigisthos only after he has defied Jupiter by proclaiming his own liberty, and murders his mother after a long scene with Electre that leaves him in no doubt about the moral objections to this act. Hugo looks Hoederer straight between the eyes and tells him that he now has no hesitation in pulling the trigger. Goetz kills the soldier as part of a deliberate and necessary policy of establishing military discipline. And Frantz von Gerlach admits to his father that it was during 'une minute d'indépendance' (Act V, Scene i, p. 217) that he decided to torture the partisans. Yet while Oreste and Goetz have no difficulty in assuming responsibility for their acts, Hugo and Frantz are each placed in a situation where they can claim their act as their own only by denying an essential aspect of their personality. If Hugo insists that he killed Hoederer for motives of political idealism, then he can no longer continue to work with the Proletarian Party, the only valid political force that he acknowledges; but if he wishes to remain a member of the Proletarian Party, he must abandon the cult of truth and political honesty which originally led him to undertake the difficult but meaningful task of assassinating Hoederer. Frantz is in an even worse dilemma, for if he faces up to the truth about the real state of Germany in 1959, the acts which he committed in 1944 to stave off Germany's defeat become not only appalling crimes but dangerous political blunders. It is only because Germany was defeated in 1945 that she now enjoys a prosperity unrivalled by that of any other European country, and the defeat which he had tried so hard to avoid has become providential. Yet he can recognise this fact only by denying the acts which he freely chose to commit, and neither the Protestant tradition of personal responsibility nor the existentialist idea that we define ourselves by our acts will allow him to do this. Like Hugo, he is caught in a trap from which the only escape is the non-solution of suicide, and both men seem, on this reading of the plays in which they appear, to be frustrated by History itself of the possibility of proclaiming, like Goetz or Oreste, 'Je le ferais encore si j'avais à le faire'. Had the party line not changed in the sense anticipated by Hoederer, Hugo's action would have been acceptable both in his own eyes and in those of the party he wished to serve. And had the whole of West Germany been reduced by Stalinist depredations to the level of desolation which so long characterised the area now governed by the Pankow regime, there might have been more said for Frantz's argument that he had tortured to defend his country. Yet neither of these two things, both political possibilities when Hugo and Frantz committed their acts, became the political realities which would have enabled them, like Oreste or Goetz, to fit their crimes into a satisfactory ideological and political framework.

The plot of these two plays is also much more complicated than the relatively straightforward presentation of events in *Les Mouches* or *Le Diable et le Bon Dieu*. Goetz and Oreste can claim their crimes as authentic acts because they are the culmination of a process which leads to their discovery of themselves and to their free invention of their own ethic. There are no flashbacks in either of these two plays – any more than there are in *Kean* or *Nekrassov* – and this depiction of events in the order in which they occur has the effect of diminishing the importance of the past, indicating how it can and should be transcended towards a more dynamic future. In contrast, *Les Mains sales* and *Les Séquestrés d'Altona* are marked by a concern for the past which reflects itself in their technique, and this is an example of how Sartre's remarks on Faulkner's narrative technique can after all be applied to his own plays. In each case it is the acts which the hero has already performed which prevent him from moving forward into the future with the same conviction of his righteousness that characterises Goetz and Oreste, and in *Les Mains sales*, this concentration on the past is accompanied by a fundamental ambiguity as to the political meaning of the play. This ambiguity produces complexities of a different type from the ones created by the various but interwoven strands of political allegory in *Les Séquestrés d'Altona*, and the two plays must now be analysed separately. Their fundamental similarity will nevertheless re-emerge when they are placed in the political atmosphere of the time when they were written.

Les Mains sales is at one and the same time the only one of Sartre's plays that he has refused to have freely performed, and the only one which can be interpreted as a criticism of the methods and ethic of the Communist Party. These two facts are undoubtedly connected, and Sartre has been reported as saying that critics and audiences in the West will be led by their own prejudices to see the play in a distorted light (see *The Times*, September 24, 1954). This certainly seems to have been what happened when the play was produced in New York under the title of *Red Gloves*, and it is not difficult to imagine an interpretation which puts the play almost on the same level with George Orwell's *Nineteen Eighty-Four*, or Arthur Koestler's *Darkness at Noon*, as a denunciation of the power-hungry cynicism which has so long characterised Communist Party policy. Hoederer, the deviationist leader of a local communist party, defies the Moscow-dominated party line by trying to arrange a temporary alliance with the Royalists and Liberals. His opponents, the hard-line doctrinaires, decide to prevent this alliance by arranging to have Hoederer murdered by Hugo, a young idealist who serves throughout as little more than their cat's paw. In conversation with Hugo, Hoederer reveals that he has no objections either to political assassination or to telling lies when it serves his purpose to do so, and the subsequent action of the play shows Hoederer being killed and betrayed – as Koestler's Rubashov is killed and betrayed – in strict accordance with his own principles. Although Hugo finally shoots him for motives whose exact nature he decides only at the end of the play, the use to which Hoederer's death is put by the party leadership underlines how wastefully the Communist Party casts its best representatives on 'the rubbish-heap of History'. Hoederer, we discover in the last act, had been not wrong but merely premature. Indeed, the policy he advocated had been so right that it is now being carried out on Moscow's orders. The decision to have him killed had been a wrong one in the circumstances, but only he had had the foresight to realise what the real needs of the situation were. Louis, who had given the order for his death, had been wrong. But Louis is still in power, still ready to do his masters' bidding without question, a living proof that those who survive in the world of Communist politics are the organisation men whose main talent lies in never showing sufficient initiative to appear dangerous. Hoederer, in contrast, has been killed on the party's orders and in strict accordance with his own acceptance of murder as a normal political weapon. His death is now being used as a basis for another collection of lies to prove that the Party is always right, and this again can be justified by his readiness to 'mentir comme il faudra' (Tableau V, Scene iii, p. 209) which he mentions in his conversation with Hugo.

It is, paradoxically, because Hoederer is so admirable a character that *Les Mains sales* is so powerful an indictment of the methods and history of the Communist Party. Like the Brunet of *Les Chemins de la liberté*, he is at home in the world of things, and Hugo's conviction that 'le vrai goût du café est dans sa bouche' (Tableau IV, Scene i, p. 132) echoes Mathieu's admiration for his friend Brunet's solidity and physical authenticity. Hoederer and Brunet are virtually the only characters in Sartre's imaginative universe who do not feel disgust at the very fact of being alive, and Hoederer goes much further than Brunet in taking decisions on his own responsibility rather than blindly following the party line. Indeed, it seems to have been Sartre's intention to present Hoederer as a model for the authentic existentialist man of political action, and a letter from a Monsieur Jean Biermez of Brussels which *Les Temps Modernes* published in 1948 (Vol. IV, pp. 574–576) almost certainly reflected Sartre's own views when it contrasted Hoederer's maturity with Hugo's failure to grow up.

This is certainly a justifiable reading of the play if the main question at issue is the superiority of Hoederer over Hugo. What it totally neglects is the fact that the person who wins is not Hoederer but Louis, and from the moment we realise that it is the Stalinists, the party bosses, who emerge triumphant, Hugo's desperate attempt to assert some kind of political ethic at the end of the play outweighs the lack of enthusiasm we feel for him as a person. It is he who defends Hoederer as a political thinker in his own right and not simply as a statue to be exploited, and at that moment in the play he becomes a far more admirable character than the adolescent idealist of the earlier scenes. The tragedy is, however, that neither he nor Hoederer can actually achieve anything, either as individuals or as members of a political party. While Hugo's sacrifice achieves nothing, Hoederer becomes virtually an Orwellian 'non-person', and the extent of their failure becomes even more marked when they are compared, respectively, with Oreste and with Goetz. Whatever the final inadequacy of the former's attitude may be, he does liberate Argos; and the whole implication of the last scene in *Le Diable et le Bon Dieu* is that even if Goetz does not win, he will have fought and died in the service of the right cause. The plot of *Les Mains sales* has entirely different connotations, and the way in which the play twists back upon itself, biting its own tail, points to a much closer relationship between form and content than the rather contrived device of the flashback originally seemed to promise. In *Les Séquestrés d'Altona*, where the theme of sequestration recalls the claustrophobic, introverted world of *La Chambre*, the possibility of right political action seems equally remote, and the construction of the play is equally linked to a basic pessimism about history which quite contradicts the admittedly difficult hopes extended by the ending of *Le Diable et le Bon Dieu*.

Les *Séquestrés d'Altona* is, of course, a very different play from *Les Mains sales* in a number of important ways. To begin with, in so far as it is a fairly clear allegory of the futility of French policy in Algeria, it is a much more openly committed play. It is surely no accident that it should be a character called Frantz who tries to win a war by the use of torture before discovering that his actions have merely postponed a defeat whereby his country becomes very rich, and the neatness with which Sartre brought together both the moral and the economic arguments against the policy known as *L'Algérie française* showed how efficiently the unofficial censorship of the Fifth Republic could be turned, as the German censorship of 1943 had been turned, by the use of allegory. Indeed, the similarity between Frantz's behaviour and the attitude of successive French governments towards the use of torture was so close that it is remarkable that no attempt was made to suppress performances of the play. Like these governments, Frantz varies between denying that his tortures ever took place and maintaining that they were necessary to avoid a disaster in which he only half pretends to believe, and his bad faith exactly mirrors that of the right-wing French press between 1954 and 1962. But Frantz is no straightforward fascist villain, and his situation offers a much more tragic and realistic expression of the problems inseparable from violent political action than the attitudinising of Oreste or Goetz. It appears to make a great difference to Sartre that Frantz should have tortured while Goetz and Oreste 'merely' killed, but not all moralists would agree with him in seeing so immense a gap between the two actions. What distinguishes Frantz most clearly from Goetz is that he tortured for a side that lost, whereas Goetz killed for a side that Sartre obviously wants to win. Take away the implied historical guarantee that Goetz is doing the wrong deed for the right reason, and in fifteen years' time his act too may become as difficult to justify as Frantz von Gerlach's. For a Marxist, of course, such an assumption is impossible, for History is moving in a direction that does enable us to say that some crimes are necessary and others not. But history, as Hugo learned, is not predictable. Louis, an impeccably Marxist leader, told him that he would be right to shoot Hoederer because the latter's policy constituted objective treason, but a twist in the road that History was taking showed how misguided Hugo was. To rely, as Marxist existentialism inevitably does, solely on the historical process to provide moral justification for acts not guaranteed by 'des valeurs . . . dans un ciel intelligible' (*L'Existentialisme est un humanisme*, Paris: Nagel, 1951, p. 35), is an extremely chancy business. The obsession with the past that characterises Hugo and Frantz has overtones which Sartre's formal political opinions would almost certainly not admit, but it is nevertheless by referring to a number of fairly specific political events that the fundamental difference between the two sets of plays, *Les Mouches, Le Diable et le Bon Dieu, Kean* and *Nekrassov* on the one hand, *Les Mains sales* and *Les Séquestrés d'Altona* on the other, can best be understood.

When Sartre began his theatrical career with the production of *Les Mouches* in 1943, the French left-wing was in one of its rare periods of political unity. The readiness of the Communist Party to collaborate with the German invader had disappeared with Orwellian rapidity on June 21, 1941, and the schisms later produced by Stalin's policy in Eastern Europe as well as by the Communist attempt to take over the French Resistance movement were not yet glaringly visible. The ease with which Oreste shook off his hesitations and committed his crime reflects the relative optimism of left-wing thinkers during this period, just as his readiness to assume that a country could and should be liberated by the once and for all defeat of one reactionary government showed a certain naivety about politics in general and twentieth-century politics in particular. By 1948, however, both the optimism and the naivety had disappeared. In the coldest year of the Cold War, the policies of the French Communist Party were suspect to even the most enthusiastic of fellow-travellers, and the plot of *Les Mains sales* expressed what many left-wing sympathisers undoubtedly felt about the dangers of a new Popular Front. But at the same time, no democratic French left-wing party seemed even remotely likely to obtain political power, and the ambiguity of *Les Mains sales*, where Hugo's opposition to Hoederer's opportunistic realism is both justified and futile, and where Hoederer's eminently reasonable attitude produces nothing profitable either for him or for his party, gave perfect expression to this particular period in French left-wing political history.

The French Communist party was the only party with a large and reliable working class following, and enough determination to carry through a clearly defined policy; but it was also the party that had supported the Nazi-Soviet pact of 1939, and which still gave every sign of doing everything that Moscow told it. On the other hand, the SFIO never looked as if it had the ghost of a chance of wielding power, and was as impotent to influence the final outcome of events as Hugo himself.

To all appearances, it had never been Sartre's intention to give expression through Les Mains sales to the contradictory situation in which the French Left found itself in the immediate post-war period. Had his mind worked as crudely as this, the play would probably not have been the success it has always proved, and it does seem, from his subsequent refusal to allow any more performances in the West, that he may have been somewhat surprised by the 'objective' meaning attributable to this particular play. If that is so, then it could be argued that Sartre the playwright is both more astute and less conscious of what he is doing than Sartre the political essayist. In some cases, imaginative literature tells the truth more frequently than political philosophy, precisely because the writer cannot exclude his subjective apprehension of events quite so ruthlessly as can the essayist, and is therefore less blinded by his preconceived notions. And while it is the long essays in Situations IV and Situations V which suggest how the political ethic expressed in Le Diable et le Bon Dieu came to be developed, it is only in an imaginative work of art, Les Séquestrés d'Altona, that this ethic is seriously called into question.

The outbreak of the Korean war in June 1950 apparently took Sartre somewhat by surprise. He could not, Simone de Beauvoir tells us (La Force de l'âge, Paris: Gallimard, 1963, p. 251), reconcile his instinctive sympathy for the North Koreans with the awkward fact that it was their troops who actually began the fighting, and his own account, in the essay Merleau-Ponty vivant, of how he came to make up his mind on this particular issue, throws a most interesting light on the relationship between his political ideas in the early nineteen-fifties and the plot of Le Diable et le Bon Dieu. It was, he explained, the reading of the manuscripts submitted to Les Temps Modernes which convinced him that it was right to support the North Koreans and oppose the Americans (Situations IV, Paris: Gallimard, 1964, pp. 245–49). From this, it was a relatively short step to his presentation of his ideal political man of action in the Goetz who throws in his lot with a revolutionary army, and his subsequent description, in Les Mots, of how he too had had to liberate himself from a passion for absolutes, underlines the semi-autobiographical nature of *Le Diable et le Bon Dieu*. In addition to being a companion volume to *Saint Genet, comédien et martyr*, it was a statement of how he, Sartre, now hoped to be able to behave, and the position he adopted towards the Communist Party in May 1952, only six months after the first performance of the play, indicated how seriously he took his alliance with the twentieth-century equivalent of the peasants' revolt espoused by Goetz. It was then that he declared himself in agreement with the Communist Party as far as its immediate aims and basic methods were concerned, and the linear presentation of events in *Le Diable et le Bon Dieu* anticipates and reflects this solution to the dilemma expressed in *Les Mains sales*. As far as Sartre was concerned, the only political organisation capable of representing the interests of the French working class in 1952 was the Communist Party, and the implication of *Le Diable et le Bon Dieu* was that any self-respecting left-wing thinker would inevitably give his support to the organisation which, in his day, best defended the interests of the oppressed.

The two plays which immediately followed *Le Diable et Le Bon Dieu*, *Kean* and *Nekrassov*, run parallel to the support which Sartre gave to the Party up until 1956, especially in articles such as *Les Communistes et la paix*, his *Réponse à Albert Camus* and the *Réponse à Claude Lefort*. *Nekrassov*, in particular, is by far the most one-sided political play he has ever written. It depicts the right-wing journalists who work for *Soir à Paris* as being the only people responsible for the existence of the Cold War, and presents any attempt to criticise the Soviet Union as inspired solely by the most cynical of motives. However, what is perhaps more interesting than this highly partisan approach to a very complex issue, is the new pattern which seemed to be emerging in *Kean* and *Nekrassov* in Sartre's treatment of sexual relationships. For all its optimism on political matters, *Les Mouches* is essentially pessimistic in its treatment of personal relationships. Oreste may well declare that 'derrière ces collines, il y a un autre Oreste et une autre Electre qui nous attendent', but his sister shows singular reluctance to follow him. As might be expected, *Les Mains sales* reveals even greater pessimism about male-female relationships, for Jessica can do nothing at all to help Hugo, and Olga is interested in him only in so far as he is 'fit for salvage'. Even in *Le Diable et le Bon Dieu*, Goetz goes forward alone, leaving Catherine dead and Hilda still devoting herself to the sixteenth-century equivalent of Christian Aid, and it is only in *Kean* and *Nekrassov*, written during the period when Sartre seems to have felt most at ease in his political attitudes and alliances, that there is the promise of a successful partnership between a man and a woman. Kean is actually going to marry Anna Damby, and while nothing quite so bourgeois seems likely to mar the relationship between Valera and Véronique, they do pair off at the end in a surprisingly musical-comedy fashion.

In *Les Séquestrés d'Altona*, however, first performed in September 1959, both personal and political relationships seem equally doomed to failure. Leni proclaims her love for Frantz, but prefers to kill him rather than let him belong to Johanna. Frantz is horrified at the thought of how real his incestuous relationship with his sister has become, and Johanna recoils from him in horror when she discovers what he really did at Smolensk in 1944. The long scenes between Johanna and Werner show how, in Sartre's world, even a successful marriage immediately breaks down under strain, and the intense love which Werner has for his father is doomed to remain unsatisfied. We are back with a vengeance in the black world of *Huis clos*, where Hell is other people and *vice versa*, and only the final scene between Frantz and his father – ending, however, in their death – depicts people who are not indulging either in emotional blackmail or the desire for absolute possession. Yet this return to the patterns of frustration which made *L'Etre et le néant* so gloomy an introduction to atheistic existentialism is very much a reflection of the political atmosphere of *Les Séquestrés d'Altona*. Just as Frantz can find no solution to his own political and moral dilemmas, so the world in which he and his family live is one where all paths to a more satisfying personal future have been closed. In what now looks as if it might be Sartre's last play, both Communism and capitalism are equally incapable of providing a satisfactory framework within which man can solve his problems. Admittedly, it is only the second form of political and economic organisation that is openly discussed, and it is typical of Sartre's fundamental hostility to all forms of bourgeois society that the economic miracle of Western Germany should be associated with cancer, incest, frustration and suicide. It is nevertheless the disappointments of Communism which seem to have had the greatest influence on the plot of the play, and which are mirrored in the alternative reading which can be given to its essentially allegorical nature.

The most obvious interpretation of *Les Séquestrés d'Altona* is, of course, as an allegory expressing the futility of the policy pursued by the French government in Algeria between 1954 and 1962, and the very fact that Sartre decided to write a play on this theme implies a fundamental optimism on political matters. In a broader context, however, the implications of *Les Séquestrés d'Altona* are less reassuring, and the parallel which Frantz von Gerlach's experience presents not only with France but also with Russia suggests that Sartre is calling into question the forward-looking approach suggested in *Le Diable et le Bon Dieu, Kean* and *Nekrassov*. The report which Krushchev made to the twentieth party congress in 1956 must have placed a number of loyal communists in a situation strongly similar in many ways to that of Frantz von Gerlach, and the type of defence which these men had earlier put forward to justify Stalin's policy could only have strengthened the parallel. Whenever the question of Soviet forced labour camps, of the Moscow State Trials, of the treatment of the Kulaks or the activities of the OGPU were raised in European left-wing circles between 1935 and 1956, the supporters of the party line would give one of two answers, and sometimes a mixture of both. They either denied that anything wrong was being done, just as Frantz and the French government denied that they or anyone under their authority had tortured – and as Sartre, in *Nekrassov*, implied that all criticisms of Russia were based on lies spread by professional anti-communists; or they admitted what was happening, but argued that you can't make an omelette without breaking eggs; or they switched alarmingly between these two contradictory theses, just as Frantz alternates between denying that he has tortured and claiming that the tortures were necessary. Common to all these defences, however, was a horrified evocation of what would happen if the Soviets lost power, and this again anticipated Frantz's basic position that the defeat of Germany had reduced everything to rubble.

Such arguments might have continued to be put forward for many years after Stalin's death had not Krushchev's speech in 1956 placed all such left-wing apologists in a position very similar to that of Frantz von Gerlach discovering that Germany owed its prosperity to the defeat he had striven to avoid. Stalin, Krushchev argued, had been much less necessary to the building up of socialism than had once been believed. Far from being indispensable to the defence of the Soviet Union, the 'cult of personality' made necessary by his vanity had been a major obstacle to the creation of the kind of society socialists wanted. Indeed, the whole impression of the speech was that Stalin had done more harm than good, with the result that those who – like the Sartre of *Nekrassov* – had implicitly defended him by pouring scorn on his critics, had merely postponed the providential day when his crimes would be recognised for what they were. To many socialists Krushchev's speech undoubtedly came as an immense relief: at last it was no longer necessary to burden oneself with the hopeless task of defending indefensible policies. But for others, who had staked their reputation on the view that the number of eggs broken did not matter so long as the omelette was made, the speech must also have read like a denial of all the ideas on which they had lived. Like Frantz von Gerlach, they found themselves in a position where what had seemed, in one context, justifiable acts of political ruthlessness – like

Goetz stabbing the mutinous soldier – became merely pointless crimes. Like Hugo, they were left stranded by a change in the party line. But unlike Hugo, they had no sooner accustomed themselves to the shock of discovering that their crimes were unnecessary, than another incident forced them to call this newly-acquired belief into question: the repression, in October and November 1956, of the Hungarian revolt by Russian troops acting on Krushchev's orders.

In common with many other left-wing thinkers, Sartre protested against this repression, and he linked with his protest a long analysis of how it was necessary, for the future of socialism, for the present Russian leadership to rid itself of 'Stalin's Ghost' (the article entitled 'Le Fantôme de Staline', published in the January 1957 number of *Les Temps Modernes*, was reprinted in *Situations* VII). His protest also contained a long explanation of why Stalin had been necessary to create the discipline required by the process of primitive socialist accumulation completed by Russia between 1930 and 1950, and the repetition in this context of something very like the arguments actually put forward during this period makes it seem at first sight as though Sartre was little concerned with those who, like Frantz von Gerlach, had wagered on one interpretation of events and been put in the wrong by what was now considered really to have happened. Once again, however, Sartre the playwright is more interesting that Sartre the political philosopher. Whatever may have been his conscious intentions in *Les Séquestrés d'Altona*, the play certainly takes on additional dimensions when seen in the context of the events that shook the Communist world in 1956, and its concern for the past, expressed both by the flashbacks and by Frantz's permanent attempt to reject the present, also reflects the more pessimistic ideas which Sartre was elaborating in the late nineteen-fifties. In this respect, *Les Séquestrés d'Altona* is not only a play about politics, but a play about political philosophy as well. And the political philosophy which it mirrors is the one put forward in 1960 in the *Critique de la raison dialectique*.

The similarities between this attempt to existentialise Marxism and the general atmosphere of *Les Séquestrés d'Altona* are most apparent in Frantz's last speech. 'Le siècle eût été bon' exclaims Frantz, 'si l'homme n'eût été guetté par son ennemi cruel, immémorial, par l'espèce carnassière qui avait juré sa perte, par la bête sans poil et maligne, par l'homme', and this is either an echo or an anticipation of a central argument put forward in the *Critique de la raison dialectique*.

Rien, en effet, – ni les grands fauves ni les microbes – ne peut être plus terrible pour l'homme qu'une espèce intelligente, carnassière, cruelle, qui saurait comprendre et déjouer l'intelligence humaine et dont la fin serait précisément la destruction de l'homme. Cette espèce, c'est évidemment la nôtre se saisissant par tout homme chez les autres dans le milieu de la rareté. (*Critique de la raison dialectique*, Paris: Gallimard, 1960, p. 208)

In both the philosophical essay and the play, there is no possibility of human beings living together on the basis of mutual co-operation and trust, and even the love which the Father feels for Frantz has its sources in the desire to enslave which Sartre depicts in *Les Mots* as the essence of fatherhood. (See *Les Mots*, Paris: Gallimard, 1964, p. 11: 'Eût-il vécu, mon père se fût couché sur moi et m'eût écrasé. Par chance, il est mort en bas âge; au milieu des Enées qui portent sur le dos leurs Anchises, je passe d'une rive à l'autre, seul et détestant ces géniteurs invisibles à cheval sur leurs fils pour toute la vie'.)

There is, however, another concept in *La Critique de la raison dialectique* which plays an important part in the plot, atmosphere and technique of *Les Séquestrés*, and that is what Sartre calls the 'pratico-inerte'. One way of interpreting this idea in the more prosaic language favoured by Anglo-Saxon philosophy would be to speak of the unintended consequences of conscious acts, and the major example which Sartre himself gives to illustrate this concept, that of the Chinese peasants who expose their land to the danger of recurrent flooding by cutting down all their trees to provide timber, exactly fits this reading of the idea. However, the real importance of the pratico-inerte is perhaps less in the realm of the dichotomy between intention and achievement than in the relationship it assumes between past, present and future. When Sartre was writing *Les Mouches*, it was against a background of the arguments put forward in *L'Etre et le néant*, which all insisted on the idea that man defines himself by what he is trying to do in the future. Oreste, Goetz, Kean and Valera do in fact transcend their present situation towards a more open future, and there is no question of their being weighed down by what has happened in the past. In *Les Séquestrés d'Altona*, however, the situation is entirely different. While Frantz cannot escape from the past for the obvious reason that he is dominated by his guilt for the tortures he committed, Johanna is equally obsessed by the memory of how she was alienated from her own beauty by the very success which she attained as an actress. Werner's attempt to create an independent life for himself collapses as soon as his father decides to reassert the authority he had over him in his childhood, and even Leni, the most determined and self-conscious character in the play, finally chooses to return to the past by remaining in the attic where she had alternated between despair and delirious happiness with Frantz. It is the Father, however, the person who seems to exercise the most authority, who is most incapable of escaping from the past, whether this takes the form of the cancer produced by the cigars he has smoked, the vast industrial empire he has built up and which is now escaping from his control, or his ambitions for his son. He has enslaved both himself and Frantz to the vision of a past which was already dead when he was seeking to reproduce it in the present, and his fate illustrates the double paradox which runs through the whole play. 'Qui perd gagne' is a phrase which recurs again and again, and which links together, on the most obvious level, the political parallel between the recent history of Germany and the present relationship between France and Algeria. But it is equally true that the winner loses, and this idea does not apply solely to the fact that le Père is totally alienated by his own success, driving his favourite son to despair by the very riches and power which he had hoped to offer him as a present. On this level, his fate is symbolic of the capitalism which nowadays generates its most violent young rebels through the very affluence that it provides. But it is also a more general reflection of any society which finds that a particular policy works so well that it cannot be abandoned – Krushchev's Russia, for example, which had such difficulty in liberating itself from Stalin's Ghost precisely because it was through Stalin's policies that it had become the second most powerful nation in the world. The events in the Communist world which immediately preceded the first performance of *Les Séquestrés d'Altona* in 1959 – Krushchev's speech to the twentieth party congress, the suppression of the Hungarian revolt, the execution in 1957 of Mr. Nagy, the threats against West Berlin, the general failure of Russia to break away from Stalinism – are all factors which throw light on the atmosphere in which the play was conceived and written, an atmosphere in which the greatest triumphs lead to the worst results, and where man is imprisoned, as much by his successes as by his failures, in what Sartre called 'l'enfer du pratico-inerte.' (*Critique de la raison dialectique*, p. 286.)

One of the most noticeable features in Sartre's experiments with new narrative techniques in his novels was an acute awareness of what he was doing. Thus he told the readers of *The Atlantic Monthly* (August 1946, pp. 114–116) that it was while reading a novel by Dos Passos that he thought of writing a book whose different characters did not know one another, but who all contributed to the formation of a historical period, and he is quite open about his debt to the Americans. Yet although the third volume of *Les Chemins de la liberté*, *La Mort dans l'âme*, is very much more conventional in its basic technique of narration, it would be difficult to argue that this reversion to more normal modes of story-telling reflected a fundamental change in Sartre's political attitude. The French defeat of 1940, he suggests, was due to the inefficiency of the high command and the lack of enthusiasm of the troops, just as the decision to surrender Czechoslovakia to Hitler in September 1938 stemmed from the cowardice of Western bourgeois politicians and the general popular disinclination of English and French people to involve themselves in another war. Sartre's career as a novelist is much shorter than his long association with the theatre, and it is therefore perhaps natural that his novels should reflect less varying political attitudes than his plays. The two published extracts of the fourth volume of *Les Chemins de la liberté* appeared in 1949, only four years after the first appearance of *L'Age de raison*, and it is significant that he did not go on to complete the rather optimistic ending which Simone de Beauvoir summarises in *La Force des choses* (pp. 213–14). By the time he had published the extracts entitled 'Drôle d'amitié', his political thinking had already begun to move in another direction, and the theme of Brunet's betrayal by the party reflects Hugo's experience, while in no way anticipating the Goetz who was to represent the attitude put forward during the most optimistic period of his political thinking, the years during which he published *Le Diable et le Bon Dieu, Kean* and *Nekrassov*.

It is, indeed, in the recurring patterns of his plays rather than in the apparently more original technique of his novels that the closest relationship betwen Sartre as a man of letters and Sartre as a political thinker is to be found. Yet this relationship, as I have already suggested, is in no way to be seen as a conscious one. Whereas Sartre deliberately imitated Dos Passos's technique of moving rapidly from one character to another because he wanted to express certain features of modern society, he did not deliberately introduce flashbacks into *Les Mains sales* and *Les Séquestrés d'Altona* because he wanted to write plays stressing the power of the past over the present. Everything that he has said about his work encourages us to read it as an account of a steady movement towards the Left, and it is only by going deliberately against his own indications that we can see his different styles of dramatic construction as having political implications of which he would not approve. Yet the search for unintended meanings follows a well-established tradition in critical theory, and one that Sartre himself at least partially practised in his essays on Faulkner. Valéry's remark that whatever the writer wanted to say 'il a écrit ce qu'il a écrit', and that there is no such thing as an 'autorité d'auteur', runs parallel to G. K. Chesterton's statement that the object of literary criticism should be to say something that would make the author 'jump out of his boots', and the only problem in this approach is to know where to stop. An author may very well argue that he is quite comfortable in his boots as they are, and point out to critics that he did not write left-wing plays in order to provide right-wing evidence against himself. But if that is the case, then studies in the technique of narration should restrict themselves to purely literary matters, and Sartre's own remark, that the task of the critic is to find the metaphysics implicit in the technique before appreciating the technique for its own sake, will become subject to a certain revision.

Select Bibliography

SARTRE, JEAN-PAUL
  Théâtre (*Les Mouches, Huis clos, Morts sans sépulture, La Putain respectueuse*)   Paris, Gallimard, 1947
  (Uncollected plays):
  Les Mains sales   Paris, Gallimard, 1948
  Le Diable et le Bon Dieu   Paris, Gallimard, 1951
  Nekrassov   Paris, Gallimard, 1956
  Les Séquestrés d'Altona   Paris, Gallimard, 1960
  (Adaptations):
  Kean (after Alexandre Dumas)   Paris, Gallimard, 1954
  Les Troyennes (after Euripides)   Paris, Gallimard, 1966
  (Scenarios):
  Les Jeux sont faits   Paris, Nagel, 1947
  L'Engrenage   Paris, Nagel, 1948

ALBÉRÈS, R.-M.   *Jean-Paul Sartre* Paris, Editions Universitaires, 1961
CRANSTON, MAURICE   *Sartre* Edinburgh and London, Oliver and Boyd, 1962
DESAN, WILFRED D.   *The Marxism of Jean-Paul Sartre* Garden City, Doubleday, 1966
KERN, EDITH, ed.   *Sartre: A Collection of Critical Essays* Englewood Cliffs, Prentice-Hall, 1962
THODY, PHILIP   *Jean-Paul Sartre, A Literary and Political Study* London, Hamish Hamilton, 1960; New York, Macmillan, 1961
  Sartre, A Biographical Introduction London, Studio Vista, 1971

CAMUS   *B. G. Garnham*

Albert Camus was himself well aware that his dramatic works were considered the least successful part of his literary output. His reply was characteristically direct: 'Ce n'est pas mon opinion. Je m'exprime là autant qu'ailleurs' (*Théâtre Récits Nouvelles*, p. 1687). He always saw the theatre as a natural mode of expression and his dramatic enterprises were among his first incursions into the world of literature. In 1936 he collaborated in the writing of *Révolte dans les Asturies*, he founded in Algiers the 'Théâtre du Travail' (to be succeeded in 1937 by the 'Théâtre de l'Equipe'), and in the years preceding the second world war he was responsible, fully or in part, for the adaptation and production of works by Malraux, Ben Jonson, Gorky, Pushkin, Fernando de Rojas, Aeschylus, Gide and Dostoyevsky. It was here that Camus enjoyed the comradeship and the working of a group towards a common end which he found to be among the great joys of the theatre, and which he never ceased to describe with affection and gratitude: the theatre, he said, was one of the few places in which he could be happy. His attachment to the theatre was in part physical, for he saw clearly that the dramatic art is one of movement, gesture and presence as well as one of dialogue and ideas. He therefore became playwright, actor, producer, translator and adapter in order to understand in all its aspects what he considered to be the greatest of the literary arts.

Beside this instinctive love, however, lies an attachment altogether more reasoned, for Camus appreciated the role of the theatre in the examination of contemporary problems. He approached it first of all on the level of a precise political commitment: the 'Théâtre du Travail' was conceived as a popular theatre, uniting revolutionary intellectuals, with Marxist sympathies, in pursuit of the following objectives: 'prendre conscience de la valeur artistique propre à toute littérature de masse et démontrer que l'art peut parfois sortir de sa tour d'ivoire' (*Théâtre Récits Nouvelles*, p. 1688). But with his disillusionment with Communism and the creation of the 'Théâtre de l'Equipe' Camus envisaged a more general commitment: in his essay *Le Mythe de Sisyphe* he emphasises the relationship between the theatre and the absurd. The absurd, which issues from the conflict between man, with his desire for knowledge and power, and the world, which refuses them, renders an ethic of quality impossible; the only substitute is an ethic of quantity. Man must *battre tous les records*, multiply his experiences, and live in the present with only indifference for the future. The actor, with the variety of his experiences, or different roles, and the brevity of their duration, is, for Camus, one example of the *homme absurde*.

Moreover, the two elements which are the source of the absurd are the two elements which Camus sees as being in conflict in Greek tragedy. The essential qualities of tragedy, for Camus, are tension and ambiguity, in that the forces in conflict are equally legitimate and at the same time both good and evil. Thus, whereas the formula for the ideal melodrama would be 'Un seul est juste et justifiable', the formula for tragedy would be 'Tous sont justifiables, personne n'est juste' (*Théâtre Récits Nouvelles*, p. 1703). Above all the confrontation must be constant and equal; otherwise tragedy is destroyed. Camus sees the twentieth century as the age when the confrontation is constant and equal. Tragedy, in his view, flourishes when the pendulum of civilisation stops mid-way between the extremes of a society based on the sacred and a society based on the human, and modern man, after a long period in which reason and science had been worshipped as the supreme gods able to explain the world, has begun to doubt, to recognise his limits, and has found that once again there is a hostile destiny which he must challenge. This destiny – the indifference of the world and the certainty of death – calls forth a revolt, a refusal to accept it as just, and it is in this climate that tragedy will be reborn:

> Après avoir fait un dieu du règne humain, l'homme se retourne contre ce dieu. Il est en contestation, à la fois combattant et dérouté, partagé entre l'espoir absolu et le doute définitif. Il vit donc dans un climat tragique. Ceci explique peut-être que la tragédie veuille renaître. L'homme d'aujourd'hui qui crie sa révolte en sachant que cette révolte a des limites, qui exige la liberté et subit la nécessité, cet homme contradictoire, déchiré, désormais conscient de l'ambiguïté de l'homme et de son histoire, cet homme est l'homme tragique par excellence. (Lecture delivered in Athens on the future of tragedy, 1955; *Théâtre Récits Nouvelles*, p. 1707)

Camus sees in Greek tragedy one constant theme: 'la limite qu'il ne faut pas dépasser', and throughout his works he sought to establish what the limits of his revolt were, which actions were defensible, and which were not, in the name of the human identity which was challenged.

It was therefore natural that Camus should turn to the theatre to express his ideas, and that he should seek to create a modern tragedy. In his search he uses different techniques and different styles, but the whole of his work is characterised by a mistrust of explanatory psychology. He wrote in his *Carnets*: 'La psychologie est action – non réflexion sur soi-même' (I, 48). He preferred Aeschylus and Sophocles to Euripides because they give less weight in their tragedies to the interior motivation of the individual, and place greater emphasis on pathetic situations. In Camus's work the emphasis will be the same. In a *prière d'insérer* to *Les Justes* he was explicit:

> Bien que j'aie du théâtre le goût le plus passionné, j'ai le malheur de n'aimer qu'une seule sorte de pièces, qu'elles soient comiques ou tragiques. Après une assez longue expérience de metteur en scène, d'acteur et d'auteur dramatique, il me semble qu'il n'est pas de théâtre sans langage et sans style, ni d'œuvre dramatique valable qui, à l'exemple de notre théâtre classique et des tragiques grecs, ne mette en jeu le destin humain tout entier dans ce qu'il a de simple et grand. Sans prétendre les égaler, ce sont là, du moins, les modèles qu'il faut se proposer. La 'psychologie', en tout cas, les anecdotes ingénieuses et les situations piquantes, si elles peuvent souvent m'amuser en tant que spectateur, me laissent indifférent en tant qu'auteur. (*Théâtre Récits Nouvelles*, p. 1827)

Camus's characters are always in a limited situation in which they are forced to react, and they define themselves not by introspection, but by action. The spectator is not faced with the question as to what inner compulsion makes them act in any particular way, but as to whether they are right in what they do. In this way Camus's theatre is a moral theatre. He always uses the individual situation to evoke a universal problem, and such emphasis on action and principle, rather than on psychological make-up, means that human relationships are not properly speaking central to his plays. External circumstances force individuals to respond in their separate ways, and they react to one another only in relation to the external circumstances. The problem of the disproportion between the specific and the general, whereby characters tend not to live in their own right, but to exist as attitudes, faces Camus throughout his dramatic works, and is only finally resolved in satisfactory fashion in his last play, *Les Justes*.

Camus's other great problem in the creation of a modern tragedy was, as he saw, one of language:

> . . . le grand problème de la tragédie moderne est un problème de
> langage. Des personnages en veston ne peuvent parler comme
> Œdipe ou Titus. Leur langage doit être en même temps assez simple
> pour être le nôtre et assez grand pour atteindre au tragique. (*Théâtre
> Récits Nouvelles*, p. 1857)

Camus's awareness of the difficulty led him to avoid situating his plays in
a contemporary setting; with the exception of those in his earliest work,
Révolte dans les Asturies, his characters never are *en veston*. *Caligula* is
taken from Roman history, *Les Justes* from early twentieth-century Russian history, *L'Etat de siège* is set in a Spain which is, superficially at least,
medieval, and *Le Malentendu*, set in a European country (probably
Czechoslovakia), is deliberately timeless. In four different ways Camus is
establishing a distance between the spectator and the action, in terms of
time and space, so that the whole dimension of the problem depicted may
be more readily discernible. The gulf is bridged, and the spectator is
implicated by means of language which tends towards simplicity interwoven with moments of passionate lyricism. Camus's language adds
urgency to the confrontation between man and his destiny because, with
its clarity and its directness, it brings the forces at play into greater relief.

Camus's first play, *Révolte dans les Asturies*, is in fact the work of
four authors: Camus himself, who appears to have contributed the major
part, Jeanne-Paule Sicard, at the time a student and later to become a
chef de cabinet of President Pleven, and two writers who have disappeared
from view, Poignant and Bourgeois. Because of the sensitive political
climate prevailing in North Africa at the time, the play was banned and
was never performed, as had been intended, by the 'Théâtre du Travail'.
Only a limited number of copies was printed, and the play was virtually
unknown, at least in Europe, until the publication of Camus's complete
dramatic works in 1962.

The play depicts the uprising by miners of the Asturias in 1934 and
their massacre by the Government and its troops. The miners enjoy a
brief victory and seem to be on the verge of achieving at least some small
social justice, but are crushed by the brutal force of the authorities. The
play has, then, a precise political aim – to commemorate a particular
workers' uprising – but it shows at the same time Camus's awareness of
the absurd as the basic condition of human existence. In a foreword to
the play he wrote: 'Il suffit d'ailleurs que cette action conduise à la mort,
comme c'est le cas ici, pour qu'elle touche à une certaine forme de grandeur qui est particulière aux hommes: l'absurdité' (*Théâtre Récits Nouvelles*, p. 399). He represents the absurd in this play by civil war and the
crimes it can drive men to commit: both sides in the conflict are cynical

in their brutality, and by extending guilt to the heroic workers Camus offers an implied criticism of communist politics, which accepts the death of the innocent as necessary to the salvation of mankind (a theme to which he will return in *Les Justes*).

There is great violence and rapidity of movement on the stage, but the play keeps its dramatic unity. Each of the four acts concentrates on one phase of the rebellion in a gradually accelerating rhythm: the insurrection, the provisional victory of the workers and their repression of the bourgeois, the massacre of the miners by the troops, and the abandoning of the dead beneath the snow (the original title of the play was to have been *La Neige*, symbolising forgetfulness). Much use is made of crowd movements, the expression of crowd feeling and music (the play begins with a popular song and ends with its nostalgic echo). This music is used to contrast with other sounds heard throughout the play – the explosion of grenades, the bugles of the troops, the combat chants of the miners and the radio loudspeaker, which puts out false news, showing the true face of propaganda.

There is no one dominant character: Sanchez, the revolutionary, and Pilar, the owner of the café where the action takes place, although they direct much of the insurgents' activity, are not the heroes. The heroes are the People, those who suffer in oppression. The specific event is transformed into a symbol of revolt against injustice, both metaphysical and political. Thus there is a mixture of historical realism and lyricism, and the play in its language varies between the tautness which will characterise *Les Justes* and the effusiveness with which Camus in his essays *Noces* sings the glories of life.

Révolte dans les Asturies is a work of Camus's youth (he was twenty-three at the time of its composition), and it is a dramatic enterprise which is collective in every sense of the word. It is with *Caligula* that Camus's career as a dramatist in his own right properly begins.

He began work on *Caligula* in 1936, although the play was not completed until 1939 and not performed until 1945. He acknowledges as his source Suetonius's *The Twelve Caesars*; he uses many details of the historical Caligula's life and many of his reported remarks, but his object is far removed from that of reproducing a faithful portrait. In a note to the play he writes: 'En dehors des "fantaisies" de Caligula, rien ici n'est historique. Ses mots sont authentiques, leur exploitation ne l'est pas' (*Théâtre Récits Nouvelles*, p. 1745). Camus has substituted for the apparent madness of the historical Caligula the lucidity of a man who, on contemplating the dead body of Drusilla, his sister and mistress, discovers that life is unbearable. Caligula sees the implications of the fact that men are destined to die; he recognises the limitations and injustices of such an existence, and resolves to use his limitless authority to change the human condition. Having found that the moon is beyond his grasp, he cannot rest until he has it; he is prepared to sacrifice all order that now exists, because it does not express the reality of the human condition. Caligula assumes the form of destiny; thanks to his position of power he is able to change the standards by which men live. He issues a decree stating that all his subjects are guilty because they are his subjects; they have been living in lies, and now truth is an inescapable necessity. Happiness, individual or collective, must accommodate itself to the true nature of things.

Caligula conceives it to be a scandal that men die and are not happy; from this he draws conclusions which for him are inescapable. The first step in his reasoning comes when he asserts that everything is on the same footing: everything is equally important because nothing has any importance. Death is a cruel event which renders equivocal everything which precedes it: if our existence is bounded by inevitable death, then, with no future for which to create, or on which to base one's life, it is apparent that it is of no consequence with what each life is filled, and thereby each life is meaningless, since it cannot have any lasting quality beyond death.

Caligula's system of government rests upon a faith, a faith in the sovereignty of this one life (in the same way that Camus says in *Noces* that the value of life is increased by the realisation of its meaninglessness), and it is a system which cannot be taught by logic, but which must be lived. It is Caligula's intention to make his subjects live in an excess of meaninglessness, in order to impress upon them, by its introduction into their lives, that the society in which they live is false, and that the only ruling factor can be the indifference of the world which he himself assumes. At the end of the first act he goes to the mirror and effaces the image upon it – the image of all that has gone before. All that remains is Caligula and what he represents, with limitless power to govern the lives of those around him.

Caligula is defeated in his undertaking. He sweeps aside everything that does not proclaim the absurd, in the belief that the scope of the human condition will be enlarged, and what is now impossible will be found on earth. He succeeds in destroying Roman society, but the impossible still eludes him. All that the mirror reveals is the image of Caligula the man. He recognises that he in his turn is guilty; he has not followed the right path, and the liberty he has assumed is not the right one. During his reign he assumes a metaphysical liberty, emphasising his rejection of any transcendent authority, and translates it into a social liberty. At this moment Cherea, a patrician, raises his objections. Caligula's conduct removes all apparent logic and purpose from life; Cherea desires peace and coherence. He feels that Caligula's attempt to create out of negation can end only in destruction, and that it would be unbearable to live in a world where he has no way of choosing his happiness.

Caligula's acceptance of his own guilt adds an important dimension to the play, because with it comes his acceptance of the inevitability of rebellion and death. As early as the second act Caligula gives implied approval to a revolt against him. Later, he takes no action against the conspirators, and at the moment of his death he offers no resistance. Camus writes:

> *Caligula* est l'histoire d'un suicide supérieur. C'est l'histoire de la plus humaine et de la plus tragique des erreurs. Infidèle à l'homme, par fidélité à lui-même, Caligula consent à mourir pour avoir compris qu'aucun être ne peut se sauver tout seul et qu'on ne peut être libre contre les autres hommes. (Preface to the American edition of Camus's theatre; *Théâtre Récits Nouvelles*, p. 1728)

Caligula's conduct is thus seen to have a double edge: not only does it force his subjects to live in an excess of meaninglessness, but it also attempts to rouse them from their lethargy. Since the emperor is separated from the rest of mankind by the crimes he has committed, the only hope is that he in his turn will be destroyed by opponents as high-minded as he, so that his reign will stand as a terrible example. Caligula comes to accept Cherea's point of view regarding the sanctity of human life and the need for peace and order. It is Cherea's revolt he approves.

In terms of structure *Caligula* brings to the stage a basically static subject, in that the play, following Caligula's insight into the human condition, is an illustration of the various types of disorder which he chooses to introduce into the life of Rome. The play is episodic: the spectator sees Caligula at various moments confronting his court with examples of his own form of logic. The exposition of various points of his philosophy, expressed at different moments throughout the four acts, is followed by their illustration. In this way ideas on the human condition are seen to be translated into actions. Caligula is essentially a character of movement, acting positively and pertinently; his restlessness is conveyed by his frequent use of epigrams, the rapidity of the dialogue and the extended use of scenes in which his fantasy is given free reign. Such scenes include those which illustrate the humiliation of the patricians, culminating in the death of Mereia, in Act II, that of Caligula's appearance as Venus in Act III, and that in which poets are required to compose a poem on death in Act IV. In these scenes, which provide the practical application of a theory, Camus makes full use of the stage to show violent action, and fully exploits the visual potentialities of the situation. Here

Caligula becomes alive, and here the play makes its greatest impact on the spectator. 'Il fait penser' Cherea says of Caligula; he makes the spectator think when he is seen in action.

The final climax of the play is in a sense muted in that it arises merely from the discontent of the patricians at such an accumulation of violence; the end comes when they can stand no more. Progression in Caligula's apparent irrationality is strictly speaking absent: at the end his violence is no more refined and no more cruel than at the beginning. This is not to say that the play lacks tension, which is provided by the enormity of the design and the scope of his vision. Nor is Caligula a mere puppet. At various moments he shows that he is capable of a passionate involvement in the affairs of men, he describes his disgust at life in terms of physical sensations, he cannot sleep at night, he is not without humour, and delights above all in the theatrical elements of the education of his subjects. He is intensely aware of the burden which he is carrying; he has need of companionship and understanding (shown by his various attempts to convince his mistress, Caesonia and the poet, Scipion). The total effect is to render Caligula more sympathetic, but he still stands apart, lord of the world, attempting to implement a grand design.

As might perhaps be expected, the other characters in the play exist only in reaction to Caligula, and in themselves do not present detailed psychological studies. What is important is the attitude each one represents and the light each one casts on Caligula. Cherea, the leader of the conspirators, is a man of restraint, courage and nobility. He understands the emperor, and even sympathises with him, but judges him harmful. His attitude shows most effectively the immediate destruction which Caligula brings about, whereas it is Scipion who is even closer in his understanding of Caligula's motives. Caligula and Scipion share the same sensuous appreciation of the beauty of nature and the innate glory of life. Scipion's poem of death, which is in effect in praise of life, corresponds to Caligula's view. Despite the torture inflicted on his father, Scipion will take no part in the assassination; he appreciates the nostalgia for beauty, the desire for true order which lies behind Caligula's actions, although he cannot countenance bloodshed. Caesonia is dismayed by Caligula's apparent illogicality, and even on occasion takes up the arguments of Cherea and Scipion. Yet under the spell of Caligula she supports him in his reign of terror, torn between her love and her desire for security. Her love persists; she offers no resistance when he strangles her.

Camus writes of *Caligula*:

> ... je cherche en vain la philosophie dans ces quatre actes. Ou, si elle existe, elle se trouve au niveau de cette affirmation du héros: 'Les

hommes meurent et ils ne sont pas heureux.' [. . .] Non, mon ambition était autre. La passion de l'impossible est, pour le dramaturge, un objet d'études aussi valable que la cupidité ou l'adultère. La montrer dans sa fureur, en illustrer ses ravages, en faire éclater l'échec, voilà quel était mon projet. Et c'est sur lui qu'il faut juger cette œuvre. (Preface to the American edition of Camus's theatre; *Théâtre Récits Nouvelles*, p. 1728)

Camus was clearly at pains to convince the public that *Caligula* was more than a mere *pièce à thèse*, but he did accept that the play has its place within the development of his ideas at the time:

Avec *Le Malentendu* et *Caligula*, Albert Camus fait appel à la technique du théâtre pour préciser une pensée dont *L'Etranger* et *Le Mythe de Sisyphe* – sous les aspects du roman et de l'essai – avaient marqué les points de départ. (*Prière d'insérer* for the 1944 edition of *Le Malentendu* and *Caligula*, written by Camus, but not signed; *Théâtre Récits Nouvelles*, p. 1742)

Camus rejected the label 'théâtre philosophique' for both *Caligula* and *Le Malentendu* and preferred 'théâtre de l'impossible'. This serves to cover two very different plays, for while *Caligula* is remarkable for its movement and spectacle, *Le Malentendu* (begun in 1941 but brought to the stage a year before *Caligula*, that is in 1944) is striking because of its stifling atmosphere and the strictly linear development of its plot.

In *Le Malentendu* Camus depicts four characters caught in a trap: Martha and her mother, who keep an inn in a remote region of a sunless land and who dream of escape to the sun and the sea; Jan, the son, who, after a long absence during which he has found happiness in a land of sunshine, returns to help his mother and sister; and Maria, Jan's wife, who with great misgivings follows her husband to his strange and inhospitable country.

The reunion is characterised by misunderstanding: Jan does not reveal his identity, and, unrecognised, suffers the fate of travellers who have spent the night at the inn before him. In order to steal his money, Martha and her mother drug him and throw his body into the river. When they learn the truth, they both commit suicide.

This sombre play, the story of which has many sources in legends not only in Europe but also in North and South America, was referred to specifically by Camus as 'une tentative pour créer une tragédie moderne' (*Théâtre Récits Nouvelles*, p. 1729). He clearly seeks to preserve both an equilibrium and a sense of moral ambiguity in the play: by 'going beyond their limit' Martha and Jan precipitate the crisis; they are both guilty, but can at the same time offer a counterbalancing innocence.

F.M.F.—5*

Martha, longing for the sun and the sea, hopes to escape to a country where she may find happiness. A world of splendour and light, in which man seems able to achieve some degree of happiness, is always in the background, contrasting sharply with the cold, dark Europe, where all serves to remind man of the finality of death and the refusal of the world to grant him contentment. Martha has stifled all tenderness and love within herself, and indeed seeks to maintain a certain purity – the purity of unrelenting hatred. She has knowingly chosen crime as a means of achieving her dream, and goes beyond her limit with frightening single-mindedness. But her crimes are not merely the indulging of egocentric fantasies: she, like Caligula, but in more muted fashion, is expressing a revolt against the human condition. Life for her is unbearable, because in the routine and habit of her dark existence, a full communion with the world is impossible.

As with Caligula, Martha's cry of protest is understandable, but the path she takes is not the right one. Jan's attitude too is ambivalent: on the one hand he has found harmony with life, and has come from a land of sun and sea where the human identity has a value and gives meaning to life. He recognises the responsibilities of the individual and the fact that he cannot for ever live in isolation. But on the other hand he compromises his position by insincerity and his liking for play-acting; his persistent refusal to reveal his identity and his lack of positive will create doubts as to the authenticity of his filial love. His failure to begin the dialogue with Martha and with his mother betokens a fundamental egoism which is itself destructive.

The other two characters in the tragedy, the mother and Maria, are victims of Martha and Jan: they offer only fatal passivity in the face of danger. The mother is above all resigned: she longs for peace and rest. Maria has nothing to offer but her love and instinctive simplicity, which cannot dissuade her husband from his charade.

The play clearly possesses, then, the qualities of tension and ambiguity, and to these may be added others which place it in the tradition of tragedy. Above all the play is remarkable for its sobriety: the simplicity of its action and the absence of all external movement and forces are complemented by the purity of its language, and successive versions of the play written by Camus between 1944 and 1958 all seek to reduce lyricism or effusiveness. The play has a fundamental dramatic unity, not only in that its action spans less than twenty-four hours, but also in that there is no deviation from the linear course of its plot. There is an overwhelming sense of fatality; in this case the gods are replaced by the absurd which in the last analysis seems to make any human happiness impossible. This **fatality is accentuated** by the characterisation: the characters in

Le Malentendu are neither human types (the Mother, Son and so on), nor are they well defined as individuals. They are representative of attitudes to the human condition in general and to human happiness in particular. The situation does not arise from the characters: they are placed into it. Martha and Jan are each locked in their private responses to the world, and do not directly challenge each other: the tragedy is not so much one of misunderstanding as one of non-communication.

Everything contributes towards a sensation of immobility. The four characters are paralysed; they are free, but their freedom has become an agony. Even when the one decisive action – the murder – is performed, it is seen to be sterile, since in committing it, Martha and the mother are forfeiting their last chance of any happiness. In this immobility the ironies of the situation are readily apparent: death comes to Jan in the place where he was born, and is brought by the woman who gave him life; the two women kill Jan in an attempt to seize what he himself has come to bring them. There are moments when it seems that fate is toying with the characters, allowing them to brush against the truth without recognising it: the mother calls Jan 'mon fils', and Martha does not look at the passport which would establish Jan's identity.

This use of irony accentuates the mechanics of the plot and further reduces the stature of the characters; it shows that it is not Camus's intention to examine the characters' inner selves, but to exhaust the dramatic possibilities of the situation and to make a final statement (after *Caligula*, *L'Etranger* and *Le Mythe de Sisyphe*) on the absurd. The play ends with the refusal of the servant, who has hitherto been silent, to come to Maria's aid: the *Non!* of the servant is that of the heavens answering man's call for help. The absurd is inescapable, and a mere cry of protest is not enough; the problem is now one of the implications of that protest and its situation in historical time.

L'Etat de siège was first performed in 1948, one year after the publication of Camus's second novel, *La Peste*, but although the play is centred upon the theme of a city besieged by plague, there is no attempt to adapt the novel dramatically. The plague which assaults Cadiz in *L'Etat de siège* is not a mysterious force which broods unseen: now it is seen by all men, and when it assumes control over the city it does so with the compliance of the authorities, and brings to its duties the organisation and the bureaucracy of a totalitarian government. It is a power of human appearance, whose interest lies in marshalling men into a particular order. It seeks to rob men of their awareness of their condition and to rob them of their lucidity by taking from them their human identity. Their only function is to be one of obedience. The plague sets out to destroy the values by which men have lived: its watchword is *supprimer*.

Its office marks the end of communication between men, and the end of their feeling of solidarity. It marks the end of love, of the couple, of honour; crime has become law, and cannot therefore be crime. Justice and happiness are replaced by silence, organisation and absolute justice, which is, more properly, tyranny.

The new government marks moreover the end of the individual's innocence, and here Camus raises a question which he has not previously discussed: if the plague is a form of government, to what extent is it inspired by an evil inherent in man himself? The problem of evil perpetrated by man is one which causes Camus great anxiety, and his tendency at this point is to believe in man despite his view of the twentieth century as a century of terror. He said in an interview with Emile Simon, published in the *Reine du Caire* in 1948:

> L'obstacle infranchissable me paraît être en effet le problème du mal. [. . .] Il y a la mort des enfants qui signifie l'arbitraire divin, mais il y a aussi le meurtre des enfants qui traduit l'arbitraire humain. Nous sommes coincés entre deux arbitraires. Ma position personnelle, pour autant qu'elle puisse être défendue, est d'estimer que si les hommes ne sont pas innocents, ils ne sont coupables que d'ignorance.

Men are guilty not of evil, but of ignorance, ignorance of the fact that the meaninglessness of life intensifies the meaning of man. This is the limit of the significance of *L'Etat de siège*. Although the plague is a form of government, Diego, who leads the revolt against it, does not place that revolt in historical time. Camus is not using the figure of Diego to illustrate the attitude of the terrorist: Diego is one for whom the evil of the time is expressed in the effects, not the causes, and his revolt places emphasis upon the fact of human suffering and the need to avoid despair at man's condition, which lies at the root of totalitarian regimes and their injustices.

Camus presents *L'Etat de siège* as a collective work and acknowledges his debt in the writing of the play to Jean-Louis Barrault, who, as we have seen, was working on an adaptation for the theatre of Defoe's *Journal of the Plague Year* at the time Camus was working on *La Peste*, and it was he who persuaded Camus to bring the theme of the plague to the stage. Barrault conceived the idea in terms of a lyrical allegory, and made certain suggestions concerning its staging; Camus is responsible for the entire text.

The play offers a deliberate mixture of styles; in a foreword to the play Camus stresses the fact that he was seeking to avoid a traditional structure and was using all forms of dramatic expression 'depuis le monologue lyrique jusqu'au théâtre collectif, en passant par le jeu muet, le simple dialogue, la farce et le chœur' (*Théâtre Récits Nouvelles*, p. 187). Gone is the static theatre of *Le Malentendu: L'Etat de siège* is character- ised by movement and variety of character. Camus has brought to the stage the figure of the Plague, complete with secretary (both wearing, in the original production, Nazi uniform), a Chorus, who warn of danger and sing the praises of liberty, the People, who provide a human decor and with whose suffering the spectator can sympathise, as well as charac- ter-types, such as the Governor, the Judge and the Priest, who each offer different instances of baseness and mediocrity. Camus makes use of simultaneous action: the scene comprises the market, the palace and the church of Cadiz. The market is the place where people meet to go about their innocent business; the palace and the church are those places where authority takes advantage of the prevailing circumstances.

The particular models for *L'Etat de siège*, in terms of structure, are the *autos sacramentales* belonging to the religious theatre of the Spanish Golden Age, which Camus greatly admired. The *autos* represent in drama- tic form abstract ideas in order to illustrate particular aspects of dogma. Much use is made of allegory, with characters, who represent human types, facing forces such as Pity, Charity or the Devil. The plays are essentially didactic, and have other recurring characteristics which Camus makes use of: tendentious speeches, grandiloquence, alternation in style between lyricism and the language of propaganda, elements of farce and an easily discernible morality. Camus is using the concept and the form of the *autos sacramentales* to defend what he calls the only living religion in a century of tyrants and slaves, that is, liberty. His characters are, he admits, symbolic: once again this play shows his wish to avoid any psychological speculation and express instead 'les grands cris qui courbent ou libèrent aujourd'hui des foules d'hommes' (*Théâtre Récits Nouvelles*, p. 1730).

The mixture of styles is particularly striking in the prologue and the first act of *L'Etat de siège*, which describe the foreshadowing and eventual arrival of the Plague. Here full use is made of diverse forms of dramatic expression to convey an atmosphere of expectancy and imminent danger. The second and third parts, which show the particular form of govern- ment established, the cowardly reaction of the authorities, and the revolt of Diego which brings, provisionally at least, some victory, are altogether less varied and closer to simple didacticism. Here the disproportion be- tween the individual situation and the general problem becomes appar- ent. For example, Diego and Victoria, as individuals, speak to each other of their love, but also express ideas on the role of men and women in the world in general; the judge's wife passes in the same scene from con- tempt for her husband, for specific shortcomings, to generalisations on the true nature of law. There is an inharmony between the two levels: the stage is crowded, and there is a great deal of movement and spectacle to hold the attention of the spectator and direct it to the specific, and yet, in order to express the eternal relevance of the theme, Camus seeks to create a timeless atmosphere. The play, in its attack on totalitarianism, implicates all authorities, civilian, military and religious, and concentrates all the evils into one figure who, it must be said, is verbose rather than active. *L'Etat de siège* does reveal, then, certain weaknesses: a structure which is contrived and disparate, characters who are too overtly representative of attitudes, and above all a philosophy which weighs down too heavily upon the scene.

Les *Justes*, which was first produced in 1949, is set in Russia during the revolutionary activities of 1905, and insomuch forms a contrast with *L'Etat de siège* and its stylised decor. It is now a question of situating Diego's revolt in positive action; Diego had been a dissenter, and now the stage is filled by revolutionaries. The five members of the terrorist group have planned to assassinate the Grand Duke Serge, but at the vital moment Kaliayev, who is to make the attempt, cannot throw his bomb on the Grand Duke's coach, because it contains two innocent children. After passionate debate as to what limits, if any, must be set on revolution, Kaliayev succeeds in a second attempt, is captured and condemned to death.

In this play the climate of oppression is the same as in *L'Etat de siège*: it destroys love, happiness, liberty, justice, but there is no examination of the cause of this oppression. What the spectator learns about the human condition he learns from the sight of revolutionary activity, of which the most remarkable aspect is that it is possible for man to choose willingly to commit murder in the spirit of revolt. The revolutionaries are killing, they are meeting oppression on its own terms, so that men in the future may be happy. In this way they commit the same crime as their oppressors: revolutionary activity becomes the servant of an ideology. Kaliayev says that he came to revolution because he loves life, but if his actions are inspired by metaphysical revolt they have betrayed their principles, since the life he upholds is a projected one, and he has become divorced from present reality. When Kaliayev says in prison that he threw his bomb upon tyranny, Skouratov, the chief of police, points out that it fell upon a man.

Les *Justes* portrays, then, men and women living the destiny of the *révolté*, and expressing in their lives the paradox of their situation. Stepan, one of the revolutionaries, while asserting his solidarity with those who suffer, by saying that liberty is a prison while there is a single enslaved man on earth, declares that they cannot impose limits of action upon themselves, since the ends of the revolution are too great. While they fight for justice and the preservation of man's innocence, they must themselves become guilty. In Stepan terror has begotten terror; he is the complete servant of the revolution. Kaliayev, with the approval of the other revolutionaries, asserts that there is a limit. If they must perpetrate evil, that evil must be directed only at those who are guilty. He cannot throw bombs on innocent children. He realises that in rebelling against indiscriminate injustice they are obliged to commit murder in the name of a human identity which of itself forbids such conduct. For him the conflict is intolerable, and he desperately seeks to regain his innocence by sacrificing his own life.

In *Les Justes* Camus adopts the dramatic structure of classical tragedy, and was indeed specific concerning his aims in the play:

> J'ai essayé d'y obtenir une tension dramatique par les moyens clas-
> siques, c'est-à-dire l'affrontement de personnages égaux en force et
> en raison. Mais il serait faux d'en conclure que tout s'équilibre et
> qu'à l'égard du problème qui est posé ici, je recommande l'inaction.
> J'ai seulement voulu montrer que l'action elle-même avait des limites.
> Il n'est de bonne et juste action que celle qui reconnaît ces limites et
> qui, s'il faut les franchir, accepte au moins la mort. (*Théâtre Récits
> Nouvelles*, pp. 1826–7)

The play is remarkable for its symmetry: after the exposition of the situation in Act I, there are secondary climaxes in Act II (Kaliayev's failure to throw the bomb) and Act IV (Kaliayev's exposure to the threats of Skouratov), the central climax in Act III (the successful assassination attempt) and the denouement, Kaliayev's death, in Act V. There is a symmetry in the disposition of the characters: not only do the five terror-ists represent carefully differentiated attitudes to revolution, represent-ing shades of opinion between the extremes of Stepan and Kaliayev, but two other characters are used to counterbalance these extremes. Skoura-tov is a Stepan risen to power, and the Grand Duchess is a Kaliayev with Christian faith. The play is built on a series of contrasts, which can be seen in terms of conflicts of ideas – guilt and innocence, or terrorism which recognises limits and terrorism which does not; or in terms of conflicts of personalities – Stepan confronting Kaliayev or Kaliayev confronting the Grand Duchess.

The spectator is constantly caught between hope and fear; the ten-sion of the play gradually rises after each climax. There is an undeniable intensity throughout the play, which is underlined by the style: Camus makes every effort to achieve directness, conciseness and simplicity. All the violent action takes place off-stage, and *Les Justes* is built around the debates between the revolutionaries, but Camus has moved a long way from the immobility of *Le Malentendu*. The characters have a basic sincerity and nobility, and the paradox of their situation is in itself more moving than the private anguish of Martha and Jan. But more significantly, the revolutionaries are committed to action on the historical level: their response to the human condition and their response to the particular circumstances of the moment coincide. They live their anguish in action, not in static contemplation, as in *Le Malentendu*, nor in stylised attitudes as in *L'Etat de siège*. In this way *Les Justes* is reminiscent of *Caligula*; ideas are translated into actions and the disproportion between the general and the specific has been overcome.

What finally makes *Les Justes* Camus's most satisfying play is the reality of the characters. Camus is able to give them a truly living quality, and he achieves this primarily through the warmth of the love between two of the revolutionaries, Kaliayev and Dora. In previous plays the love of the couple had been marginal, a faint reminder of happiness which is doomed, a glimpse of emotion quickly destroyed; in *Les Justes* it occupies a central place. In Act III there is a moving love scene between Dora and Kaliayev, which gives a sharp edge to their political anguish; after Kaliayev's death, Dora continues revolutionary activity in the hope that one day she will be reunited, in death, with her lover. The moving quality of this emotion suffuses the whole play and brings it fully to life.

Les Justes is Camus's last original creation for the theatre. In the years between its presentation and his death in 1960 he adapted for the French stage works by six different authors: Pierre de Larivey's *Les Esprits* and Calderón's *La Dévotion à la Croix* (both produced at the Angers drama festival in 1953, although much of the work on *Les Esprits* had been completed as early as 1940), Dino Buzzati's *Un Cas intéressant* (1955), Faulkner's *Requiem pour une nonne* (1956), Lope de Vega's *Le Chevalier d'Olmedo* (1957, again at Angers) and Dostoyevsky's *Les Possédés* (1959).

The reasons for Camus's turning to adaptation and production over an extended period are in part philosophical and in part theatrical. The conflict between revolt and revolution which was expressed in *Les Justes*, and discussed in great detail in *L'Homme révolté*, Camus's essay published in 1951, left him at an *impasse* which he could not satisfactorily resolve. The years following the essay mark a period of crisis for Camus; in his third novel, *La Chute* (1956), and his collection of short stories, *L'Exil et le royaume* (1958), he returned to his earlier themes of guilt, innocence and revolt. Man's involvement in history was not considered; Camus is examining once again the individual's response to life.

On the theatrical level Camus was able to enjoy again the contact with actors and the direct involvement in stage presentation which he had greatly valued in his days in Algiers. But, more significantly, the adaptations show Camus's continued attempt to create a modern tragedy; the prefaces and the interviews which he gave during this period show his preoccupation with the subject. For example:

> Il nous reste un thème antique mais toujours actuel qui est peut-être la seule tragédie du monde: l'homme aveugle, trébuchant entre son destin et ses responsabilités. [. . .] Un secret donc. Et un conflit. Celui qui oppose les protagonistes à leur destin et qui se résout dans leur acceptation de ce destin. Voilà les clés de la tragédie antique. (*Théâtre Récits Nouvelles*, pp. 1870–71)

Thus, in turning to the works of this disparate group of authors, Camus remains constant in his search for a tragic substance and a tragic form fitting to the twentieth century. The adaptations are an extension of his own work as a playwright, and it is not unnatural that he should choose to adapt plays of such differing styles. *Les Esprits* by Larivey is itself an adaptation of an Italian play by Lorenzino de Medicis, and has many of the qualities of the commedia dell'arte – mascarades, pantomime, dance – and Camus states that his version of the play should be played in the style of the commedia. With *La Dévotion à la Croix* Camus returns to the theatre of the Spanish Golden Age and to a variety of styles: the play's religious melodrama and theme of grace are interwoven with comic and burlesque elements. *Le Chevalier d'Olmedo* also issues from the Spanish Golden Age, and Camus's adaptation stresses the primacy of action and rapidity of movement, whereas with *Un Cas intéressant*, a sombre story of one individual's journey towards death, Camus was able to bring to the French stage a tragic theme in an austere framework. Camus's other two adaptations are of novels, the one, *Requiem pour une nonne* dramatised in a simple decor, and with a directness which gives it great dramatic force, the other, *Les Possédés*, a much more expansive work, comprising seven decors, twenty-two tableaux and a multiplicity of characters.

Variety of form and consistency of theme: the qualities of the adaptations are the qualities of the whole of Camus's theatre. This theme – the human condition, the place and purpose of man in the world – shows how Camus the dramatist and Camus the moralist meet. His is a theatre of ideas, but one which is brought alive by the compelling simplicity with which problems essential to the well-being of mankind are discussed. If on the level of the individual characters, Camus's plays lack a certain warmth and life, this is compensated for by the heroic situation, the confrontation between man and his destiny. It is this which makes them noble and moving.

Select Bibliography

CAMUS, ALBERT   *Théâtre Récits Nouvelles* Paris, Gallimard (Bibliothèque de la Pléiade), 1962

COOMBS, ILONA   *Camus, homme de théâtre* Paris, Nizet, 1968
CRUICKSHANK, JOHN   *Albert Camus and the Literature of Revolt* London, Oxford University Press, 1959
GAY-CROSIER, RAYMOND   *Les Envers d'un échec. Etude sur le théâtre d'Albert Camus* Paris, Minard, 1967

GENET   Richard N. Coe

The theatre of Jean Genet is a 'théâtre du scandale'. And 'scandal' in the drama, as Jean-Louis Barrault has argued, is justified only if it is the outraged and instinctive riposte of a writer who is totally *sincere*. In Genet's case, what needs to be proved is the sincerity; the scandal begins at the beginning. The illegitimate child of a common prostitute, he was abandoned by his mother and brought up by the *Assistance Publique*; and it was some anonymous official of that organisation who decreed that he should spend his childhood among the black mountains of the Morvan, in central France. Still hardly conscious of his own identity, he was detected by his peasant foster-parents in the act of stealing; and it was their ill-judged attempts publicly to shame him out of this scandalous lapse that led to his rapidly becoming a juvenile delinquent. Much of his adolescence was spent in Reform Schools, where his latent homosexual tendencies were given every encouragement to develop into a life-long neurosis; later, he touched the very depths of misery and degradation as a male prostitute, petty gangster, army deserter, pickpocket and burglar. France became dangerous for him, and he lived mainly in Barcelona and Antwerp, with excursions – a sort of parody of the Grand Tour – to North Africa and Central Europe. And each time he returned to France, the sight of a police-car made his heart beat faster. 'La Renault de la police' became the very image of Nemesis.

In spite of this, however, his phenomenal intelligence early brought him into contact with intellectual and left-wing circles, and with books – at the age of twenty-three, he was already writing to Gide. He was still an adolescent when he started writing poetry, perhaps under the influence of René de Buxeuil; a few years later, he had exchanged this somewhat chancy mentor for Baudelaire and Rimbaud, Verlaine, Lautréamont and Jammes . . . and (unexpectedly) Voltaire. Being destitute, homeless and constantly on the move – more often than not with the police at his heels – he seems to have had the habit of leaving his manuscripts with friends for safe-keeping; but many of these friends were subsequently dispersed and murdered by the Nazis, and the papers scattered or lost.

Genet's first published poem, *Le Condamné à mort*, was written in Fresnes prison in 1942; but almost immediately afterwards, Genet turned to the novel as a form of expression, beginning with *Notre-Dame des Fleurs* (published in 1944) and *Miracle de la Rose* (1945–6). His first experiments with the drama would appear to date from the period when he was writing *Miracle de la Rose* (*ca.* 1944), and his earliest extant play, *Haute Surveillance*, is in fact a development, both of the situation and of one of the main themes, of the novel. It is evident also that Genet, during this early phase, wrote a further play, entitled *Splendid's*, which seems never to have been published, although it is described in a checklist issued in 1949 as being already in print. Recently, he has given hints that he has resumed work on this play, and that it will eventually be published under the title *Le Bagne*, or else *La Rafale*.

The first play to be performed, however, was *Les Bonnes*, a long single act that had originally been conceived as a four-act tragedy. The first version was produced by Louis Jouvet at the Théâtre de l'Athénée on April 19, 1947. (A revised version, published in 1954, has since become definitive. *Le Balcon* exists in three versions, of which the last has become definitive. All references in this essay are to the definitive versions. It is worth noting that the published English translations are mostly based on variant versions.) The techniques of *Les Bonnes* – interchange of identity, stylised movement, ritual gestures, and a deliberate, highly disconcerting contrast between the passionate lyricism of the dialogue and the sordidness of the theme – caused a considerable stir in a year which marked the high-point of post-war naturalism in the theatre; nonetheless, it was sufficiently successful to encourage Genet to polish up his earlier dramatic experiment, originally entitled *Préséances* but now re-named *Haute Surveillance*, which was produced by Jean Marchat in collaboration with Jean Genet himself at the Théâtre des Mathurins on February 26, 1949. Although the weakest of Genet's five published plays, it caused a memorable scandal followed by an impassioned controversy in the press. In the course of this debate, François Mauriac published, on the front page of *Le Figaro Littéraire*, a lengthy and heated article entitled 'Le Cas Jean Genet'. Although hostile in the highest degree to everything that Genet stood for, the very fact that a writer as distinguished as Mauriac should have taken the trouble to hurl himself into action against this new *poète maudit* was in itself sufficient to establish Genet's reputation as a significant dramatist.

These first two plays, strongly influenced in form and technique by Sartre's *Huis clos*, are written in a compact, quasi-neoclassical idiom, with the main stress laid on the intimate psychological tensions between a trio of characters inseparably bound together by physical and emotional bonds, and still retaining, especially in the case of *Haute Surveillance,* a fair element of naturalism. In the eight years, however, which separate *Haute Surveillance* from Genet's next play, *Le Balcon,* this technique is completely revolutionised. Under the combined influence of Brecht and Artaud, Genet turns to a much more open or 'epic' type of theatre, dealing with broad social and political themes on an ideological level, reducing individual psychology to a minimum, eliminating any form of self-sufficient plot, and relying far more heavily on non-linguistic effects: visual spectacle, music, sound, mime and movement. He also exploits the whole stage area (thereby fulfilling Artaud's ideal of the drama as 'poésie en espace') by separating his actors into groups evolving on different levels in relation to the stage-floor.

Le Balcon was originally given in an English translation at the Arts Theatre Club in London (April 22, 1957), produced by Peter Zadek. Plans to have the French premiere in Paris immediately afterwards, however, were brought to a halt by the Prefect of Police, who informed the directors of the Théâtre Antoine that, if they allowed Peter Brook to produce the play as announced, the ensuing 'scandale' would force him to shut down the theatre. Such was the fear, by this time, that Genet's name evoked in official circles that the play was effectively banned, and it was not given in French until this ban was tacitly lifted some three years later.

Meanwhile, Genet had written his fourth play, *Les Nègres,* which was produced in Paris by Roger Blin at the Théâtre de Lutèce on October 28, 1959 with an entirely coloured cast. *Les Nègres* is probably Genet's best play, Blin's production was impeccable, and the occasion of the premiere was perhaps Genet's greatest triumph in the theatre. Later an English version, *The Blacks,* ran for over three years at the St Mark's Playhouse in New York. The French version was awarded the *Prix de la Critique* for 1959; and it was this unqualified success, coupled with the comparative absence of large-scale scandal, that caused the ban on *Le Balcon* to be lifted. *Le Balcon* was finally given at the Théâtre du Gymnase on May 18, 1960, produced, as arranged three years earlier, by Peter Brook.

By this time, however, Genet had already completed what has so far proved to be his last play, *Les Paravents.* In a programme note to the Schlosspark-Theater production, *Les Paravents* was described as being, 'according to its author, the first of seven dramas on the subject of death – apparently the opening play in a cycle based on the Seven Deadly Sins'. (To date, the six other plays in the cycle have not materialised.) *Les Paravents,* the most flagrantly 'scandalous' of all his dramas, showing as it does the ignominious defeat of French paratroopers and colonials by the Arab insurgents in Algeria, was composed at the very height of the Algerian war-hysteria, and a production in Paris was out of the question. It was given for the first time in a truncated version in German at the Schlosspark-Theater, Berlin, on May 19, 1961; subsequently, the first twelve scenes were produced experimentally in London, and the entire play was created in Swedish at the Alléteatern, Stockholm (1964). Not until nearly four years after the end of the war in Algeria was it thought that passions had sufficiently cooled to permit a performance of the play in Paris, and the French premiere was given at the Odéon–Théâtre de France on April 16, 1966, produced by Roger Blin. The first few performances passed off quietly, but by April 30 the opposition was organised and there were violent scenes both inside and outside the theatre. Actors and spectators were injured, arrests were made, the whole Place de l'Odéon was cordoned off by riot-police: and at last the great dramatic scandal which had been brewing for nearly twenty years really did boil over.

Jean Genet has the reputation throughout the world of being the most 'scandalous' of all post-war French dramatists; and unquestionably this reputation is deserved. The problem to be decided, however, is whether these 'scandalous' qualities which exist in his plays are essential to his basic concept of theatre, and hence to his ultimate stature as a dramatist, or whether they are merely gratuitous sensationalism which, being necessarily ephemeral, will eventually relegate his position in the history of French drama to that of a rather noxious oddity.

In the main, the more traditionalist critics had little doubt about the answer. 'A travers chaque phrase', wrote Christine Garnier, reviewing *Les Paravents* in the *Revue des Deux Mondes* (June 1, 1966), 'percent une rancœur aiguë, le désir d'avilir, la haine de la société, de l'ordre établi . . . de tout!'; while some seven years earlier, Gabriel Marcel had thundered some of his more sonorous invective at *Les Nègres*:

> C'est le reniement, non pas proféré mais *expectoré*, mais *vomi*, de tout ce qui a fait l'honneur et la dignité de l'occident chrétien, et cela à la faveur d'une confusion délibérément entretenue entre l'action civilisatrice dans ce qu'elle a eu d'irrécusablement bon, et des abus, des excès, qu'il ne saurait être question de nier ou d'excuser. (*Les Nouvelles Littéraires*, December 17, 1959)

Yet the closer we look at the actual nature of the scandal, and at Genet's motives for exploiting the drama as a means of provocation, the more elusive the answer becomes. To begin with, his use of shock-tactics is unexpectedly selective. There is readily available to the modern

dramatist a very wide range of well-tested techniques deliberately calculated to provoke an audience to fury or disgust; yet many of these techniques, which are freely exploited by Arrabal, say, or by the Living
Theatre, Genet neglects completely. He appears, for instance, to be quite
content with a proscenium stage, even for *Les Paravents*, which is
theoretically destined for open-air performance, and he does very little
indeed to involve his audience *physically* in the action of the drama.
There is nothing in all his work, say, to compare with the original draft
of Ionesco's *La Cantatrice chauve*, which was intended to end with the
actors literally and violently expelling the audience from the theatre. He
makes no use of nudity (his whores, if anything, tend to be over-dressed),
no use whatsoever of the physical act of sex; more surprisingly still, even
his use of violence is extraordinarily restrained.

There *is* violence of course, but it is curiously muted and at times
even abstract – a dream-of-violence at two removes from reality, rather
than the awareness of violence as an immediate experience, chalk scrawls
on a screen rather than naturalistic massacre. There is murder but there
is no torture, and those who die – Claire in *Les Bonnes*, for instance, or
the White Woman in *Les Nègres* – die quietly and resignedly, as though
'half in love with easeful death'. Genet's murderers, too, murder for the
most part with a kind of sleepy absent-mindedness, an economy of movement which at times suggests tenderness. Lefranc's strangling of Maurice
is a series of somnambulistic gestures performed *pianissimo* (*Haute Surveillance*, p. 129); Saïd's Mother croons what might almost be a lullaby
as she gently coaxes the life out of Pierre, the young French paratrooper
(*Les Paravents*, pp. 160–3). By comparison with the intensity of violence
we find in Arrabal and Ionesco, or for that matter in Sartre and even in
Ghelderode, death steals softly across the stage in Genet's drama. Claire
(*Les Bonnes*, pp. 90–93) drinks her poisoned 'tilleul' in a mood of controlled ecstasy; the hushed repetitions of the closing litany suggest the
solemn stillness of a cathedral rather than the sordid hysteria of a cheap
boudoir; and whereas, at Le Mans in 1933, the original Papin sisters, the
models of Claire and Solange, had murdered in a welter of blood, axes
and maniacal screaming, Claire dies conscious only of the ritual beauty
of the best tea-service: 'Et tu l'as versé dans le service le plus riche, le plus
précieux.'

If the violence is muted and stylised in Genet's drama, so also is that
other element which traditionally constitutes material for scandal:
pornography. In his early poems, in his novels (most characteristically in
Pompes funèbres) and in the *Journal du Voleur*, Genet uses pornography
as an intrinsic and essential part of his subject. Nor does he attempt to
conceal this fact. Referring to Armand, one of the many brutal lovers he

half-remembers, half-invents in the *Journal du Voleur*, he observes: 'Ses impudiques attitudes, je ne puis dire qu'elles sont à l'origine de ma décision d'écrire des livres pornographiques, mais [j'en] fus certainement bouleversé' (p. 150). Of course, 'pornography' itself is a vague, blanket-like term, richer in highly-charged emotional overtones than in precise significance as an aid to critical assessment. Save perhaps in some of the earlier poems (*Le Condamné à mort*) and in one or two passages in *Notre-Dame des Fleurs*, Genet is never a pornographer in the sense that he is concerned to titillate the pleasurable sensibility of the reader. On the contrary, he deliberately exploits the most humiliating aspects of his own experience as a passive homosexual, combining them with the most degrading and nauseating realities of his life spent searching for scraps of food in dustbins or emptying latrine-buckets in prisons, to shock and horrify the reader into a reaction of appalled disgust with the human body and the human condition. In a sense, his eroticism is that of an ascetic: sexuality is one of the gruesome, Dantesque tortures reserved for the damned, and every marriage-bed – recall that of Divine and Mignon in *Notre-Dame des Fleurs* – stinks of death and putrefaction.

In the plays, however, singularly little remains of this grotesque, nauseating yet indescribably powerful vision of a writhing sexual Inferno. As with the violence, the sexual realities and perversions of Genet's characters are stylised almost into gentleness – a gentleness against which what are now purely *verbal* obscenities contrast all the more startlingly. Claire and Solange in *Les Bonnes* may have originally been conceived as a pair of aging homosexuals, like Charlie and Harry in *Staircase*. Indeed, prompted by a somewhat vague and inconclusive hint from Genet in *Notre-Dame des Fleurs* –

> S'il me fallait faire représenter une pièce théâtrale, où des femmes auraient un rôle, j'exigerais que ce rôle fût tenu par des adolescents, et j'en avertirais le public, grâce à une pancarte qui resterait clouée à droite ou à gauche des décors durant toute la représentation (Gallimard ed., p. 119),

the Living Theatre, among other groups, has actually attempted to perform the play with an all-male cast. Yet in the drama as it stands in the text, Claire and Solange are nothing more 'perverted' than a pair of middle-aged, neurotic sisters bound to each other by a ferocious and tortured love-hate relationship. The nauseous exhalations are still there, but they are those of the kitchen-sink – 'le rot silencieux de l'évier' (p. 26). The sink is a reality; Solange's affair with the milkman is not: it belongs to the stylised dream-world of Claire-as-Madame and of Solange-as-Claire:

Claire [*playing Madame, to Solange, playing Claire*]. Evitez de me frôler. Reculez-vous. Vous sentez le fauve. De quelle infecte soupente où la nuit les valets vous visitent rapportez-vous ces odeurs? La soupente! La chambre des bonnes! [. . .] La fameuse lucarne, par où le laitier demi-nu saute jusqu'à votre lit! (pp. 19–20)

This subtle transformation of the brutalised realities of sex into a remote ritual of make-believe is equally typical of all the other plays: the odour of corruption subsists, while the corruption itself is transmuted into poetry. Even when the scene is set in a brothel – as it is partly in *Les Paravents*, almost wholly in *Le Balcon* – these brothels are never literal whore-houses; and the whores themselves – Warda, Malika, even Vertu in *Les Nègres* – are even more splendid: 'symbols laden with symbols'. So completely effective is this transformation, that when Genet saw Peter Zadek's production of *The Balcony* in London (April 22, 1957) he was himself 'scandalised' by the unwarranted degree of sexual naturalism that Zadek – even under the then prevalent regime of the Lord Chamberlain – had contrived to introduce. Back in Paris three days later, it was he himself who protested, more forcibly than anyone else, against the 'eroticism' of his own 'scandalous' play:

Ma pièce, *le Balcon*, se passe dans une maison close, mais les personnages appartiennent aussi peu à la réalité des 'maisons' que les personnages de *Hamlet* appartiennent au monde des Cours.
L'univers de la chaumière, de l'usine, du palais porte en soi une signification morale. La description d'une 'maison' peut avoir un sens immoral, *qu'il faut transposer*. (*L'Express*, April 26, 1957)

Zadek's naturalistic sexuality in *Le Balcon* was (as we can now see in retrospect) as inappropriate as Piscator's politico-revolutionary naturalism applied to the same play. In the last analysis, the 'scandal', in particular of the later dramas, results not from any pornographic display of sexuality, perverted or otherwise, but rather from a juxtaposition of incompatibles which is the exact reverse of the technique that Genet had exploited in the novels. In *Miracle de la Rose*, for instance, he achieved some unforgettable effects by taking the most brutally unpalatable objects of natural experience and decking them out in a language of deliberately conventional 'poetic' beauty: the thuggish murderer is visualised as a 'Mystic Rose', and when Mignon (in *Notre-Dame des Fleurs*) picks his nose, 'de ses narines il arracha des pétales d'acacia et des violettes' (*Notre-Dame*, p. 138). In *Les Bonnes*, traces of this technique still remain. 'Mon jet de salive,' declares Solange, 'c'est mon aigrette de diamants' (p. 34); and it might be argued that the bank-clerk from the Crédit Lyonnais who, in *Le Balcon*, transforms his paid prostitute into a vision of the Virgin Mary, is indulging in a similar process of anomalous transposition. None the less, the primary shock-technique of the plays in this particular respect consists, not in poeticising the unpoetic, but in using the crudest, vulgarest and most barbaric language of the latrines and the barrack-room to describe situations that, in themselves, are not devoid of poetry or of purity, and which could equally well be formulated in the language of a rational dialectic.

This technique is most highly developed in *Les Paravents*, and its efficacy as a shock-producer is evident from the reactions of the original audiences. In those sections of the play where Genet uses his old novelist's technique, the poetic glorification of the obscene and the vulgar – for instance, in the bejewelled and be-hair-pinned figure, rich and wondrous as a goddess from some oriental temple, of Warda-the-Whore – Genet's poetry emerges triumphant: the sordidness of the 'real' object beneath the glittering crystals of the vision is forgotten, and forgotten far more completely than it ever can be in *Notre-Dame des Fleurs* or in *Miracle de la Rose*. But the scenes which had the young Saint-Cyriens, the neo-nazis of *Occident* and the veterans of Indochina and Algeria beside themselves with fury, hurling steel bolts and Bengal lights at the stage and twice bringing the performance to a full stop (April 30, 1966) were above all those in which a heroic or poetic situation was 'defiled' by being accompanied with the gestures and the language of a dirty-minded schoolboy. For this is in fact the characteristic of Genet's shock-language in most of his more notoriously 'scandalous' scenes: it is not adult obscenity, it is cheap, juvenile smut. (Recently, a twelve-year-old, having pestered his father to be allowed to read the *Screens*, remained utterly absorbed for half an hour. Then gradually disillusionment became evident on his face. 'Just like scout-camp', he muttered, and put the book down.) And there is no doubt whatsoever but that this is deliberate. When the heroic French Lieutenant in *Les Paravents* (pp. 197–9) lies dying, his men surround him and salute him with a last breath of the air of his beloved native land . . . by farting over his face:

> Jojo (*d'une voix très douce*). Bien sûr, il ne sera pas en terre française, mais enfin, on peut tout de même. Puisqu'on n'a que ça . . . il aura l'illusion de s'éteindre dans sa cabane natale . . . (*il hésite*). Toi, Roger, si t'as des gaz de rab, et les autres aussi . . . on pourrait lui en lâcher une bouffée.
>
> Roger: Moi . . . J'ai pas plus que ma ration.
>
> Jojo: Y a pas longtemps, tu disais . . .

Le Lieutenant (*d'une voix mourante*):   A boire...

Nestor: C'est un devoir qu'on doit remplir. S'il n'est pas enseveli en terre chrétienne au moins qu'il respire en mourant un peu d'air de chez nous...

Dulce et decorum est pro patria mori . . . In this scene of course, Genet is gleefully and spitefully debunking the standard values of the traditional French Establishment, together with all its ideals (however shabby in reality) and all its culture. But if this were all, there would be little or nothing to justify Genet's inclusion among the major dramatists of modern France – certainly nothing to incite J.-J. Rinieri to compare him with 'Racine, Baudelaire et Proust' (*La Nef*, March 1949), or Maurice Saillet with Shakespeare (*La Quinzaine Littéraire*, May 15, 1966). The extraordinary quality of this scene (and of most of the other scenes that remain in the memory) is that Genet, strange as it may seem, is not primarily making value-judgements. He is making poetry. If the situation appears as a vile insult to noble values (or, alternatively, as a revolutionary assault on bourgeois conformism: it depends on one's point of view), this is because the audience, on its own responsibility, *chooses* to make such an interpretation. But Genet is not fundamentally concerned with interpretation; he is concerned with one thing only: to create archetypes in the theatre. For him, an archetype – an aesthetically perfect, therefore self-justifying creation – is a being in whom outward mask (appearance, words, gestures) corresponds exactly to inner reality. He 'is what he is'; in a Sartrian sense, he is 'authentic'. All Genet's dramatic characters have this desperate sincerity of purpose, this tormented longing for authenticity. Claire and Solange want to *be* maids; Lefranc wants to *be* a murderer, as totally and as perfectly as Yeux-Verts or as Boule-de-Neige; the Bishop, the Judge and the General of *Le Balcon* want to *be*, to all eternity in the immutable solitude of absolute existence, the archetypes that their regalia proclaim them; the Blacks want to *be* black: '*Archibald*: Je vous ordonne d'être noir jusque dans vos veines et d'y charrier du sang noir. Que l'Afrique y circule. Que les Nègres se nègrent' . . . (p. 76) And so it is with the most notorious of all Genet's obscenities. The heroic Lieutenant, whose 'mask' hitherto, throughout the play, has been one of ranting, caricatural, incredible, absurd heroism, *does* die heroically, and so he becomes what he is: an archetypal hero . . . but none the less absurd for that. And the soldiers, vulgar and absurd in the senseless obscenity of their gesture, realise their essence as archetypal soldiers, for *THE* Soldier (the anonymous, mindless, foul-mouthed automaton of any army) *is* vulgar, stupid and obscene. And so two archetypes are created, and Jean Genet sincerely loves them both, just as he had loved the 'inégalable bêtise' of the convicts at Fontevrault. For him, the theatre is 'un art poétique, non un spectacle'; and the dying-officer scene, together with all others like it, '[sont] destinées à exalter – je dis bien *exalter* – la vertu majeur de l'Armée, sa vertu capitale: la bêtise' (*Lettres à Roger Blin*, p. 63).

'Mes pièces sont écrites contre moi-même.' In his famous essay, Jean-Paul Sartre coined the name 'Saint Genet', but perhaps without realising quite what a degree of self-mortification there is in this particular brand of sanctity. And this too, perhaps, is one of the significances of Genet's pornography. It is his own aesthete's passion for delicate beauty, his hypersensitive need for poetic form, which is bruised and insulted by these archetypes of shoddy obscenity that he has created. And it is certainly his own 'intelligence foudroyante' which is tortured by the 'inégalable bêtise' of his characters.

But Genet is a complex character, and of course no one explanation will ever wholly suffice. He may not *specifically* set out to scandalise his audience, yet the fact remains that scandalisation is an essential part of his dramatic method. It is scandalous to make poetry out of the sort of language that, by rights, has its place on the walls of public lavatories; it is, in a more subtle way, equally scandalous to make a negress off the streets (Vertu) talk like the Princesse de Clèves. It is scandalous to show a Bishop 'realising his authenticity' with a whore in a brothel, however stylised. The exaltation of stupidity at the expense of intelligence is in itself a 'scandalous' statement, no less for a progressive and rationalistic Left than for a well-educated and privileged Right. It is scandalous to make a pantomime for ballet out of racial violence; it is scandalous to make the wrong side win, or, as an alternative, to make the right side win for the wrong reasons. It is scandalous to make good plays out of bad politics (even *Les Bonnes* was interpreted by the early critics as a 'scandalous' revelation of the appalling social conditions of domestic servants); it is scandalous at all events to be the sort of anarchist that Genet undoubtedly is.

In other words, to the scandal of violence and the scandal of obscenity, Genet adds, particularly in his last three 'Brechtian' plays, the scandal of unpopular political opinions. If the Right was offended by the opening scenes of *Le Balcon*, the Left was equally insulted by the sight of a revolutionary hero castrating himself in the presence of the Chief of Police, thereby acknowledging with a gesture of irremediable defeatism the failure of the revolution and the impotence of its ideals. 'C'est un traître à la révolution', proclaimed Claude Olivier after seeing *Le Balcon* (*Arts*, May 26, 1960). In *Les Nègres*, Genet shows the ruthless victory of Black Power over White values, and foretells with smug satisfaction the downfall of the West, its most exquisite beauties, its noblest intellectual achievements:

> . . . vierges du Parthénon, ange du portail de Reims, colonnes valériennes, Musset, Chopin, Vincent d'Indy, cuisine française, Soldat Inconnu, chansons tyroliennes, principes cartésiens, ordonnance de Le Nôtre, coquelicots, bleuets, un brin de coquetterie, jardins de curés . . . (p. 69)

– all these are ground to dust beneath the blind and arbitrary forces of black racialism. *Les Paravents* not only exults in the prospect of an Arab victory over French forces, but did so originally in the period 1959–60, when almost every family, bourgeois and proletarian alike, had a relative or a friend obliged to fight in Algeria, and thus felt Genet's attack as a personal, gratuitous and unforgivable insult.

On the other hand, the precise purpose of this calculated scandalisation of the audience is as hard to determine as the precise motivation of Genet's flagrant exploitation of obscenity. It is, in fact, quite possible to argue: (i) that Genet, in the violence of his political provocation, is not making a political statement at all, but a dramatic or aesthetic statement; (ii) that even if he is making a conscious political statement, he is not expressing in any way his personal opinions, but is simply revealing, without comment, the harsh but true realities of the modern world; and (iii) that even if he is making a sincere and personal 'profession de foi politique', he is not only justified in so doing, but is in effect one of the most far-sighted and perspicacious observers of our time – the forerunner of Marcuse and Che Guevara, the one true herald of the *événements de mai*, and the most effective debunker of Establishment values and Establishment programmes that France has seen since the Commune.

It is this ever-present ambiguity, this constant presence of conflicting political and moral significances on different levels simultaneously that gives the text of Genet's drama its intellectual density, in almost exactly the same way as the constant juxtaposition of mask and reality, of identity and make-belief, gives these same plays their dramatic intensity. For, to take the second of our three broad categories of interpretation first, it is equally true to affirm and to deny that Genet is 'personally sincere' in giving his characters the opinions they periodically express.

Genet is frequently accused of being a fascist, largely on account of his glorification of the French *Milice* under the Nazi occupation in *Pompes funèbres* and in the *Journal du Voleur*. But fascist or crypto-fascist implications have been read into the plays as well, even into *Les Nègres*, which Maurice Régnaut, for instance, sees as a sort of Enoch-Powellish piece of racist hysteria, 'un manichéisme apocalyptique . . . une révolte contre l'histoire' (*Théâtre Populaire*, No. 36, 1959), and as a bourgeois-fascist 'betrayal of socialism'.

Yet there is little or nothing in Genet's own life, as far as it is known, to justify this accusation. We have Simone de Beauvoir's evidence (*La Force des choses*, p. 14) that Genet disliked and despised the German troops that were occupying Paris; even more precisely, we know that, between 1936 and 1938, Genet frequented and was accepted by a whole circle of actively anti-fascist, left-wing intellectuals in Czechoslovakia; that, from his prison-cell in Katowice, he wrote a letter lamenting the fall of Léon Blum and the Front Populaire; and that in Berlin in 1937 he was welcomed with cordiality by Wilhelm Leuschner, the self-educated trade-union leader who, some seven years later, was to organise the 'Generals' Plot' to assassinate Hitler and was hanged in consequence. [The evidence for these statements consists: (i) of an unpublished correspondence dated 1937–8; (ii) personal communications from surviving members of the group; (iii) the 'Pringsheim documents', published in my *Theater of Jean Genet: A Casebook*. The *facts* concerning the months that Genet spent in Brno prove how unwise it is to accept the *Journal du Voleur* as valid autobiography.] Everything therefore suggests that Genet began his career politically in the nineteen-thirties on the moderate Left – radical, radical-socialist or social-democrat – and has since moved progressively further and further left, abandoning socialism in the end for a brand of anarchism so intransigent, so uncompromising and so totally negative that it can only express itself by paradox: where *all* organised political parties of whatever complexion are equally unacceptable, then it is possible for Genet, with complete sincerity, to glorify the efficiency of the police state in one play (*Le Balcon*) and to exult in the destruction of the armies of that same state in another (*Les Paravents*); to show an oppressed race conquering its temptation to assume the values and the culture of its oppressors in *Les Nègres*, and, in the final scenes of *Les Paravents*, to show another oppressed race gaining the victory over its oppressors precisely through the efficiency with which it imitates them.

Clearly, then, politics constitute a third major element in the 'scandal' of Genet's dramas; yet here again, nothing is clear, nothing is straightforward. There are no easy answers. Genet himself was so upset by unwarranted politico-sociological interpretations of *Les Bonnes* that, in all editions after 1954, he included in his preface a categorical warning against them: 'Une chose doit être écrite: il ne s'agit pas d'un plaidoyer sur le sort des domestiques. Je suppose qu'il existe un syndicat des gens de maison – cela ne nous regarde pas' (p. 11). Nevertheless, the combined influence of Sartre, Brecht and – more problematically – of Antonin Artaud has been so strong that, of the five plays he has published, *Haute*

Surveillance alone can be said to be wholly free of commitment. War and colonialism, the oppression of minorities, race-hatreds, revolt and revolution: these seem hardly the ivory-tower topics of a mystic and an aesthete. And yet in fact – most brittle of all Jean Genet's many paradoxes – they are precisely this. Genet's *engagement* is not in itself a sham, nor are his plays merely the ingenious technical triumphs of a splendid craftsman. Emotionally he is always on the side of his heroes – for the right or for the wrong reasons. 'Pourquoi êtes-vous du côté des Algériens?' his friends would ask him as early as 1954; and invariably he would reply: 'Parce que je suis toujours du côté du plus fort' (*Le Monde*, April 16, 1966). The fact remains, however that Genet is *engagé malgré lui*. His politics are never an end in themselves. Like his violence, like his pornography, they are a means to an end. And the same thing is true of his scandalisation of the church.

> L'idéal religieux est peut-être d'ailleurs celui qui m'a le plus ébranlé, et je crois en effet que tout n'est 'pas perdu' puisque j'ai encore cette naïveté d'avoir la foi. Dieu la donne aux enfants. Et puis, n'a-t-il [pas], comme le dit Mauriac, 'sauvé ce qui était perdu'? (*from an unpublished letter*)

– these sentences were written by Genet in the winter of 1937–8; and there is no evidence to suggest that he has ever changed his opinions. His plays and his novels alike are dominated by an intense mysticism which, for all its curiously inverted corollaries, is in fact much closer to traditional Catholicism than to any form of rationalistic deism. The democratic God of social equality is completely foreign to Genet's far more primitive and intense religiosity. The emphasis is never on God's nearness, but always on the immense, the inconceivable distance that separates the terrible power and beauty of the Divine from that miserable and abject being that is man. God is unpredictable, unjust, tyrannical and frightening – the God of Calvin or of Jansen rather than that of Rousseau. As François Mauriac quite correctly concluded when he saw *Haute Surveillance*, Genet's people long for the gift of Grace as fervently as did Pascal: but there is nothing they can do about it – it cannot be acquired or merited, either it is given or it is not given, and if it is not given, then there is no escape from damnation.

But herein lies the scandal – a scandal so outrageous that, in *Miracle de la Rose*, it drives Genet to one of his most frenzied cries of despair and revolt: 'C'est proprement la sainteté [. . .] de vivre selon le Ciel, *malgré Dieu*' (*Miracle de la Rose*, p. 216). For there is no escape from damnation even when the gift of Grace *is* given. The first quality of the Grace that is given by God is the intuition to know God. God is all that man is not:

and man can only know God, therefore, by knowing himself to be different. If God is immense, glorious, powerful or (just conceivably) good, then man's knowledge of God begins with his knowing himself to be abject, insignificant, mean and evil. And to be all these things – in the eyes of the world, the Church and even of most Christian mystics excepting Dostoyevsky – is to be on the road to damnation. The argument is most clearly set out in *Haute Surveillance*, but it can be sensed beneath the surface in *Les Paravents* and perhaps also in *Les Nègres*. In all three plays, the essential dramatic conflict on a spiritual, but also on a real and visible level, lies between two groups of beings: those who have received the gift of 'Grace' – Boule-de-Neige, Yeux-Verts; Saïd, Leïla and the Mother (the 'Children of the Nettle'); and all the Blacks except Samba Graham Diouf – and those to whom it has been denied. The difference between the two levels of damnation lies in a kind of spiritual richness: those who do not have the gift grow arid, intellectually tormented by the fact that they have done nothing to deserve their casting-out; those who have it submit almost joyously to their own degradation and annihilation, knowing that, even without realising exactly what has happened, they are somehow working out a purpose and lending significance to the absurdity and the 'scandal' of death.

It is this concept of 'sanctity through abjection' – a concept explored with unremitting persistence in the novels – that occasions the 'scandal' of the plays on a religious level; but it requires a certain degree of religious susceptibility in the spectator – in a Gabriel Marcel or a François Mauriac – to be appreciated. By contrast, in so far as Genet indulges at all in the more obvious means of shocking the *bien-pensants*, he does so only with the mildest of squibs and allusions. Apart from the repetition of the phrase 'voici l'homme' or 'tu es l'homme', vaguely suggestive of the 'Ecce Homo' of the Christian tragedy, there is, in the whole of *Haute Surveillance*, hardly more than the most fleeting reference to the traditional concept of God, for all that the play is entirely about Grace:

> Yeux-Verts . . . Je n'ai rien voulu. Tu m'entends? Je n'ai rien voulu de ce qui m'est arrivé. Tout m'a été donné. Un cadeau. Du bon dieu ou du diable, mais quelque chose que je n'ai pas voulu. (p. 131)

In *Les Bonnes*, Claire (as Madame) refers with biting sarcasm to the little altar on the chest-of-drawers up in the maids' attic, and to their pathetic devotions, their genuflexions to the plaster statuette of the Virgin, with her decor of paper flowers (pp. 19–21). The Blacks sing their *Litanie des Blêmes* to the tune of *Dies Irae*, while the Missionary utters the inane professional platitudes that are to be expected of him. In the brothel known as 'Le grand Balcon', one customer dresses up as a Bishop, while another indulges in the sensuous luxury of communing with the Virgin Mary . . . all this is really so tame, so un-scandalous, so devoid moreover of the least trace of derision (save in the case of the Missionary) directed against religion as such, or even against the Church. Genet the believer is constantly tempted to invert the *moral* values conventionally associated with his beliefs, but he never seems to question these beliefs in themselves, still less does he deny the intensity of authentic emotion to be derived from them.

On analysis, therefore, the 'scandalousness' of Genet's dramas is revealed as something which is rarely, if ever, gratuitous. In those aspects where the temptation of sensation for sensation's sake might be strongest – in the portrayal of violence on the stage, as in the calculated use of blasphemy and irreligion – Genet consistently refuses to exploit the full potential of his explosive material. In the other two cases – obscenity and political or racial provocation – the scandalising power of the themes and situations is used far more deliberately: but even here (and this is true of religion also), the 'shock-effect' results, not so much from the questioning of creeds or ideologies in themselves, as from the reversal of certain concomitant moral values traditionally associated with them. As an anarchist, Genet does not query the value of revolution, although in *Le Balcon* he may doubt its effectiveness in the face of modern police methods of repression: he simply inverts the distribution of values. For a Brecht or for a Gorky, the revolutionary proletarian hero is 'good', the bourgeois-capitalist exploiter is 'bad' (which is of course why both dramatists have committed so much third-rate drama); with Genet, almost invariably, it is the socio-political 'villains' who embody the traditional qualities and virtues of a sophisticated civilisation, while his revolutionary 'heroes' (unless they are just cardboard figures like Roger-le-plombier in *Le Balcon*) are cruel and sadistic, abject and evil.

This transposition, on the politico-ethical level, exactly mirrors the transpositions of identity (from Black to White, from maid to mistress, from looking-glass Bishop to real-life prelate) which form the basic dramatic material in three out of the five plays. Moreover, the effect of these transpositions in combination is to force the spectator into a position where he is compelled, by the intensity of the dramatic situation and the sheer power of the language, to identify himself emotionally with certain characters on the stage – and thus to respond authentically to Genet's own authentic fervour – without being able to justify this identification by any rational argument. He can identify emotionally with Solange, but not rationally, since 'Solange' is an identity so unstable that she may at any moment become Claire or even Madame. He can identify emotionally with Saïd as a revolutionary hero, but not rationally, since this 'hero' gradually accumulates in himself every vice known to the puritanical code of archetypal revolution. In other words, he is left suspended in a kind of vacuum, in which all reasoned arguments and certainties cancel each other out, leaving nothing but a stormy chaos of irrational hatreds.

And this is the real motive that lies behind Genet's technique of 'scandalisation'. The spectator is to be stripped of his rational faculties; he is to be provoked into taking sides for or against – above all, *against* – characters who do not exist and arguments which cancel each other out; his reason and his emotion are forced into contradiction, and he is obliged to agree and disagree with himself simultaneously, to believe and not to believe in the actions he is witnessing. And this conflict of opposites which confronts both play and spectator with a contradiction of evidence which is logically impossible, lies at the very root of Genet's concept of the theatre, and of his whole understanding of 'poetry'.

Genet's use of the term 'poetry' is unusual. It is not a literary art: it is a spiritual or metaphysical experience. 'Sous la poésie des textes', wrote Artaud, 'il y a la poésie tout court, sans forme et sans texte' (*Œuvres complètes* IV, p. 94). 'Poetry' is the actual *experience* of a certain type of situation, to which the words merely lend form; as words, they are in the last analysis superfluous – and therefore, since the 'poetry' is not in them, they are not bound by any intrinsically 'poetic' laws. They can be banal, precious, conventionally pretty – or obscene. It is the wordless experience that is, in essence, 'poetic', and, for Genet, this experience has much in common with the mystic's ecstatic awareness of being simultaneously in the presence of two realites, of existing in two incompatible dimensions: the finite and the infinite.

As a man, Jean Genet may well accuse himself of possessing 'la naïveté d'avoir la foi'; as a writer, his mysticism is all-pervading, and anything rather than 'naïf'. The most specific and the most persistent theme in his work is the relating of a particular spiritual experience: not that of human dimension ('le réel'), nor that of a superhuman dimension ('les anges'), but that of a point at which the two meet, coincide, contradict and exclude each other, and yet exist simultaneously. In a more purely metaphysical sense, it is this experience that Genet attempts to describe as 'sanctity'. It *is* a mystical experience, in that it is the simultaneous realisation of two mutually exclusive realities; but it can also be a literary experience, in that it is a spiritual and emotional interpretation of the precise implications of symbolism.

A 'symbol' is a phenomenon which concentrates in itself simultaneously two conflicting dimensions of reality. A rose is on the one hand a well-categorised botanical specimen, dicotyledonous, having a given number of stamens and pistils, corollas and bracts, arranged according to a pattern established by an evolutionary process; on the other, it is the damask cheeks of the beloved, the enmity of York and Lancaster, the Jewel of Sharon, the bride and victim of Blake's 'invisible worm that flies in the night', the Heart of Christ. In everyday life, as in literature, those who use or react to symbols tend to neglect the real and literal nature of the material object, and to concentrate upon its transcendental significance. Few Israelis, faced with an Arab attack, reflect on the chemical composition of the fibres and dye-stuffs that compose the flag under whose emblematic support they go into action; few Catholics at communion ponder deeply over the working conditions and trade-union disputes at the bakery which produced the Bread of the Eucharist.

Genet is fundamentally a symbolist: but he differs radically from the great figures of earlier symbolist literature, from Blake to Mallarmé, in that his 'poetry' (which includes, of course, his drama) does not simply *use* the objects of everyday experience as a means to transcendental intuition, but springs directly from the contrast between the two simultaneous realities: the vile, material root, and the mysterious, ineffable flower. And the more violent the contrast between the one and the other, the more vulgar, obscene and loathsome the matter and the more exquisite the symbol, the more intense, for Genet, is the experience and the more vivid the poetry.

In the novels, this 'poetry' is expressed, among a thousand other examples, in the contrast between the reality of Adrien Baillon, a moronic, homosexual, adolescent gangster who murdered an old man for a few francs, and his nickname: Notre-Dame des Fleurs. But in the plays, the working out of this basic theme is more complex, because the theatre, by its very nature, adds several additional layers of conflicting reality: the actor and the hero he incarnates; stage-dimensions, measurable in cubic feet, and the dimensions of the drama, immeasurable save in terms of intensity and emotion; mask and reality, illusion and brute fact. But at whatever level the conflict takes place, the essence of a truly 'poetic' theatre, in Genet's interpretation, is that *both* elements should be granted an equal measure of simultanous belief and disbelief. 'Il faut à la fois y croire et refuser d'y croire', he notes in *Les Bonnes* (p. 10); and elsewhere: 'Toute représentation est vaine si je ne crois pas à ce que je vois qui cessera – qui n'aura jamais été – quand le rideau tombera' (*Lettre à Pauvert*, p. 146). Only when illusion and reality are known and experienced simultaneously will the theatre cease to become a *divertissement* and become a symbol.

Genet uses two illustrations to clarify his conception of the ideal theatre: the first is the ceremony of the Holy Mass; the second, a tale of small boys playing at soldiers:

> Un jeune écrivain m'a raconté avoir vu dans un jardin public cinq ou six gamins jouant à la guerre. Divisés en deux troupes, ils s'apprêtaient à l'attaque. La nuit, disaient-ils, allait venir. Mais il était midi dans le ciel. Ils décidèrent donc que l'un d'eux serait la Nuit. Le plus jeune et le plus frêle, devenu élémentaire, fut alors le maître des combats. 'Il' était l'Heure, le Moment, l'Inéluctable. De très loin, paraît-il, il venait, avec le calme d'un cycle, mais alourdi par la tristesse et la pompe crépusculaires. A mesure de son approche, les autres, les Hommes, devenaient nerveux, inquiets ... Mais l'enfant, à leur gré, venait trop tôt. Il était en avance sur lui-même: d'un commun accord les Troupes et les Chefs décidèrent de supprimer la Nuit, qui redevint soldat d'un camp ... C'est à partir de cette seule formule qu'un théâtre saurait me ravir. (*Lettre à Pauvert*, pp. 147–8)

What these two illustrations have in common is that, in both cases, the participants believe simultaneously in two levels of reality. There is no disguise and no illusion to cause material reality to disappear: if the officiating priest serving bread and wine is *felt* to be the Servant of Christ offering the Body and Blood of Christ, if the small boy is *felt* to be Night even while, to every observer, he is nothing else but a very ordinary small boy, this is because it is not illusion, but the *wish to believe* in the mind of the observer that transmutes reality into symbol, even while this same mind is still unrelentingly and lucidly conscious of the real. If the bread were disguised as flesh, this would be nothing but 'une triste frivolité'; if the bread, visible as bread, is *believed* to be flesh, then this is drama.

On the other hand, no normal adult can believe (in the fullest positive sense, as opposed to the conventional 'suspension of disbelief') in two conflicting evidences, unless he is in the grip of some emotion powerful enough to cause him both to accept and to ignore the contradiction. In the case of the Mass, there is the faith and fervour of the communicants; in the case of the war-game, there is the total absorption of children in a world of passionate make-believe. But Genet's audiences, all in all, are neither ecstatic Catholics nor children, and so some different stimulus is needed to involve the onlookers in so furious a ferment of participation that they themselves will 'wish to believe', and in consequence themselves transform the painted flats and professional gestures of the theatre into a universe of archetypes.

But contemporary audiences are pretty blasé; they have seen too much and believe too little, and few of them are uncomplicated enough to share Genet's own 'naïveté' in Faith. Not many stimuli are left, in this middle twentieth century, which can evoke the blind and passionate responses – the instinctive, violent, irrational reactions – that were once accorded to a John Knox or a Savonarola. Religion – except perhaps in Ireland – awakens scarcely an echo of its ancient hatreds. But the hatreds themselves are not extinct; they *can* be roused up, and with them, the intensity of emotion needed to transmute simple play-acting into poetic experience. And these stimuli are: sex, with all its perversions, obscenities and sensational degradations; politics, with its corollaries of revolution and repression, mass-lies and mass-hysteria, conformism and corruption; and racial confrontation, accompanied by ritual murder, ambush, massacre and war. Actors acting the murder of Thomas à Becket will need to disguise themselves in medieval costume if they are to be believed today, for what they are creating is illusion; but actors acting – to a black audience at all events – the murder of Martin Luther King will have no need to disguise themselves in any way whatsoever. The spectators will transform them from individuals into archetypes by the very violence of their own reaction, and they will be creating not illusion any more, but symbols.

Thus it follows that Genet's 'scandalisation' – his muted violence, his sexual obscenities, his provocations offered alike to White and Black, to Colonial and Arab, to communist and bourgeois – is not an accidental, but a fundamental and necessary part, not only of his dramatic technique, but of his very vision of the theatre, its purpose and its poetry. From *Les Bonnes*, with its poisonous lyricism composed of garish finery, hysteria, saliva, bad breath and rotten teeth, to *Les Paravents*, with its heroes painted like whores and its whores arrayed with the bravado of heroes; from Lefranc, who murders the defenceless Maurice in order to merit a halo of sanctity, to Village who murders a White woman in order to give his hatred the final perfection of a Mozart minuet – every act of violence, every calculated obscenity, every cynical paradox that calls good evil and worships evil as good, every stab of political cynicism or racialist incitement is introduced and handled with the controlled dexterity of a master. 'Scandal' is the means, poetry is the end: and poetry is also – in Genet's view – the ultimate justification.

To discuss whether this justification-through-poetry is ultimately valid is to raise once again, and in its acutest form, the whole problem of the relationship between art and ethics, and the whole thorny, disreputable question of censorship. The most serious accusation that can be levelled against Genet is not so much that he is an immoralist, as that he is a fanatic: a poet who, in his quest for poetry, is prepared to sacrifice *all* other human values and achievements and yet who, as his ideal, is proposing a spiritual experience so rare and remote that perhaps not one spectator out of a hundred in any given audience will be able to share it. In this case, it could be held that the end no longer justifies the means, consequently that the scandals are in reality what they have always seemed to critics such as Jean-Jacques Gautier and Gabriel Marcel: just so many gratuitous gestures flung out by a dangerously corrupt and sadistic being bent on committing a maximum of evil among his fellow-creatures during the span of time allotted him on this earth. 'Now that I am getting old,' says the hero of Italo Svevo's *Confessions of Zeno*, 'and begin to approach the patriarchal state, I too feel that it is worse to preach immorality than to practise it. One may be driven to commit murder by love or hatred, but one can only advocate murder out of sheer wickedness.'

Yet for every critic who feels like Zeno Cosini about Genet's scandals, there is another who leaves the theatre with his brain on fire from the effects of an experience so profoundly moving that only the greatest dramatists in the world – a Shakespeare, a Chekhov, a Racine – have created anything to compare with it. It is of course far too early as yet to hope to give any categorical value-judgements concerning the plays as literature. Nonetheless, there is one danger that any dramatist who, like Genet, bases his whole concept of the theatre on the dramatic effects of scandal must envisage, and that is, that what is scandalous today may not necessarily be so tomorrow. *Les Paravents* is already less effective now than when it was written; what will remain of it when the Algerian War is as distant as the Crimean, or even the South African? When there are no more racial hatreds, no more servants, no more brothels and no more revolutions, what will be left of *Les Nègres*, *Les Bonnes*, *Le Balcon*? It is a real danger, and Genet's true stature will only become known once his scandals no longer reflect the more urgent and immediate preoccupations of his audiences. But one suspects, watching the daily press, that the Utopian society, which will permit this final and exact assessment, is not exactly due to dawn tomorrow. And meanwhile, these dramas which Mauriac had once castigated as 'l'Excrémentialisme' are hailed by Maurice Saillet as 'scandals to put an end to scandal' – and if there is no longer an Algerian war to be put an end to, there is always a Vietnam war to take its place:

> Car s'il faut que le scandale arrive – et il va sans dire que l'interminable et multiple scandale que fut la guerre d'Algérie arriva et perdura sans que Genet y soit pour rien – il faut surtout qu'il cesse. Et pour que se résolve cette formidable vague de fond, il ne s'agit pas de se

laisser porter par son écume [. . .] mais il s'agit d'aller au fond du scandale, et de traiter par le fond les forces mystérieuses et souvent monstrueuses qui l'animent. Or *Les Paravents* atteignent ce fond, et prouvent par là même qu'il n'est pas, aujourd'hui, *de dramaturge moralement plus qualifié* [. . .] pour exorcer les fantômes du drame franco-algérien. (*La Quinzaine Littéraire*, May 15, 1966)

Select Bibliography

GENET, JEAN

   Les Bonnes, précédé de Comment jouer les Bonnes   Décines, L'Arbalète, 1963²
   Haute Surveillance ('ed. définitive')   Paris, Gallimard, 1965
   Le Balcon   Décines, L'Arbalète, 1962³
   Les Nègres   Décines, L'Arbalète, 1958
   Les Paravents   Décines, L'Arbalète, 1961
   'Lettre à Pauvert sur *les Bonnes*' (1954), in *Les Bonnes et l'Atelier d'Alberto Giacometti*   Décines, L'Arbalète, 1958
   Lettres à Roger Blin   Paris, Gallimard, 1966
   Le Journal du Voleur   Paris, Gallimard, 1949
   Œuvres complètes, vol. II (*Notre-Dame des Fleurs, Le Condamné à mort, Miracle de la Rose, Un Chant d'amour*), vol. III (*Pompes funèbres, Le Pêcheur du Suquet, Querelle de Brest*)   Paris, Gallimard, 1951, 1953

BATAILLE, GEORGES   *La Littérature et le mal*   Paris, Gallimard, 1957, pp. 185–226
BONNEFOY, CLAUDE   *Jean Genet*   Paris, Éditions Universitaires, 1965
COE, RICHARD N.
   'Jean Genet. A Checklist of His Writings in French, English and German', *Australian Journal of French Studies*, VI, no. 1 (1969), 113–30
   The Vision of Jean Genet   London, Peter Owen, 1968
   The Theater of Jean Genet: A Casebook   New York, Grove Press, 1970
DRIVER, TOM F.   *Jean Genet*   New York, Columbia University Press, 1966
KNAPP, BETTINA L.   *Genet*   New York, Twayne, 1968
MCMAHON, JOSEPH H.   *The Imagination of Jean Genet*   New Haven, Yale University Press, 1963
SARTRE, JEAN-PAUL   *Saint Genet, comédien et martyr*. In *Œuvres complètes de Jean Genet*, vol. I   Paris, Gallimard, 1952
THODY, PHILIP   *Jean Genet: A Critical Appraisal*   London, Hamish Hamilton, 1968

9

IONESCO   *James R. Knowlson*

For the past twenty years, Eugène Ionesco has written almost exclusively for the stage. His only non-dramatic writing in that time consists of a volume of notes and essays, *Notes et contre-notes*, which are primarily reflections on the theatre in general and on his own plays in particular, a collection of *nouvelles*, entitled *La Photo du colonel*, upon which several of his plays were based, and two volumes of his journals, *Journal en miettes* and *Présent passé, passé présent*, which go back to the years before the war in Rumania, but which throw considerable light on the memories and dreams, obsessions and fears that provide some of the raw material for his later work.

One of the main reasons why Ionesco has devoted so much attention to the theatre is clearly because it has offered him a medium in which he could best explore his own most fundamental concerns in ways quite distinct from those of conceptual thought and discursive language. By creating a highly individual form of theatre in which the surprising, the fantastic, the irrational and the paradoxical play a large part, and in which dream sequences, and visual, as well as verbal, images also figure prominently, he has been able to express aspects of existence (and particularly of the inner life of man) that, in purely rational terms, might appear difficult to reconcile, even totally contradictory. Ionesco has said that many of his plays were created at times when there was the least semblance of equilibrium and coherence in his thought and feelings, at times indeed when he came nearest to a state of inner chaos. And yet the dramatic world which results from the materialisation and exteriorisation of these conflicts and contradictions possesses a much greater degree of internal coherence and unity than might at first appear to be the case.

For a play is not, or in Ionesco's view, should not be a demonstration of something already formulated. It is, or again should be, *itself* the means of exploration, in which dialogue, movement, and scenic images are all used as important instruments of discovery. 'Toute pièce est pour moi', he wrote in *L'Impromptu de l'Alma*, 'une aventure, une chasse, une découverte d'un univers qui se révèle à moi-même, de la présence duquel je suis le premier à être étonné . . .' (*Théâtre* II, p. 13). Ionesco's creative writing springs basically then from the urge to seek, within the dramatic forms he adopts, for some understanding of the world of 'reality' and of the self. Writing of the activity of the dramatist, and comparing it with that of the philosopher or the painter, he wrote that 'Le dialogue et le mouvement du théâtre sont sa façon même d'explorer le réel, de s'explorer soi-même, de comprendre et de se comprendre' (*Journal en miettes*, p. 218).

But the exploration of 'reality' may take innumerable forms. Though Ionesco ranges over an extremely wide terrain, he is concerned with social and political problems, for instance, almost exclusively in their effects upon the inner life of man. And if the form and the style of his plays have changed considerably in the course of his career, his central concern has remained that of the relationship between the 'self' and the 'non-self', looked at through his own awareness of existence and his fundamental responses to it. Though, in a philosophical sense, his investigation may appear to have led only to the most banal of everyday truths, his dramatic world is, by contrast, highly original, compelling and, at its best, rich in verbal and visual poetry. Though the later plays sometimes suffer from too great a complexity in thematic or dramatic structure, there is, as I hope to show in this brief study of the most important plays, little that is gratuitous (unless it is deliberately so), since every element in an extremely wide theatrical 'vocabulary' has its part to play in Ionesco's central exploration.

Though once considered highly controversial, Ionesco's early one-act pieces are now widely acclaimed and have been performed probably more often throughout the world than any other modern plays. Ionesco came somewhat fortuitously to the theatre with the writing of *La Cantatrice chauve*, first produced by Nicolas Bataille in the little Théâtre des Noctambules in May 1950. The story of how he found the inspiration for his play in the incredible banality, yet astonishing truth, of certain phrases in the Méthode Assimil English course, is now extremely well known. Yet far from merely borrowing phrases from the English textbook or transposing the clichés, the platitudes and the proverbs that he had observed in everyday speech, Ionesco's imagination arranged, grouped, and above all radically transformed these elements into a dense, comic dialogue in which rhythm, pattern, and movement matter almost as much as sense, half-sense, or lack of sense. In this way, an 'Alice in Wonderland' type of world is created in which our own world is reflected in a distorted and yet revealing form.

La Cantatrice chauve, described as an *anti-pièce*, is, most obviously, a parody of the 'family drama' of the naturalistic theatre in its bourgeois interior, English middle-class characters, traditional recognition scene, intruding visitor, and lengthy monologues on subjects of minimal importance. The form of theatre parodied here reflects, however, a whole way of life, so that in ridiculing the one, Ionesco inevitably mocks the other. For the world of accepted truths and of comprehensible cause-effect patterns is neatly undermined by what Richard N. Coe has termed 'a kind of dialectic of anti-logic' (*Ionesco*, p. 30). The Smiths and the Martins try hard to be logical, but reality constantly proves too complex for them to succeed; their questions receive no answers; they contradict themselves gaily as they talk, without noticing anything in the least odd; and they act in the most paradoxical and inexplicable ways. But most of all, they reveal the mechanical, empty nature of their daily lives by the emptiness of their language.

Ionesco has recently drawn attention to certain misconceptions which arose concerning his early plays, and particularly to that in which emphasis was placed upon the solitude and the lack of communication that exists among his characters. It is important to bear in mind, first, that what Ionesco's characters need perhaps most of all is solitude, since the presence of others worries, annoys, even totally unnerves them, and, secondly, that Ionesco, like Beckett, never forgets that people believe that they are communicating, and that they do at times in fact succeed reasonably well in establishing some degree of communication. So we are offered the more disquieting picture of figures, oblivious to the strangeness of what they are doing, using quite naturally words that are almost devoid of meaning and sentences in which certain crucial connections are missing, *as if* they meant something that was readily understood by themselves and by others.

The fact that people manage to communicate at all is to Ionesco one of the most astonishing features of this extraordinary world. And it is the systematic destruction of language which provoked in him feelings of disgust and asphyxia and which, at the end of *La Cantatrice chauve*, disturbs the spectator so much, as the Smiths and the Martins are finally led by mechanical associations of sound to the final dislocation and disintegration of their speech. In the early plays, language, which is looked at from the outside with critical detachment, in Jean Vannier's words, literally 'exposed upon the stage, promoted to the dignity of a theatrical object', is shown then being emptied of meaning and controlling its users rather than the other way around. The young girl pupil in *La Leçon* (1951) succumbs to the verbal rape of an increasingly sadistic teacher, who is himself a victim, in the sense that he is unable to control the direction in which his words lead him. Similarly, though Jacques, in the brilliantly inventive *Jacques ou la soumission* (written in 1950, though not produced until 1955), at first refuses to conform to the demands of bourgeois society, represented by marriage and 'pommes de terre au lard', he is finally seduced by Roberte until he comes to accept the single word 'chat', with its erotic associations, as a name for anything and everything, a development described by Ionesco himself, in an interview with Claude Bonnefoy, as an abdication of lucidity and liberty in the face of the organic. In these plays language is actively menacing, the verbal equivalent of the wide variety of physical objects which take over the stage and threaten his grotesque characters with annihilation. In what is arguably Ionesco's most successful play, *Les Chaises* (1952), the stage becomes crowded with empty chairs and invisible guests, summoned up by the incessant chatter of the flesh and blood characters of the Old Man and the Old Woman, while in the later *Le Nouveau Locataire* (written in 1953) the stage space is completely choked with physical matter in the shape of furniture of all kinds, so that a, by then unseen, tenant can only capitulate, ask for the light to be put out, and say a polite 'thank you'.

All of these plays from *La Cantatrice chauve* to *Le Nouveau Locataire* quite clearly explore different manifestations of the same fundamental state of consciousness: unreality, vacuity, and yet weight and omnipresence of being. The subject of *Les Chaises*, Ionesco wrote in 1952, is the 'ontological void', absence, the reality of unreality, or if one prefers, the unreality of reality, a feeling which the dramatist had already experienced as he subjected himself to the profoundly disturbing, literally nauseating, proliferation of words.

Much of the strength of the early plays derives from the fact that the threatening hostility of a world of proliferating matter, or of words used as meaningless utterances or instruments of aggression, is demonstrated *directly* without any need for comment by the characters, who are themselves quite unaware of the nature of their situation. In this way Ionesco avoids being over-explicit, since the spectator, who alone is exposed to the total impact of the drama, is left to interpret what he sees, perhaps as evidence of the nothingness which may after all be the ultimate reality.

The mechanisms of invasion, proliferation, and indeed, it is clear from the journals, acceleration too, all form part of Ionesco's way of apprehending reality. But they are also crucial to the dramatic form and style of his early plays. In *La Cantatrice chauve* and *La Leçon* the underlying movement is a basically simple one: a gradual build-up of tension and an acceleration of pace, as words, used as the play progresses more and more as instruments of shock, are hurled across the stage with growing aggression and frenzy. In the structurally rather more complex *Les Chaises*, the opening calm, nostalgic evocation of a garden set in the city of light leads to nervous tension and anxiety until the all-important arrival of the first unseen guests; then a progressively mounting excitement builds up to a climax of activity, after which, with the arrival of the Emperor, there follows a further slowing down of pace. In *La Cantatrice chauve*, the clock had been used to underline, at one stage, the intensely violent nature of the dialogue, and, in *Les Chaises*, dialogue, gestures, movements, sound effects, and stage 'props' all contribute towards the increasingly frenetic rhythm of the central section of the play: chairs are brought on with greater and greater rapidity; the movements of the Old Man and the Old Woman become both more agitated and more restricted as their stage space is taken over by the unseen guests; the sounds of boats arriving and bells ringing become louder and more frequent; doors open and close by themselves; and the old couple exhaust themselves in trying to cope with the work of accommodating and conversing with so many invisible people.

In a programme note for a production of *Les Chaises*, Ionesco wrote that 'Des êtres noyés dans l'absence de sens ne peuvent être que grotesques, leur souffrance ne peut être que dérisoirement tragique' (*Notes et contre-notes*, p. 261). And in portraying man as exposed to a meaningless world that invades and proliferates, threatens and annihilates, Ionesco has created what have aptly been termed 'tragic or metaphysical farces', which are at once riotously comic and yet desperately and ineradicably pessimistic. For, as Coe has shown (*Proceedings of the Leeds Philosophical and Literary Society*, IX, March 1962), the laughter is of a particular kind, springing directly out of the dramatist's detached attitude towards the 'absurd' nature of existence. Just as in Beckett's *En attendant Godot*, knock-about action and music-hall, circus, or silent-screen 'numbers' are not superfluities, added to coat an extremely bitter pill, but an integral part of the writer's vision (the spectacle of Estragon, tottering on one leg as he imitates a tree, and asking Vladimir 'Do you think God sees me?' is in itself a ridiculous, yet poignant, image of Beckettian man), so in Ionesco's early plays, the dislocation of *cliché* and platitude, the introduction of anti-logic, the comic-pathetic dialogue and actions of the grotesque old couples in *Les Chaises*, while provoking laughter at scape-goat figures caught up in the mechanisms of farce, at the same time communicate anguish at the derisory, yet tragic, situation of man.

'Tragic' and 'comic' are then but different ways of expressing Ionesco's own fundamental reaction to the human condition. But their opposition in the plays is dramatically of the greatest importance, for, in

Ionesco's own words '. . . ces deux éléments ne fondent pas l'un dans l'autre, ils coexistent, se repoussent l'un l'autre en permanence; se mettent en relief l'un par l'autre; se critiquent, se nient mutuellement, pouvant constituer ainsi, grâce à cette opposition, un équilibre dynamique, une tension' (*Notes et contre-notes*, pp. 61–2). This tension between the tragic and the comic, together with a number of other opposites, provides the dramatist with the bases for his particular form of dramatic construction. 'Tragique et farce, prosaïsme et poétique, réalisme et fantastique, quotidien et insolite, voilà peut-être les principes contradictoires (il n'y a de théâtre que s'il y a des antagonismes) qui constituent les bases d'une construction théâtrale possible' (*Notes et contre-notes*, p. 62).

The early plays tend to take certain comic mechanisms as their starting-point, only to end in an anguish that is more commonly associated with tragedy. But, in the later and lengthier plays, the main character is far more of a human being than, for instance, are the Smiths and the Martins. As a result Ionesco's dramatic style tends less markedly towards the mechanical and becomes more directly concerned with reflecting the inner world of the dream, the obsessions, fears and personal anguish of this principal character and of the author. Nonetheless, even though, on occasion, one feels that the comic is deliberately invoked rather than arising spontaneously, the derisory nature of existence remains an essential part of Ionesco's vision and his dramatic manner reflects this by the use of exaggeration and of the grotesque, both of which are techniques characteristic of the *guignol*. Bérenger in *Le Piéton de l'air* pops his head in and out of the window, like a modern Punch in a miniature proscenium arch; the acting of Bérenger as he comes face to face with the Killer in the earlier *Tueur sans gages* should appear at once, the stage direction informs us, 'grotesque et sincère, dérisoire et pathétique'; while King Bérenger in *Le Roi se meurt*, in facing up to his death, is at once moving *and* ridiculous.

The unnamed, essential, half-forgotten reality that was first glimpsed in *Les Chaises* in the Old Man's nostalgic evocation of a garden set in the city of light, and that found oblique expression in the, ultimately, deceptive, sexual imagery of abandonment in *Jacques ou la soumission*, takes on a far more explicit form in the more complex (and, in my view, generally underrated) *Victimes du devoir* (1953). Choubert's journey which anticipates in many respects that of Jean in the much later *La Soif et la faim*, takes him through various levels of experience, re-living, as he does, many of Ionesco's own most poignant, or disturbing, childhood memories. As, forced by the remorseless detective to embark upon a search for 'Mallot with a *t*', he plunges more and more deeply into the nature of reality, Choubert confronts, on the one hand, the banality or horror of everyday life, the failure of love, the process of aging, and the fact of death, before, on the other hand, climbing back to scale, momentarily at least, new heights of joy, he comes very near to capturing the wonder of being, as he almost floats away into a world of infinite space and light, only to end his futile search with indignity in the wastepaper basket.

'Je voyage pour retrouver un monde intact sur lequel le temps n'aurait pas de prise' wrote Ionesco in the *Journal en miettes* (p. 15), and the theme of the journey recurs frequently in his plays. Bérenger in *Tueur sans gages* has, he confesses, searched for many years in vain for the 'radiant city' before, quite by chance, he comes upon the apparent realisation of his dream. His namesake in *Le Piéton de l'air*, finding that he possesses the power of flight, sets out on an aerial journey as far as the edge of 'le néant'. Finally, Jean in *La Soif et la faim* undertakes a fruitless quest for the absolute, only to recognise, when pressed to relate what he has witnessed in the course of his travels, that he can name only the most banal and unimpressive of everyday sights and sounds. From these examples it will be clear that the road taken by these twentieth-century pilgrims represents no path to the intellectual understanding of reality. For the dominant impression, both from the plays and the journals, is of a world that constantly eludes definition, of a vast enigma to which rational solutions are by their very nature – and the nature of existence – inevitably incomplete or false. 'Je n'ai rien résolu; depuis toujours dans le même état d'interrogation', commented Ionesco in the *Journal en miettes* (p. 66). And an image that recurs frequently in the journals is that of the 'wall', understood, in this particular context, to represent an impassable barrier to understanding.

Instead, the goal of Ionesco's solitary traveller – and the search is one that must be conducted in solitude – appears to be the realisation, or rediscovery, of a state of astonishment, wonderment, joy, fullness of being, which, once experienced, alone seems to have any true significance (though exactly how and in what sense it is significant becomes one of the main problems of the later plays). The experience of this privileged state of consciousness is one which has most profoundly marked both Ionesco himself and the rather weak, down-trodden, dissatisfied, yet sensitive and sympathetic character who has aptly been termed 'a hero in spite of himself' and who, from *Victimes du devoir* onwards, is a major figure in Ionesco's longer plays, whether he is called Choubert, Amédée, Jean or, most often, Bérenger. For, at rare moments of his life, this highly unglamorous hero experiences a sense of deep wonderment at the sight of a world which suddenly seems as if it had been newly created, created especially for him, a source of astonishment, yet at the same time delightfully familiar. 'Un monde nouveau, toujours nouveau, un monde de toujours, jeune pour toujours, c'est cela le paradis' (*Journal en miettes*, p. 15). This enchanted view of the world is accompanied by a feeling of deep harmony and equilibrium, a harmony between the inner self and the outer world and an inner sense of completeness, immutability, and permanence, yet at the same time overwhelming joy and lightness, which leads in a number of plays to the impulse, the possibility, and finally, to the realisation of levitation and actual flight. This feeling of harmony and euphoria, which, at its purest and most intense, is like a state of grace comparable to the experience of wholeness and absolute joy granted to the mystic, seems to arise out of an acute awareness of the fact, the certainty, and the wonder of being. At such moments, the self appears to exist in a sphere of infinity outside the normal dimensions of space and time. 'Un chant triomphal jaillissait du plus profond de mon être', exclaims Bérenger in *Tueur sans gages*, 'j'étais, j'avais conscience que j'étais depuis toujours, que je n'allais plus mourir' (*Théâtre* II, p. 78).

The fascination with childhood memories that is characteristic both of the plays and the journals is not then simply nostalgia for an elusive past. It is rather an attempt to recapture at its maximum point of intensity the exhilaration and lightness of a state of naivety and continual wonderment, and to chart the stages at which one became caught up in time and conscious of the fact and the finality of death. Ionesco has even gone so far as to say that literature exists for him 'pour exprimer cet égarement, cette chute, cet abandon malgré nous de l'état primordial qui est tout près de l'état paradisiaque' (*Entretiens*, p. 147). Only the child, Marthe, in *Le Piéton de l'air*, is capable of understanding the natural ease with which Bérenger takes to the air, flight being the ultimate expression of this tendency to lightness and evanescence.

What is remarkable in Ionesco's theatre is the very intensity of the longing for this state of grace and its repercussions throughout almost all his subsequent plays. It is the 'nostalgie ardente' that his central character feels for this inner Eden, and his attempts to recapture even a glimpse of it that gives him the will to live in a world that habitually appears as quite the reverse of miraculous. And it is the memory of this state of joy that inspires his later revolt against all that is grim and intolerable in creation.

> Dans mes jours de tristesse, de dépression nerveuse ou d'angoisse [confessed Bérenger in *Tueur sans gages*], je me rappellerai toujours, me suis-je dit, cet instant lumineux qui me permettrait de tout supporter, qui devrait être ma raison d'exister, mon appui. (*Théâtre* II, p. 80)

For, regrettably, sadness, nervous depression and anguish are far more common reactions to the nature and circumstances of life, and astonishment, which may, on occasion, lead to a privileged state of wholeness and joy, is more commonly experienced as 'anguished stupefaction', to use Simone Benmussa's term, rather than as wonderment. Caught up by his very mortality 'dans le temps, dans la fuite, et dans le fini', Ionesco's unlikely 'hero' is acutely aware of the intolerable nature of existence. For Choubert, Amédée, Bérenger or Jean, often presented as total failures in social terms, are superior to their fellow-men only in that they are more sensitive to the 'malaise existentiel'; unlike the Smiths and the Martins, they are conscious, for instance, of the threat of being reduced to the status of an object, of being oppressed, and perhaps annihilated, by a world of hostile matter, by words, by dogmatic systems and ideologies, but above all by death which casts its huge shadow over so many of Ionesco's plays. And if, for Ionesco as for Sartre, lucidity means anguish, it seems infinitely preferable to the denial of one's very existence as a human being.

Ionesco's theatre is, in fact, full of people performing the drab, ritualistic gestures of everyday living, existing without really existing, in the sense that they never face up to the crucial facts and fundamental problems that his 'hero' confronts, instinctively rather than intellectually. The only alternative then to the two states of lucid awareness of reality appears to be an attitude of stupid, unthinking, and, what is worse, unfeeling 'tired neutrality', an insensitivity best summed up perhaps in Bérenger's words in *Tueur sans gages*:

> Depuis des années et des années, de la neige sale, un vent aigre, un climat sans égard pour les créatures . . . des rues, des maisons, des quartiers entiers, des gens pas vraiment malheureux, c'est pire, des gens ni heureux ni malheureux, laids, parce qu'ils ne sont ni laids ni beaux, des êtres tristement neutres, nostalgiques sans nostalgies, comme inconscients, souffrant inconsciemment d'exister. (*Théâtre* II, p. 74)

The two states of consciousness just described are, as Ionesco himself has pointed out, at the root of all his plays. Not only in the obvious sense that they provide a central image or series of images upon which the play hinges, but also that, either separately or together, they are largely responsible for controlling their dramatic structure, rhythm, and movement, as well as such detailed features as lighting, setting and costume. In *Victimes du devoir* and Ionesco's first three-act play, *Amédée ou comment s'en débarrasser* (1954), the two states of awareness of reality find their most natural expression in imagery to which the dramatist has remained faithful throughout the whole of his work. On the one hand, luminosity, joy, evanescence, transparency, elevation and freedom are conveyed in images of intense light, enchanted gardens, brightly coloured flowers, radiant cities, bridges of silver, ladders leading to a higher plane, spheres and circles, and, of course, images of levitation and flight. Amédée's stirring words to Madeleine in *Amédée ou comment s'en débarrasser* well illustrate the brilliance and exuberant profusion of certain images of light and movement.

> Regarde, Madeleine . . . tous les acacias brillent. Leurs fleurs explosent. Elles montent. La lune s'est épanouie au milieu du ciel, elle est devenue un astre vivant. La voie lactée, du lait épais, incandescent. Du miel, des nébuleuses à profusion, des chevelures, des routes dans le ciel, des ruisseaux d'argent liquide, des rivières, des étangs, des fleuves, des lacs, des océans, de la lumière palpable . . . (*Théâtre* I, p. 298)

On the other hand, the converse experience of opacity, entombment, separation, destruction and decomposition is most frequently communicated in recurrent images of darkness and shadow, mud and water, consuming fire, and sharp, threatening, angular objects, a number of which figure in Madeleine's despairing response to Amédée's dream of light, space and beauty. 'Sombre vallée, humide, marécages, on s'enlise, on se noie . . . au secours, j'étouffe, au secours ! . . .' (*Théâtre* I, p. 286). It was in the *Journal en miettes* that Ionesco explained that fire which for others might represent light, purification and life was for him a symbol, even a premonition of death, while he saw earth, not as life-giving, but as mud, decomposition and again as evoking death. The image of water recalled not abundance, calm, or purity, but anguish, putrefaction and degeneration. In the central 'flash-back' to the honeymoon of Madeleine and Amédée in the second act of *Amédée* there are two sets of contrasting images, which suggest here sexual conflict and incompatibility and opposing views to life in general. It is worth noting, I think, that in an attempt to convey the overwhelming intensity of a sense of wonderment, fullness of being and harmony, Ionesco frequently combines images of light and movement with hostile images of water and fire in particular, so that these latter elements are not only neutralised, but are fused harmoniously into the perfect equilibrium that is the principal characteristic of the experience that they are intended to express: 'des ruisseaux d'argent liquide', 'des lacs, des océans, de la lumière palpable', and, over ten years later in *La Soif et la faim*, 'l'océan du soleil . . . l'océan du ciel' (*Théâtre* IV, p. 80).

But the poetry of Ionesco's theatre is not confined to the dialogue of his plays; nor are the visual and aural scenic images, that appear so often, added simply as reinforcements to it. They are usually quite essential to the whole conception of the work, sometimes in fact constituting the original image from which the entire play has evolved. In the case of *Les Chaises*, Ionesco has said that the first image that came to him was of the chairs themselves, followed by that of someone bringing them on to an empty stage at great speed, and it seems likely that *Le Nouveau Locataire* and *Amédée* began in a similar way. In the earliest plays, scenic images, conveying the growing oppressiveness of physical matter, tended to evolve out of an exaggeration of everyday actions performed with common-place objects. For example, chairs and furniture of all kinds are carried on to the stage, coffee-cups are piled up at a feverish pace and bread is thrust rapidly into mouths in *Victimes du devoir*, while Choubert's metaphysical search is represented visually by nothing more than a bathetic journey up, over and around the furniture of their 'petit-bourgeois' room. In Act I of *Amédée*, the wife Madeleine similarly engages in frenetic bursts of activity at a small telephone exchange, forming a contrast to Amédée's frustration at his own impossibly slow rate of progress in writing. But the same play is dominated by the presence of the huge expanding corpse, which, though still absent from the stage until the end of the first act, attracts, fascinates and troubles both Amédée and Madeleine, then, in the second act, invades and takes over the stage with its bulk, and the green light and music that emanate from it, Amédée responding like some automaton, as he rushes to measure the ground that it has covered in its 'geometrical progression'. *Amédée* marks perhaps the beginning of what Jacques Guicharnaud (*Modern French Theatre*, p. 228), has referred to as the evolution from 'armchair proliferation' to the 'cosmic proliferation' of the later plays, in which the emphasis upon spectacle, and the increasing demands that are therefore made upon set designer and lighting engineer, arise naturally out of the need to give sufficiently gigantic form to those hostile elements with which Ionesco's rather pathetic hero must struggle. *Amédée*, together with *Rhinocéros*, draws some of its inspiration from those deep inner fears of man that lie at the root of the Gothic romance, tales of mystery and imagination, or their modern counterpart, the horror film: the continued growth of a long since dead body and the guilt felt at its presence and preservation; the transformation of man into beast by changes in his appearance and behaviour. All of these elements recall numerous examples of the genre, in particular tales by Poe, Stevenson, and Wells. Yet, in *Amédée*, it is the first act that is most successful with its subtle interplay of fantastic and naturalistic elements rather than the more heavily macabre second act in which the steady advance of the monstrous corpse, with its huge accompanying mushrooms, intended to create an atmosphere of mingled horror and beauty, leads too easily to the laughter provoked by melo-drama. Taken as a whole, *Amédée ou comment s'en débarrasser* is clumsy and ill-balanced in structure. Yet the first act contains some of Ionesco's most impressive writing for the theatre, and the central image of the proliferating corpse is sufficiently enigmatic to have fascinated numerous critics, from those who seek one single precise interpretation, to those who, like Martin Esslin, feel that since it is 'in the nature of both dreams and of poetic imagery that they are ambiguous and carry a multitude of meanings at one and the same time, [. . .] it is futile to ask what the image of the growing corpse stands for' (*Absurd Drama*, p. 10). Yet, with the help of certain internal links in the play and the evidence of other plays and the journals, it is surely clear that this image reflects Ionesco's concern with the fall from grace, from a state of wonderment and joy, hence the experience of being caught up in time, of being menaced by death or nothingness. Amédée spoke in despair of the corpse as having 'la progression géométrique . . . La maladie incurable des morts' and, in the journals, Ionesco wrote that 'La vitesse n'est pas seulement infernale, elle est l'enfer même, elle est l'accélération dans la chute. Il y a eu le présent, il y a eu le temps, il n'y a plus ni présent ni temps, la progession géométrique de la chute nous a lancés dans du rien' (*Journal en miettes*, p. 15). In an interview with Bonnefoy he provided his own similar inter-pretation of the image of the corpse: 'Le cadavre, c'est pour moi la faute, le péché originel. Le cadavre qui grandit, c'est le temps' (*Entretiens*, pp. 96–7).

Of all Ionesco's longer plays, *Tueur sans gages* (1959) is the one most fully organised by the contrast between the two states of awareness of reality. The contrast is foreshadowed by the change in the lighting at the opening of the play, the light being first grey, like a dull November day or an afternoon in February, with dark silhouettes only visible, then, with the entry of Bérenger, a bright white against the dense vivid blue of the sky, recalling the 'light of Italy' combined with 'the pure blue sky of Scandinavia in June evoked by Ionesco in the *Journal en miettes*. The first and second acts are set deliberately in direct contrast one to the other, the decor of Act II being heavy, realistic and ugly to contrast sharply with the lack of decor and simple, bright, lighting effects of Act I. Even the costume is governed by this central contrast, Bérenger wearing a grey overcoat and scarf, while the Architect of this sun-filled 'paradise' sports an open-necked shirt and jacket. Both the dialogue and the sound effects of the second act are intended to produce an impression of caco-phony, darkness, horror, and yet still appear comic. The shouts of the children in the school-yard, for instance, are distorted and caricatured so that they sound like dogs yapping. And the whole of this act in which truck-drivers curse, dogs bark, people pontificate on politics and progress, call each other 'bastards', 'pimps', 'lazy old buggers' and so on, is thrown into strong relief, partly by Ionesco's favourite technique of exaggeration of characters and sounds, but also by Bérenger's earlier account of a state of joy and his delight at its apparent realisation in the radiant city.

Amédée, in the earlier play, had met with no understanding or sympathy from Madeleine, and Bérenger's enthusiasm for the radiant city, which expresses itself in a tendency to soliloquise at length and to use exaggerated exclamation and repetition to convey the extent of his enchantment, is also set in dramatic contrast with the detached, indifferent attitude of a coldly polite, somewhat impatient Architect. But, for all Bérenger's enthusiasm, there is a destructive element in this radiant city, for a Killer stalks the streets, showing his photo of the colonel to his victims and claiming them all, a fact which is 'known, assimilated, and catalogued', accepted, in other words, as inevitable by everyone in the city, except by Bérenger. He alone, with the strength of his inner dream, is not indifferent to the presence of the Killer in their midst, and it is the pathetic, naive and rather grotesque Bérenger who tracks him down and, in a final brilliant scene, comes face to face with him in a desperate attempt to explain why he destroys men, women, and children. Finally, unable himself to find reasons to substantiate life as it is, Bérenger, though remaining instinctively an 'homme révolté', is forced to lower his pistols and prepare to receive the Killer's knife saying 'Que peut-on faire? . . . Que peut-on faire?'

The Killer represents most clearly, of course, death itself. But it is at the same time everything which disfigures the world of the 'radiant city' and prevents man from savouring the transfiguration that Bérenger had described as the greatest experience of his life. His revolt is then an instinctive, irrational, even futile gesture made in the face of the absurd metaphysical situation of man. Yet doomed to failure though it may be, it is a gesture that has to be made.

Ionesco's next important play, *Rhinocéros*, first produced in Düsseldorf in the winter of 1959, then put on by Jean-Louis Barrault at the Odéon-Théâtre de France in 1960, has as its hero the same rather weak, indecisive, naive, self-effacing, yet sympathetic Bérenger. Jean, Bérenger's friend, an extremely bitter caricature of the well-organised bourgeois 'social animal', who regards life as a struggle in which it is essential that he should come out on top, and who uses such well-known slogans as 'duty' and 'will-power', is among the first to be transformed into a rhinoceros. He is soon to be followed by Botard, a demi-savant of the Left, who, while using ready-made formulas, pretends to have a critical mind, and by Dudard, the intellectual, who attempts to apply a logical, scientific, objective approach to a disease that requires prompt remedial action rather than understanding and explanation. 'Rhinoceritis' is, however, extremely contagious, and, at the end of the play, only Bérenger, who was at first too wrapped up in his own remorse, anguish, and terror at life in general to notice with any concern the appearance of the first marauding rhinoceros, is left, refusing, almost in spite of himself, to renounce his individuality and join the growing horde of rhinoceroses.

The origins of this play in Ionesco's experience of the growing nazification of his country are by now well known; it has also been pointed out that the disease to which they are all exposed possesses certain specifically Nazi characteristics. Ionesco's way of handling such a political theme, however, while retaining the Nazi 'glorification of nature', is to stress certain elements that are common to collective dogmatic ideologies: their appeal to logic and reason, which may be used to justify any position or perpetrate any crime; an outwardly rational form, hiding roots which are sunk deep in the feelings and the passions ('Toutes les idéologies, marxisme inclus, ne sont que les justifications et les alibis de certains sentiments, de certaines passions, d'instincts aussi issus de l'ordre biologique', *Entretiens*, p. 25); and, finally, their power to capture men in a web of propaganda, and transform them, making intellectual and moral resistance exceedingly difficult. And so against the arguments, slogans or prejudices of the 'rhinos' Ionesco sets no rational counter-arguments. His commitment is to no conflicting ideology, which might equally well in its turn make monsters out of men. Instead, he sets Bérenger's instinctive, irrational refusal to capitulate, a revolt expressed both as a defence and an assertion of his individual self, a revolt which, like that of Bérenger in *Tueur sans gages*, may be futile but must be made.

The transformation of men into rhinoceroses (a physical mutation representing a mental one) is an image that first occurred to Ionesco, *Présent passé, passé présent* reveals (pp. 163–70), in Rumania in the nineteen-thirties. The rhinoceros, heavy, ugly, fearsome and monster-like, is an extremely powerful image of 'massification' and, since their numbers increase rapidly, of proliferation also, which, as in *La Leçon*, provides the basic dramatic structure of the play. The first act of this 'farce terrible' and 'fable fantastique' (*Notes et contre-notes*, p. 288), with its dense and complex interplay of dialogue and feverish activity, from which Bérenger is set apart, is dominated by the repeated incursions of the first rhinoceros, which are conveyed partly by sound effects and clouds of dust, but principally by means of the automatic, comic responses of a variety of caricatured, provincial types. In the second act the epidemic is shown to be spreading, first by looking at the reactions of a small, but varied, group of characters, then, in the brilliantly handled second scene, through the individual metamorphosis of Bérenger's friend, Jean, in which dialogue and visual transformations are most successfully combined. Finally Bérenger himself is completely surrounded, hemmed in on all sides and threatened by that scenically haunting gallery and chorus of rhinoceroses.

Again, then, there lies at the root of this play the threat of invasion and possible annihilation, against which Bérenger must revolt or to which he must succumb entirely. And though *Rhinocéros* has often been considered as very different from Ionesco's other plays, the threat is essentially the same (though both its source and form are new in Ionesco's theatre), and the reason for Bérenger's revolt is the same in its inspiration as that of his earlier metaphysical insurgent in *Tueur sans gages*, namely an impulse towards freedom on the part of the individual self and an intuitive feeling that he must not bow down before those factors in existence that threaten it with annihilation.

For Ionesco is, as Ross Chambers has recently shown (in 'Eugène Ionesco, ou comment s'envoler?', *Australian Journal of French Studies*, VI, 1969), someone who defines himself by *opposition* to the world: 'd'un côté il y a moi, de l'autre côté, tout le reste. Tout est autre' (*Journal en miettes*, p. 49). And if this effort towards self-definition arises, as it appears to do, both out of the recollection of a state of joy and out of contact with the threatening, invading world of the 'non-self', what possible significance can it have and what are its implications for the individual and his life in society? Is the state of joy and wholeness of being experienced in the self any sure sign of an 'ailleurs' or other world, or must man's only possible joy be found in that very existence which at times he finds so appalling, or more rarely, so miraculous? These are a few of the extremely elusive questions with which Ionesco's later plays deal, as they pick up themes or images that have been touched upon earlier.

Le Roi se meurt, first produced by Jacques Mauclair at the Théâtre de l'Alliance Française in December 1962, treats directly the theme of death, which has been present in some form in almost all of Ionesco's plays. In spite of a marked alteration in rhythm that occurs in the middle of the play and a tendency to be over-rhetorical, which is mocked ironically in the text itself, *Le Roi se meurt* remains an impressive piece of theatre and a highly lucid dramatisation of a man's efforts to come to terms with his own death. 'J'avais écrit cette œuvre', wrote Ionesco, 'pour que j'apprenne à mourir. Cela devait être une leçon, comme une sorte d'exercice spirituel, une marche progressive, étapes par étapes, que j'essayais de rendre accessible vers la fin inéluctable' (*Journal en miettes*, p. 147).

The central figure in this moving, yet, at the same time, comic, ceremony, King Bérenger, is universal man, or Everyman, in several different senses. He is man seen through the ages with all his achievements and his failures: the inventor of the balloon, the train, the aeroplane, gunpowder and nuclear fission; the builder of magnificent cities and the author of great works of literature and art; the warrior and the executioner; the founder of revolutions and counter-revolutions. But above all, King Bérenger is Everyman in the sense that he must die. Yet, the play is concerned primarily not with the fact of death, but with the *manner* in which Bérenger faces up to its certainty and its imminence. For, from the beginning, he is caught up in an irreversible running-down process, the *terminus ad quem* of which is stated in advance as the end of the play. And as Bérenger slows down and loses his authority, his power, his dignity, even his magic, so time is speeded up and decline, decay and degeneration extend with growing rapidity throughout the whole of his kingdom and the entire universe. As he proceeds through the various inevitable stages that precede his death, Bérenger seeks comfort from his two wives: the younger Marie, who offers him, along with her warm sensuality and tenderness, a view of life as a '. . . courte promenade dans une allée fleurie . . .' (*Théâtre* IV, p. 37), in which all is sunshine and joy and where death has no real existence, and who, as a result, can neither help nor reach him; and the older, more austere Marguerite who can give him no warmth or joy, but who, having accepted all that death involves, is the only one able to assist him, by showing him a possible way of making his death into a triumph rather than a defeat. The final brilliantly conceived section of the play sees then Bérenger, with the help of Marguerite, seeking to attain, through a gradual, and sometimes painful, separation from all that is merely contingent, the essential integrality and reality of self that might perhaps survive death in a splendid transfiguration. By an enormous effort of concentration, King Bérenger does in fact reach that state of harmony and light which throughout Ionesco's theatre has been identified as the most intense awareness of the fact of being.

> L'empire . . . A-t-on jamais connu un tel empire: deux soleils, deux lunes, deux voûtes célestes l'éclairent, un autre soleil se lève, un autre encore. Un troisième firmament surgit, jaillit, se déploie! Tandis qu'un soleil se couche, d'autres se lèvent . . . A la fois, l'aube et le crépuscule . . . C'est un domaine qui s'étend par-delà les réservoirs des océans, par-delà les océans qui engloutissent les océans. (*Théâtre* IV, p. 72)

But these are oceans that Bérenger must cross, as Ionesco questions the ultimate significance of this all-important experience. And once everything else, including Marguerite, has faded away, Bérenger still has some way to go before he reaches a final immobility on his throne and disappears, leaving the stage quite empty but suffused with a grey light. This enigmatic conclusion has been interpreted both as a triumph and as a defeat for the self. Yet it is, I think, essentially ambivalent, since if the light that remains suggests the greyness of nothingness, the mist into which Bérenger disappears is no mere stage trick, but is surely a metaphorical indication as to the limits of our knowledge. The impossibility of understanding may, of course, in itself be regarded as constituting an exceedingly pessimistic conclusion.

Ionesco's next two plays were *Le Piéton de l'air*, first produced three years after *Rhinocéros* by Barrault at the Odéon-Théâtre de France in 1963, and *La Soif et la faim* which had its prèmiere in Düsseldorf in 1965, and was first produced in France at the Comédie-Française in February 1966. Both of these extremely complex and difficult plays contain themes and techniques already found in Ionesco's earlier work : the creation, for instance, of a dramatic world in which dream and 'reality' are indistinguishable since, for Ionesco, the dream may be more revealing of the true nature of reality than the waking state, and in which the most fantastic events are considered in no way exceptional; the use of *clichés* and everyday sayings, often comically underlined by repetition, gesture, or sound effects; and, in *Le Piéton de l'air* particularly, a technical dexterity and virtuosity that make demands upon the producer, designer, and lighting engineer greater than any of Ionesco's plays since *Amédée ou comment s'en débarrasser*.

Yet the controlling factors remain, as in *Tueur sans gages*, two contrary modes of awareness of existence. The opening, idyllic setting of *Le Piéton de l'air* contains almost all the elements that we have seen Ionesco associate earlier with a state of euphoria and joy : a pure, blue sky, a bright light that casts no shadow, an elevated situation, features that are combined here with other recurrent oneiric images, the bridge of silver, the *téléphérique*, and, in *La Soif et la faim*, that of the enchanted garden, first evoked in *Les Chaises*. The first episode of *La Soif et la faim* reflects, on the other hand, in its sombre, grey, worn set, the grim dissatisfaction and horror at existence felt by Jean, who longs for more light, not simply for 'le bonheur' but for a 'joie débordante, l'extase' (*Théâtre* IV, p. 82).

In neither play, in fact, can the central character accept the purely relative nature of human happiness or the destructive elements that are an inseparable part of existence. Central to *Le Piéton de l'air* is the aerial flight of Bérenger, which arises directly out of a feeling of lightness and wonderment in which he is 'enivré de certitude'. But to attain this state of being and express it in flight is not an end in itself; it merely leads Bérenger now to seek to explore an 'anti-world', which lies across the valley beyond the frontiers of 'le néant' and which seems to represent that radiant world of permanent, unalloyed joy that all Ionesco's characters are seeking. In *La Soif et la faim*, similarly, Jean, unable to bear any longer the anguish that he feels at the conditions of mortal existence, travels far in search of a land where all is freedom, lightness and joy, a land where no one ever dies.

But, as Chambers has pointed out, Bérenger's aerial flight and Jean's search for the absolute have important consequences both for themselves and for those they must leave behind. In *Le Piéton de l'air*, Joséphine, abandoned by her husband Bérenger, gives an extremely moving account of the life of someone deprived of love, in which there are no friends, simply strangers shut up in their shells, prepared only to take advantage of one's vulnerability in a world that resembles a jungle. She lives through nightmare scenes in which the innocent are judged guilty, in which children are slaughtered callously, and in which death is both a temptation and a threat. In the first episode of *La Soif et la faim*, Jean is so totally immersed in his own inner quest that he is completely lacking in understanding and sympathy for others; he behaves in fact with cruelty, cynicism and indifference. Yet in the play within the play mounted by the callous 'false monks' of the final episode, Jean finds himself no longer indifferent, but sharing in the sufferings of the victims of the 'third-degree' tortures. It is then too late, however, for he has been trapped into joining those who have themselves rejected life, only to find enslavement. *Le Piéton de l'air* and *La Soif et la faim* thus carry further that exploration of the theme of guilt and remorse which was already present in *Victimes du devoir* and *Amédée ou comment s'en débarrasser*.

Humour, according to Ionesco, is a manifestation of lucidity and liberty. 'You must arrive at a point where you can laugh at anything, as I must at the idea that I shall be a corpse. You must see things as they are and yet be detached from them. Humour helps you to achieve that detachment', Ionesco said in an interview with Carl Wildman (*The Listener*, December 24, 1964). But if the detachment that is essential to the writing of farce was a natural one for the dramatist to take, it is clear that, when it also figures as an essential part of the experience of Bérenger, his 'homme révolté' detachment seems to necessitate a solitude, an alienation from man and from life in general that Ionesco cannot happily concede. There is, therefore, at the root of Ionesco's later plays a crucial paradox. Expressed in over-simplified terms, it is that in order to tolerate the absurd, one must seek for and cultivate a sense of inner joy, wonderment, and detachment; yet detachment breeds indifference and Ionesco is never indifferent. Part of this central dilemma is expressed in discursive terms in the *Journal en miettes* :

> Quelle est la bonne voie? Peut-être l'indifférence. Ce n'est pas possible; puisqu'on est là, on ne peut pas ne pas participer... Considérons alors que tout est comique, prenons le parti d'en rire. Ce serait faire offense à Dieu ou au monde.... Ayons l'humour. Nous ne pouvons pas rejeter le monde. Alors prendre tout au sérieux : c'est ridicule également. L'esprit de sérieux tue. L'esprit de sérieux prend parti. L'esprit de sérieux fausse. (pp. 137–8)

Bérenger in *Le Piéton de l'air* sets out with the intention of reaching the radiant world across the valley. But he is unable to pass beyond the frontiers of 'le néant' and instead of the radiant world, he sees spread out below him a world of catastrophe, horror and chaos, an Inferno of the guillotined, whole continents of paradise in flames and after that 'nothing' – 'Rien. Après, il n'y a plus rien, plus rien que les abîmes illimités . . . que les abîmes' (*Théâtre III*, p. 198). The 'ailleurs' or other world to which the state of joy had seemed to point may, after all, simply lead to nothingness or to total chaos. And so, as Ionesco wrote in the journals :

> Ces murs qui s'élèvent, ces murs impénétrables que je m'acharne à vouloir trouer ou abattre ne sont peut-être que la raison. La raison a élevé ces murs pour nous préserver du chaos. Car derrière ces murs, c'est le chaos, c'est le néant. Il n'y a rien derrière les murs. Ils sont la frontière entre ce que nous avons réussi à faire de ce monde et le vide. De l'autre côté c'est la mort. Na pas franchir ces murs. (*Journal en miettes*, p. 212)

Ionesco's plays lead, ideologically, to a total impasse. For the state of joy and wonderment that is the only bearable, lucid response to existence is not only elusive and transitory; it is also finally deceptive, in the sense that it leads either literally nowhere, or back to the very existence against which it had originally inspired revolt.

Without wishing to attempt any general assessment of Ionesco's dramatic achievement, I think several things are worth saying in conclusion. First, that his plays are artistically most successful when the broad lines of his dramatic construction are at their simplest and most economical, as, for instance, in *La Leçon*, *Les Chaises*, or *Le Roi se meurt*. In a play like *Le Piéton de l'air*, on the other hand, the themes of euphoric dream, inner yearnings, disillusionment and regret, fear of age, loneliness and death are set in a subtle, ironic counterpoint that makes the play too complex to be wholly successful in the theatre. Secondly, as I suggested earlier, Ionesco is at his best when he avoids the over-explicit, allowing his extremely resonant visual and verbal imagery to affect the spectator directly. Finally, by using words as instruments of shock, scenic effects as visual metaphors, and dreams to illuminate reality, Ionesco has created a dense and highly personal form of 'total theatre' that has provided a practical demonstration of controlled freedom and has played a most important part in freeing the theatre from an ossified traditionalism of form. 'Mais je veux, moi,' he wrote, 'faire paraître sur scène une tortue, la transformer en cheval de course; puis metamorphoser celui-ci chapeau, en chanson, en cuirassier, en eau de source. On peut tout oser au théâtre, c'est le lieu où on ose le moins' (*Notes et contre-notes*, p. 84). But the point is, I think, that when Ionesco performs tricks almost as fantastic as this, they rarely fail to illuminate and explore an intensely anguished personal vision of the world.

Select Bibliography

IONESCO, EUGÈNE
  Théâtre   Paris, Gallimard, 1954 etc.
  Notes et contre-notes   Paris, Gallimard, 1962
  La Photo du colonel   Paris, Gallimard, 1962
  Journal en miettes   Paris, Mercure de France, 1967
  Présent passe, passé présent   Paris, Mercure de France, 1968

BENMUSSA, SIMONE   *Eugène Ionesco* Paris, Seghers, 1966
BONNEFOY, CLAUDE   *Entretiens avec Eugène Ionesco*   Paris, Pierre Belfond, 1966
COE, RICHARD N.   *Ionesco* Edinburgh and London, Oliver and Boyd, 1961
DONNARD, JEAN-HERVÉ   *Ionesco dramaturge, ou l'Artisan et le démon*   Paris, Minard, 1966

10

Conclusion : *TOWARDS A NEW CONCEPT OF THEATRE:
ADAMOV, BECKETT and ARRABAL*   John Fletcher

The preceding chapters have shown a remarkably rich and living theatre,
with different men writing plays for differing ends, but all clearly vital
forces in contemporary drama. In the later chapters, however, a gradual
change of tone will have been noticed. The first six playwrights, despite
their divergencies, have an *air de famille* about them: they are still very
'French', classically elegant and moralistic, in temper. 'Ce sont des
dramaturges bien de chez nous', a Frenchman might say, and he would be
quite right. With Genet and Ionesco, though, a new note is heard. Their
plays, as their world fame testifies, are less home-bred, less culturally
introverted, and more universal in appeal. And so it is not surprising that
a distinctive, if misleading, label has been stuck on to them – the 'Theatre
of the Absurd'. Now, the truly remarkable thing about this movement
is that it is international (our own Harold Pinter is a leading exponent,
and Martin Esslin, in his classic study on the subject, includes Italian,
Catalan, German, Swiss, Israeli, American and East European playwrights
within its purview), and yet its masters write in French. Of these, however, only one – Jean Genet – was born in France, and as we have seen,
he differs radically from Claudel, Giraudoux, Sartre and the others in that
he distinctly did not enjoy middle-class birth, education and prospects.
His Ecole Normale Supérieure was Fresnes jail, and his diplomatic career
that of a wandering pickpocket. As for the others, Ionesco is Rumanian,
Adamov Russian, Beckett Irish and Arrabal Spanish. The fact that these
highly gifted men chose to write in French primarily for French audiences
is a tribute to the prestige and vitality of the phenomenon we have been
examining in the course of this book. But the equally important fact that
their cultural background was not that of the *lycée* and *fonctionnariat*
helps explain both the wide appeal of their work abroad among proselytes
and public alike, and the new attitude to drama which they have helped
to develop. It is with their approaches to a new concept of theatre that
I wish to deal in this concluding chapter.

Like many other apparently 'new' phenomena, this particular manifestation has its sources in the past. It reminds us forcibly that the most
basic response to drama is one of naïve simplicity: the child, wide-eyed
with wonder and hysterical with glee at a Punch and Judy show, is closer
to the member of an Athenian or Elizabethan or contemporary Chinese
audience, to the man of the Middle Ages watching open-mouthed a
miracle play, or to a nineteenth-century Japanese spectator of the Noh,
than he is to the individual munching nuts before a television screen. We
cannot fully understand what French drama is about, what it has achieved
in the last eighty years or so, if we cannot sympathise with the child's
attitude: because French theatre since about 1890 has been reaching
back to the religious and mystical origins of the drama, in order to attempt
to recapture that precious gift of amazement, terror and glee.

The antithesis of this kind of theatre is the complacent 'bourgeois'
theatre of the later nineteenth century, which though by no means
uniformly bad (Labiche and Sardou are not nonentities), offered on the
whole undisturbing plays with well-built if artificial plots in elaborately
naturalistic settings. In England, this sort of entertainment is known as
'drawing-room comedy', complete with butler, cocktails and French windows, with Scene 1 putting the spectator literally into the picture (a
masterpiece which half subscribes to this form and half parodies it is
Wilde's *Importance of Being Earnest*). It is still, of course, a very lively
form. In France it is generally known as *théâtre de boulevard*, and throws
up regularly such hardy perennials as *Boeing-Boeing* and *L'Œuf à la
coque*, both of which are still running in Paris as I write. Against this
basically frivolous form the producers discussed in our introductory
chapter have all reacted in their different ways, but in accordance with a
shared belief in the fundamental seriousness (which need not mean
solemnity) of the drama. All take it for granted that theatre today, just
like theatre at its greatest moments in the past, must have a quasi-religious
function: it must both stir the heart and inspire the mind. It must
reveal what Giraudoux called 'these surprising truths – that the living
must live, that the living must die, that autumn follows after summer,
spring after winter, that there are four elements, and happiness, and
billions of catastrophes, that life is a reality, that it is a dream, that man
lives by peace, that man lives by blood, in brief, what they will never
know . . .' Or as Antonin Artaud put it, pithily and movingly: 'The
theatre exists primarily to teach us that we are not free and that the
heavens can at any moment fall about our ears.'

The work of the playwrights I shall be concentrating on in this
chapter (Adamov, Beckett and Arrabal) pursues this ideal in forms that
are often radically new. Nevertheless, even these were clearly fore-

shadowed earlier: at least three writers (Jarry, Apollinaire and Cocteau), by their theories and their practice, laid the foundations for the theatrical *renouveau* which was to occur from about 1950 onwards. And there were, of course, other straws in the wind, like Roger Vitrac's *Victor ou les enfants au pouvoir*, first performed in 1928 and revived by Anouilh in 1962, a play of anarchic and effective satire, and Artaud's *Les Cenci* (May 6, 1935), with its theme of the fatality of evil and the anti-realism of its decor and *mise-en-scène*, consisting of thunder, lightning and portentous dialogue. *Les Cenci* tells the terrible story of a monstrous man whose death is no less bestial than his life, and is in line with the whole movement of Artaud's violent reaction against foppish dilettantism which was discussed in Chapter 1, and which has been so influential on such leading contemporary directors as Roger Blin. But it represents also only one other aspect of the great surrealist seism, the effects of which have been widely felt in the theatre only relatively recently.

One of the writers whom the surrealists posthumously hailed as a begetter of their movement was Alfred Jarry (1873–1907). His Ubu plays, based, he claimed, on 'la déformation par un potache d'un de ses professeurs qui représentait pour lui tout le grotesque qui fût au monde' (*Tout Ubu*, p. 19), were the first to make absurdity the basis of dramatic form, in violent reaction to drawing-room comedy, which he saw as a 'leçon de sentimentalité fausse et d'esthétique fausse' (p. 148), epitomised by its mania for 'la stupidité du trompe-l'œil' which creates an illusion only for those who cannot see. The more perceptive theatre-goer, Jarry argues, will respond better if doors and windows are treated like other props, to be brought on merely as and when the action requires them (p. 141). These and other remarks, dating from 1896, reveal how forward-looking Jarry's dramatic theory was: much that seems very contemporary in the practice of Genet and Ionesco can be traced back to his thinking.

Another clairvoyant in theatre matters was the inventor of the very term 'surrealist', the poet Guillaume Apollinaire (1880–1918). He foresaw, in the preface to his play *Les Mamelles de Tirésias* (written between 1903 and 1916), that in future the former genres of tragedy and comedy would become inextricably confused,

> car il y a une telle énergie dans l'humanité d'aujourd'hui et dans les jeunes lettres contemporaines, que le plus grand malheur apparaît aussitôt comme ayant sa raison d'être, comme pouvant être regardé non seulement sous l'angle d'une ironie bienveillante qui permet de rire, mais encore sous l'angle d'un optimisme véritable qui console aussitôt et laisse grandir l'espérance. (*Œuvres poétiques*, p. 869)

Written early in the century, this is not a bad forecast of the kind of sensibility which was to throw up, for example, the works of Ionesco and Beckett. Like Jarry, Apollinaire had no time for naturalism: the theatre is no more like life, he said, than a wheel is like a leg, so that it is fully legitimate to introduce new and striking methods of presentation to underline the stagy qualities of the characters and the pomp of the production. 'Cet art', he prophesied, 'sera moderne, simple, rapide avec les raccourcis ou les grossissements qui s'imposent' if one wishes to impress the spectator and, above all, *influence* him (p. 868). He was as opposed as was Jarry to the 'idéalisme vulgaire' of later nineteenth-century dramatists, and to 'ce théâtre en trompe-l'œil qui forme le plus clair de l'art théâtral d'aujourd'hui'; he even foresaw the kind of developments Dorothy Knowles discussed towards the end of her introductory chapter, with 'Un théâtre rond à deux scènes/Une au centre l'autre formant comme un anneau/Autour des spectateurs' (p. 881), and yet he was conscious of 'renouant avec une tradition négligée' in presenting a serious message (the urgent need for French people to have large families in order to repopulate their country) in symbolic form. Adamov was to do precisely the same in situating *Paolo Paoli*, his marxist-leninist indictment of the capitalist system, in the 'Belle Epoque' with, as protagonists, an entomologist and a feather-dealer. As Cocteau succinctly put it in his preface to *Les Mariés de la Tour Eiffel* (1922), a ballet play about a comic wedding performed by dancers and narrated by two actors dressed up as phonographs, '*Ubu*, de Jarry, et *Les Mamelles de Tirésias*, d'Apollinaire, sont à la fois des pièces à symboles et à thèse' (*Théâtre* I, p. 46).

In *Notes et contre-notes* (pp. 9–10) Ionesco was, nevertheless, hostile to Jean Cocteau (1889–1963), who found himself however in good company, since Ibsen and Strindberg came in for equally scathing dismissal. Whatever may be the present status of his poetry, fiction and graphic work, in the drama Cocteau clearly foreshadowed developments in what was to be called the Theatre of the Absurd. He was fascinated by what he called 'le bon absurde' (*Théâtre* I, p. 44) which manifests itself in 'un enchaînement logique de circonstances illogiques' (p. 180): his plays tend to show a deliberate anti-naturalism subverting a naturalistic framework. In addition to this, Cocteau was a superb craftsman: his *Chevaliers de la Table Ronde* and his *Parents terribles* are gripping and fast-moving dramas, in which an impression of realism is created, while the unreal, the mysterious, and the mystical are exalted. This is in accordance with Cocteau's theory of poetry, that it is coextensive with reality but in another dimension. 'Je cherche à peindre', he declared, '*plus vrai que le vrai*' (p. 42). Because of this sincere ambition, there is nothing 'fay' about the extraordinary *jeux de scène* and complex *travestis* in his adaptation of the King Arthur legend, *Les Chevaliers de la Table Ronde*: his Sir

Galahad is the poet who embellishes all he touches, but who thereby makes himself redundant and must continually move on. 'Le Graal revenu à Camaalot', the wise Cocteau hints, 'n'est autre que le très rare équilibre avec soi-même' (*Théâtre* I, p. 74). Like his plays, his films also veer from the mundane to the mythical: in *Orphée*, for instance, Death falls in love with the middle-class, happily-married poet Orpheus and abducts him in a limousine. She broadcasts poetry on a private wavelength which only the limousine's wireless will pick up, and her gloves have the power of dissolving mirrors and stopping time. It is this sensitivity to the mystery and wonder of life, while preserving an earthy good sense (for if *Orphée* is a meditation on death, it is also a shrewd comment on conjugal love), which keeps Cocteau's work fresh and alive. His ability to recreate the great myths is impressive: it is hard not to be moved by his cinematic interpretation of the Tristan and Isolde legend, *L'Eternel Retour*, and to feel nothing when his modern Tristan dies, thinking Isolde has refused to come to him, because he has been misled about the colour of the sails on her boat. At his best, Cocteau succeeds in making us aware of the mythical dimensions of everyday experience; like Giraudoux in *Amphitryon 38*, he uses fabulous themes to project elegantly a truth about the human condition, that man often thinks himself strongest when in fact he is weakest, and is most proud when he is riding for a fall. But he has a buoyant optimism which is sometimes lacking in Giraudoux, a confidence in the power of the poetic vision and the immortality of the poet, who cannot die because the sound of his lyre pleases the gods too much.

It may seem a far cry from Cocteau's 'frivolity' (as his detractors would say), or his 'magical seriousness' (as I would prefer), to the world of Michel de Ghelderode (1898–1962), but they have in common their fascination with myth. In Ghelderode's case, the inspiration came from the legends and folklore of his native Flanders, and was more medieval than modern in quality, more brutal and earthy than the metropolitan sophistication of a Cocteau or a Giraudoux. He was a sort of primitive, peasant Maeterlinck, in fact, and shares with his compatriot an obsession with the mistily fantastical. His dramatic technique is however highly polished and subtle, as (for example) the play *Sortie de l'acteur* reveals.

This is primarily an exploration of the nature of reality, in this case the reality of the theatre. It is a play within a play, opening with a rehearsal under the direction of Jean-Jacques, an unsuccessful author of plays in which death looms large. Throughout the three acts, certain questions keep occurring to the actors whom he is directing: 'What is the nature of the thing we call "theatre"? What is it doing to us? And in any case who are "we" when we're not on stage? Have we any separate existence, in fact?' The answer to these Pirandellesque questions is negative as far as Renatus, the actor, is concerned. Fagot, the prompter, says to him that his madness lies in taking theatrical illusions for reality and in believing that all-powerful realities are illusory. For in Renatus's case reality is so confused with theatre that when his role requires that he should die, his stage death becomes a real death – a true 'sortie de l'acteur', in fact. Renatus's demise is the centre of this play's simple plot. But even death has no finality about it, since Renatus returns in the last act as a somewhat ill-at-ease ghost, pursued by four angels who remind one more of a secret police than the heavenly host. The mystery remains entire at the end, or as Fagot says, 'doorless', and so openable by no 'key'. Nevertheless, *Sortie de l'acteur* is far from being didactic and abstract; like all of Ghelderode's plays it is vivid and, above all, visual – indeed, use is made of mime, as for instance when Fagot appears at one point in the guise of Pierrot.

Jarry, Apollinaire, Cocteau, Ghelderode – these, then, were the principal forerunners and pathfinders for the 'new theatre' which emerged in Paris in the early nineteen-fifties. Two of its major exponents, Genet and Ionesco, have already been discussed. The three I shall concentrate on are possibly not of their stature, but are extremely significant (Beckett especially) nevertheless.

Arthur Adamov (1908–70) was more than brushed, first by expressionism, and then, in Paris in the nineteen-thirties, by surrealism. His literary idols were very much those one might expect: Büchner, Gogol, Strindberg, Kafka and Artaud. Later on, he came very heavily under the influence of Brecht. In fact, Adamov made much in his essays (collected under the title *Ici et maintenant*) of the fact that there were two phases in his dramatic career, an apolitical period followed by one of political commitment to the cause of the Left; and it is certainly true that *Paolo Paoli* (written in 1956 and produced by Planchon in Lyon on May 17, 1957) was the first of his works explicitly opposing a named political position. Thereafter Adamov merely stepped up his attack in plays using the familiar Brechtian devices of signboards, projections, notices, *guignol* and equal stress on a foreground of individual destinies played out against a background of political crisis. Although not very original in terms of technique, Adamov's committed plays, and especially his treatment of the story of the Commune, *Le Printemps 71*, are not ineffective. It must be said, however, that they have not had the impact which works by other *dramaturges engagés* like Césaire and Gatti have had, even in the circles which could be expected to be sympathetic to their message. Perhaps Adamov was too old a dog to learn new tricks; at his best, in *Paolo Paoli* and *Le Printemps 71*, he was old-fashioned, but at his worst, in *La*

Politique des restes (a play of 1962 about racial injustice in a southern and white-dominated community), he was naive and ineffectual. He died a sick and disappointed man.

But the distinction which Adamov sought to establish, after the event, between his apolitical and political manner will not stand up to close scrutiny. Nearly all his plays are political in one way or another, being derived from his experience as a rootless intellectual who, in a very human way, was subject to terrifying dreams of injustice and persecution. His early work, written and performed around 1950, is undoubtedly his finest achievement, since it springs with such intensity from his personal sufferings and fears. His very first play, *La Parodie* (written in 1947 and produced by Blin on June 5, 1952), is a depressing but impressively claustrophobic image of modern life: the anonymous 'Employé' is searching, like Ionesco's Bérenger, for 'une vraie ville où la vie serait gaie et les gens de bonne humeur' (*Théâtre* I, p. 28), but of course he never finds it, nor does he manage to establish any contact with any of the other characters, or they with each other. The dialogues are, in fact, monologues: the characters rarely 'get through' to each other, but are seen merely to be talking at each other. Unnerved by their inability to evoke a response in the interlocutor, they start to lose confidence and humiliate themselves. An example of this is the fifth tableau, where the journalist and N are discussing the whereabouts of the girl Lili: the journalist begins by criticising N for his laxness in seeking her, and getting no answer, he loses all assurance; N then takes up the same line, ending up by accusing himself of murdering Lili by his criminal negligence. The play as a whole shows little development (except that N, who had masochistically craved death at Lili's hands, is in fact run over by a car); it is a simple *constat d'échec*, an intense, personal, rather naked, and perhaps narrow, vision of things. In an understated, unexplicit play such as this, the dramatic power generated arises from the initial situation projected; the problem for the playwright is then to harness this energy and get it to drive the play forward. Like Genet, who is faced with a similar difficulty in some of his work, Adamov does not quite solve the problem in *La Parodie*, which remains a grey, rather drab play which Blin had considerable trouble in bringing to life, and which now seems to be destined for oblivion.

L'Invasion (written in 1949 and produced by Vilar on November 14, 1950) is clearly better; it has more of a recognisable plot, and is set in a more readily indentifiable milieu. Pierre is editing the papers of his dead brother-in-law, and himself dies in the attempt. His wife runs off with Le Premier Venu (puckishly called so in the play); this, and the chilling presence of Pierre's mother, who insinuates herself between husband and wife and proffers reactionary opinions about the immigrants she reads of in the papers, are the themes which recur in the next two plays, *La Grande et la Petite Manœuvre* and *Tous contre tous*.

Like *L'Invasion*, they are about fear, about pressure and influence, and about the weakness of the individual who attempts to resist. Whereas, though, *L'Invasion* was almost a *pièce mondaine* (not unlike Cocteau's *Parents terribles*, in fact), with only a hint about politics in the mother's remarks, these works deal explicitly with such menaces as police repression and political chicanery. So far, however, the politics remains undirected: the rhetoric of the Militant in *La Grande et la Petite Manœuvre* (written in 1950 and produced on November 11 by Jean-Marie Serreau), and of Jean, Darbon and the Radio in *Tous contre tous* (written 1952 and produced by Serreau on April 14, 1953) could be of left or right wing colouring. On becoming aware by 1963 of the open-endedness of these plays from a political point of view, Adamov wrote his auto-critique in true marxist form (*Ici et maintenant*, pp. 142–3). It is too 'commode', he there argues, to 'renvoie dos à dos les adversaires qui s'affrontent, considérant d'emblée la lutte comme dérisoire, et appliquant en toute circonstance la hautaine philosophie du "tout est foutu"'; one is tempted to reply that his recantation itself is too 'commode'. 'On sait toujours contre quoi on lutte, et pour quoi', he writes after the event; but the answer must be that one doesn't always, and that the plays Adamov later repented of are eloquent proof to the contrary. There is a moral here, similar to the one Philip Thody draws in his chapter on Sartre.

The truth is that a play like *Tous contre tous*, which is one of Adamov's best, constitutes a ruthless exposure of intolerance, cowardice, the abuse of power by racial minorities as well as by racial majorities, and of the dishonest hollowness of the kind of political rhetoric which covers such abuses and blatantly excuses self-interest. No specific enemy is mentioned in the speeches Adamov transcribes with Orwellian accuracy: the limping 'réfugiés' of *Tous contre tous* could be Jews, but they could equally well be 'long-haired louts' in a right-wing context, or 'bourgeois revisionists' in a left-wing milieu. The play, whose title is well-chosen, is in fact about the cruelty of all political life: the 'réfugiés' are alternately harried and courted, with cynical opportunism, according to the political needs of the moment. Adamov projects a world not dissimilar to that of the Hungarian cineasts Jancsó and Kósa, one in which we witness the disgusting treachery of those who are politically afraid, and in which we observe the shifting quicksands of political fortune, of anarchy and disorder, of rhetoric and menace, and the consequential spinelessness of those involved. The conclusion is lucid and detached: in such a climate only the shrewdest opportunists survive, like Darbon; the rest, both the genuine and courageous like Noémi, or the shabby and grovelling like the loathsome Mother and the refugee Zenno, go under. The play ends with one of the most effective codas in all political theatre: the stage is cleared and four shots ring out, the last of which silences the Mother.

'Whatever one does, one is crushed.' Adamov pursued this theme, and that of the individual thrown back on himself, cut off from communication with others, with great effectiveness in his next play, and his most perfect: *Le Professeur Taranne*, which he wrote in 1951 and which Planchon put on two years later (Lyon, March 18, 1953). Like other works, this play is the direct transcription of a dream of Adamov's, with only minimal alteration. It consists of only two tableaux, and is constructed with economy: the characters who enter exit immediately their function is over. This not only heightens the oneiric nature of the piece, it also makes for a crisp performance. Professor Taranne's ordeal begins when he is summonsed for indecent exposure; then it transpires that he has been leaving his papers and notebooks around in bathing-huts; and finally, he receives a letter from the Vice-Chancellor of a Belgian university telling him, politely but unequivocally, why he is not being invited again to lecture there. All the while Taranne protests his innocence before the law, his eminence as a scholar (in the face of the charge that he merely plagiarises his famous colleague Professor Ménard), and his effectiveness as a lecturer (in answer to the accusation that he bores his hearers to death). In the end, he is beaten: 'Pourquoi me dire ça maintenant, après tant d'années?' he asks, in reaction to the letter, and slowly starts to take off his clothes as the curtain falls. This exquisite one-acter is almost unbearably potent in its dramatisation of a nightmare we all have experienced, in one form or another, in our sleeping lives. The skill of the writing is most impressive; at one moment, Taranne says he cannot work as he walks, and then contradicts himself shortly afterwards: 'je travaille souvent en marchant', he says (*Théâtre* I, p. 229), betraying his growing confusion as his world starts to collapse around him.

It is clear, then, that Adamov's best work is that which arises from his personal fears and obsessions, and his worst from an over-ambitious if well-meant attempt to write plays that would turn away from those fears to the injustices of the social universe. It is a pity that such an honest and likable man, who exposes himself, without vanity if not without silliness, in *Ici et maintenant*, was not able to achieve his ambition of writing a committed drama, which would be founded 'sur la volonté très simple, très légitime, de ne pas "en remettre" sur la condition humaine, assez lourde et assez terrible en elle-même' (p. 45). The truth is that Adamov was more successful in dealing in broad symbolic terms with the human condition, its miseries, anxieties and acts of self-deceit, than he was in showing up the iniquities of a given politico-economic system.

If Adamov's contribution to the permanent repertoire should in the end turn out to be slender, there is no doubting his historical importance in vitally assisting, at a certain moment in time, in the fixing of the idiom of the new theatre we are examining. It is no coincidence that the leading producers of the day were involved in the launching of his work in the early nineteen-fifties: they recognised the originality, at least in the French context, of a dramaturgy which took 'les mots les plus simples, les plus délavés par l'usage, en apparence les plus précis, pour leur restituer leur part d'imprécision innée (*Ici et maintenant*, pp. 14–15), and were attracted by the use of anti-realism (such as the man's hair which turns white between the two parts of *La Parodie*, like the tree sprouting leaves in the interval of *En attendant Godot*) to create a sense of heightened reality. They were no doubt impressed, too, by the architectonics of Adamov's plays, by his fondness for balance and counterpoint (in the eighth tableau of *La Parodie*, for instance, the decor is the same as in the seventh, but 'les objets qui étaient à droite sont à gauche et inversement', and in the second part of *Tous contre tous*, the attacker Jean of the first finds himself attacked). Then there was Adamov's predilection for the return of certain themes: that of the smothering matriarch has already been referred to, but there were others, such as the obsessive insistence, natural enough in a writer, on the proliferation of paper (*L'Invasion*, *Le Professeur Taranne*); when Pierre, for instance, says of the man whose work he is editing, 'il parlait souvent de détruire ses papiers . . . mais c'était aux moments terribles, quand tout lui apparaissait d'avance inutile' (*Théâtre* I, p. 65), we feel he is very much his creator's mouthpiece at that moment. Finally, there was an awareness of the possibility of exploiting sound and lighting in an original way: *La Parodie* demands 'sifflets, bruits de cars, avertisseurs' to be heard throughout the performance, and for the stage to be bathed in light of a 'clarté insoutenable' as the curtain falls, in a metaphor of life and its difficulties. The purpose of all this, Adamov explains, is to 'susciter le dépaysement' (p. 10) on the spectator's part, and devices like a polyvalent decor, modified only slightly from tableau to tableau, and couples not dancing to the tune (p. 22), certainly do 'soulignent le caractère "parodique" de la pièce' and make absurd behaviour seem quite natural.

Adamov's technical originality is not, therefore, in doubt. What one misses is a certain playfulness: except at one moment in *Taranne*, when a society woman introduces the professor to her friends as 'Professor Ménard', the conception of his drama is rarely witty. Like all dream plays, Adamov's draw their strength from the power of evocation through unassigned symbols in which universal but vague anxieties are figured in stage action; this is not devoid of a certain ponderous monotony, for which, in the end, one does not feel the originality of the manner and the technical smoothness and efficiency (such as the trick of achieving transitions through a momentary darkening of the stage) really compensate. It now seems clear that for all his intelligence and sensitivity, Adamov was only a relatively minor dramatist.

As a playwright, Samuel Beckett (b. 1906) is certainly less uneven than Adamov; nevertheless his dramatic works would not place him in the very front rank of twentieth-century writers, which is where his French novels situate him. For whereas the fiction pursues single-mindedly a path that leads to one goal, silence, the silence of the form which has exhausted itself, each of the plays is *sui generis*. Beckett himself admits that they are by-products, the amusement of a prodigiously gifted and inventive mind fascinated by media (the stage, the television, the cinema, and radio) which have periodically tempted him away from the arduous wrestling with fictional prose. His dramatic writings are therefore not systematic in the way his novels are. Usually he wrote them with a particular actor in mind (Patrick Magee in the case of *Krapp's Last Tape*, for example), or in response to an invitation, such as that extended by the BBC which led to *All That Fall*.

His first play was written in 1947, a baroque three-acter involving seventeen characters and a stage split in two; entitled *Eleuthéria* ('Freedom'), it was semi-autobiographical and rather derivative, and has never been published or performed. *En attendant Godot* was written in 1949, and *Fin de partie* for Roger Blin in 1956. After *All That Fall* in the same year, Beckett also wrote in English *Krapp's Last Tape* in 1958 and the radio play *Embers* in 1959. He returned to the stage with *Happy Days* in 1961 and *Play* in 1964; *Film* was made in the same year, and 1966 saw the first production of the television play *Eh Joe*. The canon is virtually complete if mention is made of two other radio plays, *Words and Music* and *Cascando*, which show Beckett in danger of beginning to repeat himself in this medium, and two mime plays, *Actes sans paroles*, I and II, which betray his basic fascination with the formal, wordless aspect of the dramatic experience, its vital element of pure action and gesture.

Beckett has thus written over a dozen plays, but they are all fairly short, and have been getting progressively shorter. *Come and Go* (1967) runs for only a few minutes, and the most recent, *Breath*, for precisely thirty seconds: the time for a vagitus, inhalation, exhalation and second vagitus to be heard on a barren stage while the light goes crescendo and decrescendo. There is clearly plenty of the playfulness here which one misses in Adamov, but it is equally evident that, although he may joke about it, Beckett has exhausted the possibilities – for him – of the stage, as he has of the radio too. Perhaps he will write more for the cinema and for television, but even there the possibilities would soon be exhausted by such a writer.

Nevertheless, the canon extant is impressive and significant. Beckett is without doubt one of the most original dramatists to have emerged in any country in the last two decades, and since about half his dramatic output happens to have been written directly in French (the rest has been translated, mostly by the author himself), he is of considerable interest to the student of French theatre in this century. The nature of his originality as a playwright can most conveniently be discussed under four heads: structure and language, tones, characters, and themes.

Beckett's plays have a characteristic structure: whether they are in one act or two, they all rely on a basic, and rather formal pattern, which accounts for their distinctive shape. This becomes evident, for example, if one looks at the construction of *Play*: there the parts assigned to wife, mistress and husband are written out with the precision of a musical score – the counterpoint, harmony and especially the *da capo* of 'repeat play exactly' are very reminiscent of musical construction. In Beckett's drama, in fact, actors are assigned words to utter as instruments are assigned parts in a score; an example of this is the way he ends the two acts of *En attendant Godot*, the words in each case being identical: 'Alors on y va?' and the reply 'Allons-y.' At the end of Act I, however, Estragon asks the question and Vladimir answers it, but at the end of Act II it is Vladimir who asks the question and Estragon who answers it. The reason for the difference does not lie, as one might suspect, in the characterisation: there is no need, Vladimir and Estragon being who they are, for one to ask the question at the end of the first act, and for the other to ask it at the end of the second. The reason must be sought in Beckett's fascination with what he has called 'the stratum of movement which underlies the written word', with 'the kind of form one finds in music, where themes keep recurring'. For him, when in a text things are repeated, 'they ought to be made unusual the first time, so that when they happen again – in exactly the same way – an audience will recognise them from before' (*Encore*, March–April 1962, p. 44). Repetition is essential to provoke this kind of recognition, but monotony is avoided by assigning the same words to a different speaker – not symmetry, therefore, but asymmetry, the same that is not quite the same: the sameness is essential to drive home the point being made in *Godot* about the hopelessness of the ever-renewed wait, but to avoid clumsy obviousness the roles are reassigned.

Asymmetry, in fact, is a basic Beckettian structure. The two parts of the novel *Molloy* are asymmetrical; so are the two acts of *Happy Days*, and of course of *Godot* itself – the second panel of the diptych reflects the first, but does not precisely reproduce it. In a general way, indeed, recurrence is a fundamental feature of Beckett's writing. Things not only recur – with slight modifications – within one play, they also recur from one play to another: in *Fin de partie*, for example, we see Clov moving around the set at the beginning doing various jobs, all acted out in full on the stage; and in *Eh Joe*, similarly, we see Joe going round his room and sealing off all its exits, the whole again performed in full. Beckett in fact is fascinated by combinations and the changes that can be rung on them: he offers the director of *Film* what he modestly calls a 'foolish' suggestion for the eviction of the dog and cat from the room involving no fewer than seventeen different actions; and in *Come and Go*, short as it is, seven successive positions are required of the three women on their bench reminiscing and gossiping about each other. There is an element of play here, of the gratuitous that may shock serious minds; but drama is basically play, and most drama prior to the nineteenth century had an element of gratuitous activity in it. Plays by Molière, Wycherley and Marivaux, for instance, incorporated ballet interludes which had little or nothing to do with the main action. In this, as in other ways, Beckett is returning to an older tradition: except that he makes what used to be mere interlude or epilogue into the stuff of the piece. In so doing, he draws attention to the fact that drama is about play, or it is not drama. In *En attendant Godot*, for instance, he presses the music-hall and circus analogy as far as it will go in serious dramaturgy. Vladimir and Estragon go in for cross-talk like two seedy comedians; all four main characters rough-and-tumble in the tradition of circus clowns, and Pozzo is a kind of ring-master, cracking his whip and getting his minion to perform for the delight of the other two, who become spectators for the duration of Lucky's spot. Even the bowler hats are a silent tribute to Laurel and Hardy, the great archetypes of Estragon and Vladimir. All these elements from the world of popular entertainment are harmoniously incorporated into the play and give it that comic basis which the good producer should bring out, as Roger Blin did in the original production of 1953.

In *Fin de partie* Beckett is more austere. Here the stage is claustrophobic – all is contained within a cell, outside of which, we are told, is death. But once again the accent is on the visual, active element, in the games Hamm and Clov play with the step-ladder, the gaff, the dustbin-lids and the armchair on castors. Then, in *Krapp's Last Tape*, Beckett exploits the possibilities the tape-recorder gives us of storing the human voice for years: Krapp, an old man, listens with mingled fascination and exasperation to the ramblings of himself many years before. Thereby Beckett is able to say something about a subject very close to his heart, the decay of the body, of the mind, and of our ideals and illusions as we grow old. As Hamm expresses it in *Fin de partie*: 'Mais nous respirons, nous changeons! Nous perdons nos cheveux, nos dents! Notre fraîcheur! Nos idéaux!' (p. 25); but Hamm puts it in words, explicitly. In *Krapp's Last Tape* it is implicit in the action itself.

Of Beckett's radio drama little need be said, except that from the first he saw its limitations and possibilites. Radio drama is entirely a matter of voices coming out of the dark: the unheard voice has no existence. Now, in his novels Beckett is preoccupied with the problem of the voice that cannot die into silence and yet finds it infinitely difficult to carry on: in desperation, it tells stories. So does the Voice in the most recent of the radio plays, *Cascando*, which is introduced by an Opener (clearly a surrogate for Beckett himself) who like a studio technician opens the channel marked Voice and allows it to pant out its story of Maunu, which it hopes in vain will be the story to end all stories. Beckett here uses radio very appropriately to project in dramatic terms the central struggle fought out in his fiction.

Whatever he attempts, he swiftly attains mastery of his medium. Without previous experience, he was able to exploit the 'chamber' quality of television in *Eh Joe*, and to use in *Film* the possibilities the cinematograph camera gives for rapid displacement, tracking and panning. It is a silent film, which looks back nostalgically to the pre-1930 era and pays tribute to its greatest comic artist, Buster Keaton, whose performance in *Film* was one of the last he undertook before he died.

But if Beckett knows the potential power of wordlessness in *Film* and in the two mime plays, he knows too how to use language in his stage, radio and television plays. This language is an extraordinary amalgam of the demotic and the poetic. The demotic aspect is obvious: the Irishisms of the English texts, the faubourg slang of Vladimir and Estragon. But Beckett's language is also poetic, ranging from the straight verse of *Words and Music* to the less overt poetry of some of the exchanges in *Godot* (such as the one about 'toutes les voix mortes', pp. 105–6) and Mrs Rooney's extraordinary modulations from despair to happy cheerfulness, from the banal to the sublime, in *All That Fall*. Of similar resonance is Winnie's tendency, in *Happy Days*, to quote as readily from Shakespeare and Milton as she does from the libretto of *The Merry Widow*

This varied use of language permits the characteristic tone of a Beckett work to establish itself, and this is the second important aspect of his dramaturgy I wish to draw attention to. The tone is serious, and yet at the same time witty – a quality Beckett recognised when he subtitled

Waiting for Godot a 'tragicomedy' (which strictly speaking it is not). The first act, while remaining serious basically, is primarily comic: the two old men play about, Pozzo has Lucky perform his dance and thinking act, and at the end the boy comes on to say that Godot, though detained that evening, will surely turn up tomorrow. The second, and shorter, act is altogether more hopeless in tone: the tumbles are still funny, but Pozzo's tirade about birth astride a grave is less so. And when the boy comes on the second time, the message which he had delivered in a rush the first time has wearily to be dragged out of him by Vladimir, who is moved to cry out 'Miséricorde!' at the realisation of his great misery, and ours, condemned as we all are to die on a dying planet.

This is intense drama, but drama of understatement. The words uttered are not necessarily remarkable in themselves. They are made deeply moving by all that has gone before in the play, by the evident fact that not merely will Godot not come that evening, but that he will never come, that there is no hope and no escape, that the two men, having said they will go, simply do not stir, staring only blankly before them.

There is a similar collapse into wordless misery in *Happy Days*, the second act of which is also shorter, and more desperate, than the first. In a one-acter things naturally have to go faster, and how this is done can best be seen in *Play*, set in a sort of limbo where an inquisitorial spotlight picks out each character and forces him or her to narrate, in counterpoint, his or her version of this sorry tale of adultery, reconciliation and final abandonment. The point is made by having the actors repeat the play over again – why have two acts, indeed, when you can do it all so much more economically by having the actors repeat the whole piece exactly? This play thus becomes as desperate as the others; but it is not all gloom, being suffused with a very adult wit ('Adulterers', the man says for instance, 'take warning, never admit').

Beckett is very concerned that the humour of his writing should come over in production. He doesn't of course want naive playing for laughs, but he does want the humour implicit in the words and situations to be brought out. In the preface to the script of *Film* he specifies 'climate of film comic and unreal. O should invite laughter throughout by his way of moving'. Similarly, he intends that Vladimir's duck-waddle and Estragon's tussles with his boots should be funny to watch. He requires considerable fitness of the actors who play his decrepits, and a tautness and precision of performance that is not often met with. The episode of the hat-swapping in *Godot*, for instance, requires practice to get perfect; and as in the circus, his clowns must train in order to know how to provoke laughter by their pratfalls without doing themselves injury.

One of the shrewdest things ever written about Beckett's theatre was Jean Anouilh's comment that *Godot* was like the *Pensées* of Pascal performed by the Fratellini clowns. We do not usually associate the circus and metaphysics. Beckett has taught us to do so, and it is this which constitutes what is unique about the tone of his drama.

In his characterisation, the third important aspect of his art which I wish to discuss, Beckett once again links up with an old tradition, that of the commedia dell'arte. In his plays, as in the conventional plots of the commedia, roles are assigned and characters perform in accordance with them: only the improvisatory element is left out, but we have the impression at least that the role is being adlibbed. Several of the exchanges between Vladimir and Estragon could be reassigned without noticeable loss, and big Pozzo, dressed up like a prosperous Irish landowner, duly performs like one, just as Lucky performs like the browbeaten slave he is, cringing to his boss but vicious to others who come near him.

Beckett is, in fact, very conscious that his people are actors, and makes them conscious of it too. His most famous character is one who doesn't even appear: he exploits the particularly suggestive idea of the off-stage quality of the unseen Godot, who has considerable influence on the actions and attitudes of those on stage. As for Hamm, he is a ham actor, and begins by yawning, 'A moi . . . de jouer'; the reality, and at the same time the artificiality of stage drama, are emphasised by that remark. Winnie too, soon after the curtain has gone up in *Happy Days*, tells herself 'Begin your day, Winnie'. In *Play*, of course, the spot acts like a director, pointing to each actor when his moment comes, prompting the performers. And even the audience is brought in on the act in Beckett's plays. Clov points his telescope at the auditorium and declares ironically that he sees a crowd delirious with joy, and Estragon gawks at them and says 'Aspects riants' (p. 20). The audience is made an accomplice of the characters' bankruptcy, and thereby of the poverty of all theatre when it comes to reflecting the huge inexpressible dilemmas of the human race.

But the actor does what he can in the circumstances. He exploits to the full the old music-hall device of making the audience wait for its fun, the golden rule of which is to do nothing directly which can be done more deviously and after a maximum of prevarication, suspense, deliberate misunderstanding and argument. This means that everything is liable to interruption: Estragon's story about the Englishman in the brothel, for instance, and Hamm's guilty tale about the starving man and his son. Some questions which are asked in the plays are never answered, and others only pages later. Beckett's characters are vaudeville actors who know their business.

And they are all old. The boy in *Godot* stands out as an exception, but his is a minor part, as is Jerry's in *All That Fall*; the others have all been wearied by life. Some, like Henry (in *Embers*) or Krapp, are going over it all again, probing their past like a wound. Others, like the trio in *Play*, or Joe in the television play, are visited by accusing eyes or voices from the past. In *Happy Days* Winnie recalls nostalgically her first ball and her first kiss, and Mr Tyler in *All That Fall* curses under his breath the wet Saturday afternoon of his conception. Beckett's fascination with old age antedates his own experience of it by many years; he is interested in the old because they have nothing to distract them from the realities of their existential situation: they see it close and they see it entire.

This is in fact one of the basic themes of Beckett's theatre, and that brings me to the last aspect of his work I wish to consider. The most obvious point to be made in connection with his themes is that Beckett is distinctly not the author of one unambiguous statement, does not transcribe a straightforward message, but explores in his plays attitudes and issues which preoccupy him personally. Another important fact is that the focus has changed gradually over the years with the increasing tendency to write in English. *En attendant Godot* and *Fin de partie* were concerned to examine the existential dilemma of four people caught in a timeless situation: in *Godot* no end to the cycle can be envisaged, but in *Fin de partie* life is dying within and without – the planet having been smitten, Hamm sits peevish, blind and decrepit in his cell as he and it sink into nothingness. The same, rather abstract, notions inspire the two mime plays and *Cascando*, also written in French.

In *All That Fall*, however, a different note was struck. Whereas the two previous French works were set in no particular place, the BBC play is set, it seems most likely, in Foxrock, the Dublin suburb where Beckett grew up; and whereas nothing much happened – spun out to seem a lot – in *Godot* and *Fin de partie*, in *All That Fall* it is more than probable that the child's death on the railway line was caused by Mr Rooney. This is quite a new kind of problem for Beckett to tackle: people struggling with the cruelties of their individual destinies in an Irish village is a far cry from two men waiting for a third on a country road somewhere in Europe. Similarly, he shows Krapp making himself unhappy as he listens to the taped account of dead love-affairs: 'Be again, be again. All that old misery. Once wasn't enough for you' (p. 18). The middle-aged Krapp had suggested 'Perhaps my best years are gone. When there was a chance of happiness' (p. 19); as we gaze on the senile and very decrepit Krapp we realise how right he was. In this play Beckett is clearly more interested in the unhappiness of the individual with a life behind him littered with bereavements and failed affairs, with the losing battle against alcoholism and declining intellectual powers. His English plays, in fact, are chiefly concerned with human relationships: in *Embers* Henry recounts his uneasy connection with his father, and how his marriage went sour after the birth of his daughter. In *Happy Days* Winnie tries to keep some fellowship with Willie, but she is buried in the ground and he is taciturn; she tries to put a brave face on things, but the play remains a terrible portrait of a marriage gone dead. In *Play*, as we have seen, Beckett investigates the eternal triangle, and his sympathies are evenly divided: the wife is bitchy, but she is to be pitied; the mistress is proud, but rather cold; the man is weak, but he is also henpecked on both sides. In *Eh Joe* the hero is reminded of the cruelties he inflicted on the women in his life. And in *Film* – which is built around the philosophical dictum *esse est percipi* – the man is pursued by himself until he tears up photographs from his past under the gaze of that same remorseless self.

There is little consistent pattern in this, autobiographical or otherwise: for all his understanding of such human problems Beckett remains detached and objective, concerned even in these English plays not with his own but with universal problems. His immense prestige throughout the world (recognised by the award of the Nobel Prize for Literature) is ascribable in part to the fact that, in a few of his plays, he has managed (as Adamov has not) to crystallise the essential disquiet of modern man.

One of the younger playwrights on whom Beckett has had considerable influence is Fernando Arrabal (b. 1932). After Adamov's greyness and Beckett's ascetic simplicity, however, Arrabal is rich and baroque in the extreme. He is a prolific writer, of fiction, fantastic autobiography (*Fête et rite de la confusion*), and plays – by no means all of which have been performed, and the finest of which were written, in a riot of spontaneous and unpremeditated exorcism, between the ages of eighteen and twenty. His most endearing quality is the warm poetry of much of his dialogue; one of his characters, for instance, is moved to tell her lover: 'Tu as le feu et l'aube dans ton ventre. On dirait que ta hanche berce une larme qui t'emplit d'orage!' (*Théâtre* II, p. 227). His least endearing features are a tendency to self-indulgent exhibitionism, and an occasional inability to resist the facile (such as the identification of Emanou with Jesus Christ in *Le Cimetière des voitures*). Nevertheless his fluid and inventive dramaturgy, together with that extraordinary brand of sophisticated naivety which is all his own, makes him the most outstanding of the younger playwrights who are following up the innovations of Genet, Ionesco and Beckett.

Like all truly original creators, however, Arrabal has taken his distance from his predecessors: 'je crois que mes pièces viennent d'horizons plus sauvages', he has said (*Entretiens*, p. 38), and has defined his theatrical aims in these terms: 'Le théâtre est surtout une cérémonie, une fête, qui tient du sacrilège et du sacré, de l'érotisme et du mysticisme, de la mise à mort et de l'exaltation de la vie' (*Théâtre* I, p. 7); as he put it rather beautifully, the theatre should project 'les songes humanoïdes qui hanteraient les nuits d'une machine IBM'. His true masters are Dostoyevsky and Lewis Carroll, Breughel and Hieronymus Bosch, all of whom loom large in his drama; and he shows himself a continuator of surrealism in his creation of an intense poetic imagery, at once erotic and chaste. There are indications that he now feels a certain guilt over this, and aspires, in his private life, to nothing short of bourgeois normality (*Entretiens*, pp. 96–7).

Nevertheless, he makes no secret of the fact that his plays are auto-biographical in the sense that he is always the central male character, and his wife Luce – who appears as Lis, Lys, Arlys, and so on – the principal female personage (*Entretiens*, pp. 107 and 112); this is not out of vanity, he claims, but out of ironic lucidity. The dominant themes of his drama are those one might therefore expect: he writes of childhood and lost innocence, of cruelty and lust, sex and violence and death. Two figures haunt his world: that of the domineering, smothering, hypo-critical mother, who does most harm when she professes the greatest affection and concern; and that of the protean infant/virgin/whore who is capable at one moment of great adoration and at another of blatant infidelity. So Arrabal's vision is both childlike (the Tépans shield from the bombardment under an umbrella and Zépo donates an artificial flower for every comrade who dies in action), and fully adult: *Fando et Lis* is about the difficulty not only of conjugal but also homosexual relationships; it deals with terror, exploitation and brutality, and portrays the way a lover's fleeting tenderness may be swamped by an irresistible impulse to denude, chain and flog his mistress. Arrabal's most complex and subtle work, *Le Grand Cérémonial*, treats of the close relationship between love and death, mother-fixation and violence, voyeurism and impotence. *La Communion solennelle* explodes the myth of youthful innocence by revealing the little girl in her first-communion clothes as a murderess: this play is typical of the 'mi-religieux, mi-obscène' nature of Arrabal's vision, and the intimate relation, in his dramaturgy, between 'le mauvais goût et le raffinement esthétique' (*Théâtre* V, p. 189).

This dramaturgy, which is dedicated to the celebration of 'confusion', is far more rigorous than one might be forgiven for assuming. In the *Entretiens* with Alain Schifres Arrabal speaks of his fascination for the polished and well-constructed in the arts (p. 113), and at the end of his fifth volume of plays specifies that 'sous un apparent désordre, il est indispensable que la mise en scène soit un modèle de précision'. This precision is characteristic of his art: *Le Grand Cérémonial* consists of prologue and two acts, with a very dramatic break between the first and second at the moment when Cavanosa (the name, like most of Arrabal's, is a significant anagram) is strangling Sil; she is on the point of death when loud knocks are heard at the door, and the curtain falls. The second act begins a few seconds later, with the Lover storming in to rescue Sil. Moreover, the long scene between Cavanosa and his mother in Act I is handled with a psychological subtlety of which Anouilh or Giraudoux might be proud: we observe her gradually casting her spell on him. Even the screen projections which are part of *Concert dans un œuf* have a balance and order about their appearances. This might seem to restrict the freedom of the director and actors, but in fact the reverse is true: Arrabal gives them considerable latitude, which may be why, as he revealed to Schifres, he has not always approved of some productions of his plays. There are, however, certain constants with which the director has to reckon, such as the regular presence among the necessary props of cages of one sort or another, and the fact that there is usually no development of any real plot. This requires on the part of the director an acute sense of ceremonial and improvisation, so that the liveliness of theatre and the theatricality of life become indistinguishable; 'les spectacles ainsi réalisés', writes Arrabal, 'ont permis la renaissance due théâtre d'aujourd'hui et fait de la scène le moyen d'expression idéal de l'homme actuel' (*Théâtre* II, p. vii).

As for the actors, they must respond to a form of drama in which roles amalgamate (Arlys-Sylda) or invert, in which there is opposition (Sil/Lys) and balance (Lys/Cavanosa). Nevertheless, there is a basic pattern in Arrabal's characterisation: we usually find a central male-female couple with peripheral males (the *Fando et Lis* situation, for example). Some of the roles are explicitly comic, like that of the Lover in *Le Grand Cérémonial*, who is so conventional in his manner and attitudes that he serves a useful dramatic function in helping to root in reality what would otherwise be a somewhat fantastic play: 'Comment ai-je pu me fourrer dans ce repaire de fous?' he wonders when the absurdity of Act II reaches its height. Cavanosa handles him with a wit of which Ionesco would be proud: 'Comme c'est un gentleman, il sait garder son sang-froid; mais comme c'est un gentleman con, il garde son sang-froid d'une manière con' (Prologue, Tableau ii).

For Arrabal is not at all a solemn writer. Even when he is at his most horrific, he retains a playful sense of humour that is appealing. He certainly is establishing himself now as a playwright of great importance, particularly on the strength of the early writings (*Pique-nique en campagne*, a perfect one-acter, is a fine work by any standard). Recently, in fact, there has been a falling-off in inspiration: in *L'Architecte et l'empereur d'Assyrie* and *Le Jardin des délices* (both of which enjoyed an excellent press, the latter helped in part by a brilliant performance by Delphine Seyrig), one senses that the childlike fantasy is in danger of becoming mechanical. One hopes that success will not make Arrabal into a professional buffoon and pompous theorist of confusion. His kind of art can know no happy medium between spontaneous freshness and mannered self-parody; so it is to be hoped it will not slide into selfconscious 'artiness'.

Fortunately, Arrabal seems himself to be aware of the dangers that his very gifts expose him to. He told Schifres that he is keeping other options open by, for example, reading for a degree in mathematics; and in the preface to the sixth volume of his plays, he looks forward to an imminent convulsive renaissance of the theatre: 'C'est le temps du théâtre qui vit à la pointe des actes, des contestations et des rêves. Veille fascinante !' The youthful confidence of that prophecy seems an appropriate note on which to take leave of the three dramatists whose work I have been examining, and who have done so much to prepare the new dawn of which Arrabal here speaks. For though no one can predict the forms which the theatre of the next few decades will take, given such forbears the prospects for young French playwrights are auspicious indeed.

This is perhaps because the essential issue, of which – like Jarry, Apollinaire and the others who went before them – they show an almost uncomfortably sharp awareness, is that the theatre is by its very nature a *paradox* (in a famous essay, Diderot made a similar point about acting). For it's obvious that conditions in a playhouse may be stuffy, hot and uncomfortable, with too many seats crammed into the auditorium, an exiguous stage, and noises from the everyday world impinging on the action. And yet in this often far-from-ideal arena a whole universe, albeit a counterfeit one, unfolds before our eyes. A sham, in fact, which under the right circumstances – with a good play in an intelligent production – can rely on what Thornton Wilder called our acceptance of the 'permitted lie' and, by defying the distracting forces of workaday bustle without, provoke within that uniquely intense action which characterises the contemplation of the supposititious art of the stage.

In the course of this book, we have been looking at the richly varied manifestations of this 'permitted lie' in modern French drama. We have seen the prodigious inventiveness of the French mind in the field of twentieth-century dramaturgy, where its contribution may well turn out to be even more significant – because richer and more varied – than in that other golden age of French theatre, the later seventeenth century.

For it can be argued that once the best work of writers of genius like Molière and Racine is left out of the reckoning, the output of the French neo-classical period in terms of plays of lasting worth can be counted on the fingers of one hand. The *grand siècle*, in fact, produced some outstanding plays and a great deal of dross – some of it written by the most eminent, not excluding Racine and Molière themselves. The striking thing about the present age, on the other hand, is that although it has not yet thrown up a writer to rival in stature the great masters of western drama, it has shown greater evenness of achievement in its creation of numerous impressive plays at the hands of highly gifted directors. Claudel's *Partage de midi*, Giraudoux's *La Guerre de Troie n'aura pas lieu*, Montherlant's *La Reine morte*, Anouilh's *Eurydice*, Sartre's *Huis clos*, Camus's *Les Justes*, Genet's *Les Nègres*, Ionesco's *Les Chaises*, Adamov's *Le Professeur Taranne*, Beckett's *En attendant Godot* and Arrabal's *Le Grand Cérémonial* are only a few of the many French works of this century by which the theatrical repertoire has permanently been enriched, as we have continually sought to show.

The moral of this book, therefore, can be stated simply enough, and it is this. Since the eighteen-nineties and the days of Jarry and Lugné-Poe, the French have established and held a strong position in the development of the drama, that paradoxically shabby and magnificent, impure and plastic art of impermanent vitality and fragile, haunting display.

Select Bibliography

ADAMOV, ARTHUR
  Ici et maintenant   Paris, Gallimard, 1964
  Théâtre   Paris, Gallimard, 1953 etc.
APOLLINAIRE, GUILLAUME   *Œuvres poétiques* Paris, Gallimard (Bibliothèque de la Pléiade), 1956
ARRABAL, FERNANDO   *Théâtre* Paris, Christian Bourgois, 1968 etc.
BECKETT, SAMUEL
  All That Fall   London, Faber and Faber, 1957
  Come and Go   London, Calder and Boyars, 1967
  Comédie et actes divers   Paris, Editions de Minuit, 1966
  Eh Joe and Other Writings   London, Faber and Faber, 1967
  En attendant Godot   Paris, Editions de Minuit, 1953[2]
  Fin de partie   Paris, Editions de Minuit, 1957
  Happy Days   London, Faber and Faber, 1962
  Krapp's Last Tape and Embers   London, Faber and Faber, 1959
  Play and Two Short Pieces for Radio   London, Faber and Faber, 1964

COCTEAU, JEAN   *Théâtre* Paris, Gallimard, 1948 etc.

GHELDERODE, MICHEL DE   *Théâtre* Paris, Gallimard, 1950 etc.

JARRY, ALFRED   *Tout Ubu* Paris, Le Livre de Poche, 1962

FLETCHER, JOHN, and JOHN SPURLING   *Beckett: A Study of His Plays* London, Methuen, 1971

OXENHANDLER, NEAL   *Scandal and Parade: The Theatre of Jean Cocteau* London, Constable, 1958

SCHIFRES, ALAIN   *Entretiens avec Arrabal* Paris, Pierre Belfond, 1969

GENERAL BIBLIOGRAPHY

Below is a selection of general works dealing with modern French drama, or books which discuss more than one author. Material on individuals or on more specific aspects will be found at the end of each of the chapters above.

Books

ABEL, LIONEL   *Metatheater: A New View of Dramatic Form*   New York, Hill and Wang, 1963

ADERETH, MAXWELL   *Commitment in Modern French Literature*   London, Gollancz, 1967

ASLAN, ODETTE   *L'Art du théâtre*   Paris, Seghers, 1963

BÉHAR, HENRI   *Etude sur le théâtre dada et surréaliste*   Paris, Gallimard, 1967

BEIGBEDER, MARC   *Le Théâtre en France depuis la Libération*   Paris, Bordas, 1959

BENTLEY, ERIC
    What is Theatre?   Boston, Beacon Press, 1956
    The Life of the Drama   New York, Atheneum, 1964

BISHOP, THOMAS   *Pirandello and the French Theatre*   London, Peter Owen, 1961

BOISDEFFRE, PIERRE DE
    Une Histoire vivante de la littérature d'aujourd'hui   Paris, Perrin, 1964[5]
    Dictionnaire de littérature contemporaine   Paris, Editions universitaires, 1963[2]

BRODIN, PIERRE   *Présences contemporaines*   Paris, Debresse, 1955[2]

BROWN, JOHN RUSSELL, and BERNARD HARRIS, *eds.*   *Contemporary Theatre*   London, Arnold, 1962

BRUSTEIN, ROBERT   *The Theatre of Revolt*   Boston and Toronto, Little, Brown, 1964

CHAMPIGNY, ROBERT   *Le Genre dramatique*   Monte Carlo, Regain, 1965

CHIARI, JOSEPH
    The Contemporary French Theatre   London, Rockliff, 1958
    Landmarks of Contemporary Drama   London, Herbert Jenkins, 1965

COHN, RUBY   *Currents in Contemporary Drama*   Bloomington, Indiana University Press, 1969

CORVIN, MICHEL   Le Théâtre nouveau en France   Paris, Presses Universitaires de France, 1963

CRUICKSHANK, JOHN, ed.   French Literature and Its Background, vol. VI   London, Oxford University Press, 1970

DENNIS, NIGEL   Dramatic Essays   London, Weidenfeld and Nicolson, 1962

DICKINSON, HUGH   Myth on the Modern Stage   Urbana, University of Illinois Press, 1969

DIETRICH, MARGRET   Das moderne Drama: Strömungen, Gestalten, Motive   Stuttgart, Alfred Kröner, 1961

DUVIGNAUD, JEAN   Spectacle et société   Paris, Denoël/Gonthier, 1970

ESSLIN, MARTIN
    The Theatre of the Absurd   Harmondsworth, Penguin Books, 1968[2]
    Absurd Drama   Harmondsworth, Penguin Books, 1965

FECHTER, PAUL   Das europäische Drama, vols. II and III   Mannheim, Bibliographisches Institut, 1957, 1958

FLETCHER, JOHN   New Directions in Literature   London, Calder and Boyars, 1968

FOWLIE, WALLACE
    A Guide to Contemporary French Literature   New York, Meridian Books, 1957
    Dionysus in Paris   New York, Meridian Books, 1960

FRANZEN, ERICH   Formen des modernen Dramas   Munich, C. H. Beck, 1961

FREEDMAN, MORRIS, ed.   Essays in the Modern Drama   Boston, D. C. Heath, 1964

GASCOIGNE, BAMBER   Twentieth-Century Drama   London, Hutchinson, 1963[2]

GASSNER, JOHN
    Masters of the Drama   New York, Dover Publications, 1954[3]
    Directions in Modern Theatre and Drama   New York, Holt, Rinehart and Winston, 1965
    with RALPH G. ALLEN   Theatre and Drama in the Making   Boston, Houghton Mifflin, 1964

GINESTIER, PAUL   Le Théâtre contemporain dans le monde   Paris, Presses Universitaires de France, 1961

GROSSVOGEL, DAVID I.
    Twentieth Century French Drama   New York, Columbia University Press, 1961[2]
    The Blasphemers   Ithaca, Cornell University Press, 1965[2]

GUICHARNAUD, JACQUES   Modern French Theatre from Giraudoux to Genet   New Haven, Yale University Press, 1967[2]

HEIDSIECK, ARNOLD   Das Groteske und das Absurde im modernen Drama   Stuttgart, Kohlhammer, 1969

HINCHLIFFE, ARNOLD P.   The Absurd   London, Methuen, 1969

HOBSON, HAROLD   The French Theatre of Today   London, Harrap, 1953

JACOBSEN, JOSEPHINE, and WILLIAM R. MUELLER   Ionesco and Genet: Playwrights of Silence   New York, Hill and Wang, 1968

JACQUOT, JEAN, ed.   *Le Théâtre moderne: Hommes et tendances* Paris, Centre National de la Recherche Scientifique, 1958

KERR, WALTER   *The Theater in Spite of Itself* New York, Simon and Schuster, 1963

KESTING, MARIANNE
   Das epische Theater   Stuttgart, Kohlhammer, 1959
   Panorama des zeitgenössischen Theaters   Munich, Piper, 1962

KITCHIN, LAURENCE   *Mid-Century Drama* London, Faber and Faber, 1962[2]

KNOWLES, DOROTHY   *French Drama of the Inter-War Years, 1919–1939* London, Harrap, 1967

LALOU, RENÉ   *Le Théâtre en France depuis 1900* Paris, Presses Universitaires de France, 1961[4]

LEWIS, ALLAN   *The Contemporary Theatre* New York, Crown, 1962

LIOURE, MICHEL   *Le Drame* Paris, Armand Colin, 1963

LUMLEY, FREDERICK   *Trends in Twentieth-Century Drama* London, Barrie and Rockliff, 1960[2]

MARCEL, GABRIEL   *Théâtre et religion* Lyon, Vitte, 1958

MAURIAC, CLAUDE   *L'Alittérature contemporaine* Paris, Albin-Michel, 1958

MELCHINGER, SIEGFRIED
   Theater der Gegenwart   Frankfurt am Main and Hamburg, Fischer-Bücherei, 1956
   Drama zwischen Shaw und Brecht   Bremen, Schünemann, 1957

MENNEMEIER, FRANZ NORBERT   *Das moderne Drama des Auslandes* Düsseldorf, Bagel, 1961

MIGNON, PAUL-LOUIS, ed.   *Les Entretiens d'Helsinki ou les tendances du théâtre d'avant-garde dans le monde* Paris, Michel Brient, 1961

MOORE, HARRY T.   *Twentieth-Century French Literature* London, Heinemann, 1969

NORTH, ROBERT J.   *Myth in the Modern French Theatre* Keele, University of Keele, 1962

PEYRE, HENRI   *Contemporary French Literature* New York, Harper and Row, 1964

PICON, GAËTAN   *Panorama de la nouvelle littérature française* Paris, Gallimard, 1960[2]

PINGAUD, BERNARD, ed.   *Ecrivains d'aujourd'hui* Paris, Grasset, 1960

PRONKO, LEONARD CABELL   *Avant-Garde: The Experimental Theater in France* Berkeley and Los Angeles, University of California Press, 1962

PUCCIANI, ORESTE F., ed.   *The French Theatre Since 1930* New York, Ginn, 1954

QUENEAU, RAYMOND, ed.   *Encyclopédie de la Pléiade: Histoire des littératures, III* Paris, Gallimard, 1958

REBELLO, LUIZ FRANCISCO   *Imagens do teatro contemporâneo* Lisbon, Atica, 1961

ROY, CLAUDE   *L'Amour du théâtre* Paris, Gallimard, 1965

SCHNEIDER, MARCEL   *La Littérature fantastique en France* Paris, Arthème Fayard, 1964

SÉE, EDMOND   *Le Théâtre français contemporain*   Paris, Armand Colin, 1933

SEIPEL, HILDEGARD   *Untersuchungen zum experimentellen Theater von Beckett und Ionesco*   Bonn, Romanisches Seminar, 1963

SERREAU, GENEVIÈVE   *Histoire du 'Nouveau théâtre'*   Paris, Gallimard, 1966

SIMON, KARL GÜNTER   *Avant-Garde Theater aus Frankreich: Moderne oder Mode?*   Berlin, Rembrandt, 1962

SIMON, PIERRE-HENRI   *Théâtre et destin*   Paris, Armand Colin, 1959

SION, GEORGES   *Le Théâtre français d'entre-deux-guerres*   Tournai and Paris, Casterman, n.d. [ca. 1945]

SOUTHERN, RICHARD   *The Seven Ages of the Theatre*   London, Faber and Faber, 1962

STEINER, GEORGE   *The Death of Tragedy*   London, Faber and Faber, 1961

STYAN, J. L.
   The Elements of Drama   Cambridge, University Press, 1960
   The Dark Comedy   Cambridge, University Press, 1968[2]

SURER, PAUL   *Le Théâtre français contemporain*   Paris, Société d'Edition et d'Enseignement Supérieur, 1964

SZONDI, PETER   *Theorie des modernen Dramas*   Frankfurt am Main, Suhrkamp, 1959

TYNAN, KENNETH   *Curtains*   London, Longmans, 1961

VALENCY, MAURICE   *The Flower and the Castle*   New York, Macmillan, 1963

VOLTZ, PIERRE   *La Comédie*   Paris, Armand Colin, 1964

WELLWARTH, GEORGE E.   *The Theater of Protest and Paradox*   New York, New York University Press, 1964

WILLIAMS, RAYMOND   *Modern Tragedy*   London, Chatto and Windus, 1966

ZAMORA, JUAN GUERRERO   *Historia del teatro contemporáneo*, 4 vols. Barcelona, Flors, 1961

Periodicals

Esprit devoted a special issue to 'Notre Théâtre : Théâtre moderne et public populaire' (May 1965), and *Yale French Studies* No. 29 consisted of articles on 'The New Dramatists'. These and other periodicals (such as *Cahiers Renaud-Barrault, Drama Survey, Modern Drama, Plays and Players, Revue d'Histoire du Théâtre, Theatre Research, Tulane Drama Review*), are – as will have been noted at the end of some chapters – of regular interest. And for much fuller bibliographical information than can be given here, *French XX* (formerly *French VII) Bibliography* should be consulted.

APPENDIX OF ENGLISH TRANSLATIONS

Wherever possible a standard English or American translation is quoted and the translation used is indicated in brackets. Where no published translation is available a literal translation is given and is preceded by an asterisk. The first number listed refers to page; the numbers following the colon refer to lines.

INTRODUCTION

7:4   * in full awareness
8:29–30   * it is only before the footlights that a work of drama begins truly to exist
9:23–4   * scandal and provocation in the theatre are only possible when the playwright is totally sincere

CHAPTER 1   PRINCIPLES OF STAGING

11:7   * producers
13:6   * staging
    15   * bare boards
    24   * realistic painted drop
15:34   * magic box, optical box
17:35–36   * the speaking of lines is basically breathing
19:27–28   * decrepit dodderers . . . insubstantial phantoms representing nothing
20:27–28   No more masterpieces. (*The Theater and Its Double.* New York, Grove, 1958)
23:6–7   * theatre with multiple stages in counterpoint
    24   * the gamut of physical gesture
26:13   * district
    25   * theatre of protest
27:27   * the Vilar style
28:3   * document-play
    4–5   * modern awareness **drama**
30:20   * third world

CHAPTER 2   CLAUDEL

35:6–12   What a responsibility for us writers, above all, who are the leaders of men and the directors of their souls! The mere fact of our enlightenment makes us spread light all about us. We are delegated by the rest of the world to the way of knowledge and truth, and there is no other truth but Christ, who is the Way and the Life, and the duty of knowing and serving Him lies more heavily on us than upon others, and lies upon us with a terrible urgency. (*The Correspondence between Paul Claudel and André Gide*. London, Secker and Warburg, 1952)

    23–25   * I feel more and more that all feelings, all human, even universal events are only parables of the eternal drama enacted between God and man.

    35–37   * The essential conflict that Christianity awakens within us is the great source of dramatic tension as it is the great source of strength in our moral and social lives.

36:3–9   * Finally the fourth advantage is that faith comforts and relieves human nature by showing the final end for which it is suited. Through faith all our feelings, our passions assume at last their meaning and appear in the fullness of their truth. The Catholic belief, indeed, is that man is naturally destined to be happy and that no effort he makes to achieve this end is bad in itself.

    12   * even sin

    14–15   Even sin! Sin also serves. (*The Satin Slipper*. London, Sheed & Ward, 1931)

    33   * has tremendous potential

36:39–40   * total theatre

37:10–11   It's really most absorbing to work on problems of gesture, ensemble, and attitude, and then to watch it all coming alive and taking shape. (*The Correspondence between Paul Claudel and André Gide*)

    20   * mystery play

    21   * satyric drama

    22   * radiophonic extravaganza

    28–29   * The Flesh, according to what we have been told, forms desires in opposition to the Spirit and the Spirit forms desires in opposition to the Flesh.

    31–33   * This drama . . . shows us one of those conflicts in which the lovers, in spite of mutual attraction, sprung precisely from contradictions, are separated by divergent interests.

38:7–9   * from time to time the audience in the theatre needs violence, a bite, a lash with a whip

    19–21   As the actors themselves are hidden in their robes, so, as it enters each bosom, does the drama stir under the living stuff of the crowd. (*The East I Know*. New Haven, Yale University Press; London, Oxford University Press, 1914)

39:3–7   * No props, no painted sets, no cardboard sets. No picturesque effects. Everything should be subordinated to dramatic interpretation. The stage's only purpose is to provide a structure for the action and the organic construction of planes and elevations against which it should develop.

39:9 * actors permanently on stage

15–17 * a theatre of ideas? and if you can hold the audience's attention with such a spectacle, what effect can it have on them?

29–30 * congested, stifling life

33 * certainly not very pleasant

38–39 * Everything is cast in the same mould, both body and mind.

40:13–16 * I have begun to understand that what happened in *Break of Noon* and *The Satin Slipper* in its own dimension was merely an attempt to explain what happened in two human hearts.

19–20 The only play of mine which *might* be acted now . . . (*The Correspondence between Paul Claudel and André Gide*)

25–29 * The play which you, no doubt providentially, imposed on me has taken on an enormous importance for me. Hardly a day passes without my thinking deeply about it. . . . It seems to have made me seek the meaning of the whole of my life. It is certainly much more than literature to me.

41:12–17 * The State's money would be put to much better use in encouraging researchers, pioneers of a new art, rather than perpetuating those mausoleums which pass for state-controlled theatres. When one looks back, as my age allows me to do, over the past fifty years of artistic history, one finds that the role of these sinister establishments has been little more than that of a freezer.

25–26 * a sort of back drop, a kind of projection of the characters' thoughts

42:16 * similar extravagances

18 * day

42:38 to * Alas! what a failure! These old things remind me of cast-

43:2 off clothes in a forgotten cupboard which still retain vaguely the shape of the body. . . . I'm going to try to make the play suitable for the stage, using an idea I've had of completely rewriting the character of Pierre de Craon and of doing away with the architectural shifts at the end.

44:17 * swan

21 * to rape

30–32 Yes, I know he will not wed me save upon the Cross, and our souls each to each in death and night, beyond all human motive!

If I cannot be his Paradise at least I can be his cross! (*The Satin Slipper*)

39–40 * vertical direction

45:38–40 * I should like Marthe alone to seem a real woman in the midst of three sinister puppets with stiff gestures and impassive faces (masks would almost be appropriate).

46:25 * sap, proof and synthesis

40 * double shadow

47:4–7   * A work of art that generates its own world, which is in no way the world of the theologian or of the apologist, has the simple aim of pleasing the spectator.

15–18   * I have never written with the intention of proving anything, or of revealing the truth. I have written quite simply to create a whole from which spectators may draw what they wish and, as indeed I hope, spiritual advantage.

28–30   * To enter into my theatre there is definitely no need to be a Christian, one need only be, I might say, Claudelian.

CHAPTER 3   GIRAUDOUX

49:21   * preciosity
23   * understanding
50:13–14   * new science
14   * created without raw material
16   * without luggage
17   * distinctive characteristic
18–19   * to realise your intrinsic difference
21   * somewhat unholy effusions of a bourgeois couple
52:29   . . . the pleasantest planet on which to alight—but only for a brief stay (*Amphitryon 38*. New York, Random House, 1938)
53:16   * one who acquiesces
29–30   So, for one night, I offer you the hospitality of this island, set in a pure and windless ocean. ('Judith' in *Plays*. London, Methuen, 1963)
30   . . . age of gods ('Judith')
31   . . . a man completely of this world ('Judith')
35   Think of mankind entirely innocent. ('Judith')
53:42 to   How can those who wake like this each morning near to
54:1   one they love let them escape and return to life ! ('Judith')
55:12   * simple and pure
23   All-Rounder ('Intermezzo' in *Plays II*. London, Methuen, 1967)
25   * a right note
32   It's not a question of bringing her back to herself but of bringing her back to us. ('Intermezzo')
55:42 to   Life might be more beautiful than men consent to make it.
56:1   (*Fruits of the Earth*. Harmondsworth, Penguin Books, 1970)
6–7   . . . any demands but this world's ! ('Intermezzo')
58:13   * Let's not start the Trojan War again
33   * suitable
34–35   All bodies are base and contemptible. (*The Virtuous Island*. New York and London, Samuel French, 1956)
59:1–3   To the presence of Mr. Banks, even, wonderful as he is, I prefer the absence of Mr. Banks. (*The Virtuous Island*)

59 : 7–8   * Oh ! Mrs. Banks ! It isn't the question of couples that
matters here below but that of happy couples.
    10   * shame
    11   * to repent
    14–15   * this blend of Sophocles, you and Jouvet
    18   * unwedded
    28   * keywords
    32–33   * one of those rare creatures that Fate creates for its own use
60 : 11   * to declare oneself
    24   * those who acquiesce
    25   * a woman who insists on her rights
    26   * desperately determined, difficult woman, truth's house-
keeper
61 : 8   * renouncer
    16   * to tell people the truth about themselves
    25–26   * a place of light, of fine language
    38   * terrace, pavement in front of a café
    39   * a supra-terrestrial hour
    40   * a balcony of serenity ... a terrace of euphoria
62 : 18–19   Don't join the world of men ! ('Ondine' in *Plays II*. London,
Methuen, 1967)
    32–33   * The power to forget is the great secret of strong creative
lives.
    37   * Memory is an invention of evil.
63 : 17   * 'going one better'
    22   * How handsome you are !
    29–30   * virtuosity reduced almost to its essential
64 : 6   * malpractice, cheating
    9–10   * what good is a duo ?
65 : 23–24   * the death of a good-for-nothing is nothing
    38–39   On every incontinent person I see a creature. (*Duel of
Angels*. London, Methuen, 1958)
66 : 4   You've reintroduced original sin. (*Duel of Angels*)
    6   * the mafia of women
    15–18   * Madame Blanchard has herself denied her own great
speciality here below. She is no longer purity because she couldn't recognize
her own purity.
    21–22   ... man's stupidity, and coarseness, and wickedness (*Duel of
Angels*)
    26–27   Purity's not for this world, but every ten years we get a
gleam of it. (*Duel of Angels*)
    40–41   The world has purity, Paola, beauty, and light. (*Duel of
Angels*)
67 : 9   * Giraudoux in danger
    21–23   * Plays change theme and tone periodically, as snakes cast
their skins. ... The play is inexhaustible. A work of art has no end.

CHAPTER 4   MONTHERLANT

68 : 4   * pure, sober, spare
    9   * moralistic
    21–25   * a man goes into a room in which a woman he loves is cry-
ing: he has never seen her crying. At the first attempt I write: 'What's
wrong? My God! Do I see you crying!' I cross it out and write: 'What's
wrong? My God! You . . . crying . . . ?' I cross it out and I write:
'What's wrong? My God! I see *you* crying!'
69 : 1–2   * with as much sharpness of observation as possible, the ways
of human souls
    4–6   * A play only interests me if the external action, reduced to
its simplest form, is merely a pretext for the exploration of man.
    7–10   * When I read Shakespeare or Racine, I never ask myself
whether or not it is 'theatre'. I read it, seeking a deeper understanding of the
movements of the human soul, of moving situations and of those words
'which carry at their peak a curious gleam'.
    13–14   * peripeteias, sudden turns of events, misunderstandings
    20   * staging
    25–26   * total indifference to external things
    27–28   * a play that exists only through its internal action
70 : 1–2   * they seem to be a gathering of magnificent and slightly
monstrous insects
    3–4   * glittering, frightening insects—enormous insects from the
virgin forest
    7–8   * Sisters of the night
    16–17   * the chariot of fire when it skimmed the earth between
Elisha and Elijah
    18   * the threat rises with the sun
    24   * those Gates of Darkness of which God spoke to Job
71 : 22–27   * Even beyond the silence, there is the final loneliness,
between abandonment and treachery . . . When the page, the evil little angel
walks finally on tiptoe towards the crowd with a last glance at what he is
betraying and abandoning, we are at the extreme limit of what emotion is
for me—well beyond the bells, the kneeling and the prayer.
    28–29   . . . there are chimings of bells, but discreet, with no excess
('The Master of Santiago' in *The Master of Santiago and Four Other Plays.*
London, Routledge and Kegan Paul, 1951)
    39   * this is pasteboard mystery
72 : 2–3   The court is a place of darkness. In it you would have been
a little light. ('Queen after Death' in *The Master of Santiago*)
    4   . . . with shadowy eyes . . . ('Queen after Death')
    5–6   . . . those candles one extinguishes one by one, at regular
intervals on Holy Thursday, at the midnight service . . . ('Queen after Death')
    10–11   . . . they are like him: by turns dark and luminous, luminous
and dark. ('Queen after Death')

72 : 12   . . . this appalling knot of contradictions . . . ('Queen after Death')

17–18   . . . it doesn't struggle, it follows its course ('Queen after Death')

19   . . . that water, so cool, my only support all through the day . . . ('Queen after Death')

21   . . . like calm lakes . . . ('Queen after Death')

22   . . . like a boat in calm water . . . ('Queen after Death')

23–26   . . . sitting by the edge of the basin, with the fountain that sometimes sent us drops . . . that basin continually overflowing, ceaselessly filled . . . ('Queen after Death')

27–28   . . . this feeling of black rain ceaselessly ready to fall . . . ('Queen after Death')

30   The Prince is not very deep. ('Queen after Death')

32–33   . . . to try to portray the King is like trying to carve a statue out of sea water. ('Queen after Death')

37   . . . it burns me. It's as if I were eating fire. ('The Master of Santiago')

38–39   . . . only really burns any longer in the heart of your father. ('The Master of Santiago')

42   . . . 'Lion and nightingale are always athirst'. ('Malatesta' in *The Master of Santiago*)

73 : 5   . . . the Malurus bird, at the fall of evening . . . ('Queen after Death')

6   . . . a lion that's fallen into a trap. ('Queen after Death')

8–9   . . . one of those wicked flames one sees wandering over rotten pools . . . ('Queen after Death')

17–19   I have flowed away like the wind of the desert, which begins by chasing before it waves of sand like a cavalry charge and ends by being diluted and exhausted : nothing is left of it. ('Queen after Death')

22–24   Murder and Suicide, they walk about among us unceasingly, and sometimes in passing give a gentle squeeze to the tips of our fingers. ('Civil War' in *Theatre of War*. Harmondsworth, Penguin Books, 1967)

31   * rake

32–33   * I may well have suffered enough from speaking to you with an open heart, nothing will prevent me from continuing to do so.

74 : 4–5   * Classical theatre is successful only when it understates.

75 : 14   * dogma of distinct genres

21   * when these are of a certain quality

40–42   * The tragic element in my theatre is far less one of situation than one which stems from the inner life of a man.

76 : 11–14   * One dies as one is and one dies as one wishes. A moment ago I cried out 'How horrible it is,' didn't I? You won't tell anyone I cried that.

21–27   * The Infanta became ill from pride because I did just that during certain periods of my childhood. The king, whose character is barely outlined in Guevara's play, took shape, moulded by moments of me. Each of these creations became in turn a mouthpiece for some side of me . . . In short *Queen after Death* obeyed the rules that govern all my writings . . . they are nothing but fragments of my memoirs.

76 : 32–33   * Where feelings are concerned, I hit upon the diversity and changeable quality of my nature.

    36–37   * much better and much worse

    38–39   * the worst and the best man in the world

    41   * The essential characteristic of his nature is changeability.

77 : 7–8   * Theatre is based on the coherence of character and life is based on its incoherence.

    11   * An absolute fatality binds them together and draws them toward their Destiny.

    23–24   * A very strong, obsessive feeling of the inanity, the futility and the absurdity of nearly everything has overwhelmed me since my youth.

    25–26   * vanity of vanities

    26–27   * who are dead to the world or who seek to be so

    29   * weary

    31–37   He [Pompey] is tired of himself . . . [* and I am tired of devoting myself . . . Tired out from feeling that I could give my life for a man . . .] Tired out from feeling that I could give my life for a cause . . . I am tired of courage. I am tired of foreseeing and foretelling, tired of never having been wrong : tired of the lack of hope, or rather of lying hopes, tired of the contradiction . . . ('Civil War')

78 : 3   * Darkness pleases me; I feel better at dusk.

    8–9   * she has made me hear the voice of truth from out of the mouth of madness.

    24   * theatre of grandeur

79 : 7   women's nerves ('Malatesta' in *The Master of Santiago*)

    9   * the very sensitive man

    11–16   * I was writing the first act (of *Malatesta*) at Grasse, in the hotel Muraour, during the winter of 1943–4. The head waiter who was serving me said something rude. I left the room instantly, went up to my room, threw myself on to the bed and started to tremble convulsively, shuddering (I spread my coat over myself) and actually tossing jerkily on the bed.

    23–26   There is a sort of wave that has just washed over me and is plunging me into a deep—into a deep—An extraordinary sadness suddenly bearing me down and drowning me. ('Malatesta')

    30–33   Do you know how I interpret the myth of Psyche? Love flies away, all's destroyed, because Psyche has looked upon Love while he was asleep. That means that one should never touch a soul when it is uncovered and without defence. ('Malatesta')

    34–36   . . . there are always certain hours when a man is so weak, morally and physically . . . that a little push and you would make him fall over. ('Queen after Death')

80:1–2   * He dies of emotion, no doubt, but perhaps also because he has revealed the truth about himself: he has emptied himself.

6–7   * how strange to want to make oneself suffer and to create unhappiness from within oneself alone!

10–12   * You are not mine, you give me nothing, all that we do is false . . .

19–23   * Thus men of my sort will speak more and more a language that the majority of people do not understand. Their solitary thought rises and does not disperse, like the thread of smoke from nomads' fires that rises above the desert at dusk: this pure, lost thread, so slender a link between heaven and earth.

33–35   * The temptation to destroy all that one has constructed is one of the obsessions of my work. *I shall build and I shall destroy . . .* has been for a long time one of the mottoes of this work.

36   * the extreme temptation

81:7   enveloped by the hand of God ('Queen after Death')

10   * emotivity

16   * God is Nothing.

18   * His God is more nothingness than love.

23   * people *of value*

82:5   * Waiting for the king

6   * I created him, I am his father.

9   * the understanding of people

10–12   * It is you who have made me a woman. That is much more than having created me. It is you who have given me birth.

13   . . . this darling girl ('Malatesta')

15–16   I had thought it was this or that that gave my life a sense: I now saw it was loving. ('No Man's Son' in *The Master of Santiago*)

17–20   * He thought he had discovered, as in a revelation, what made his feelings for Ram so special. It was that before her he felt himself to be both lover and father.

23–24   * there is only one love

25–26   * there are not two types of love

28–29   * it is another story of education spoiled by passion

32   . . . the son I should have had ('Queen after Death')

35   * from nothing

83:6–7   * I love her more than her father and mother put together.

19   He created me, I love him . . . ('The Master of Santiago')

23   My loyal little man! ('Civil War')

28–29   * In *Queen after Death* and *No Man's Son* the children betray the adults. In *The City of which the Prince is a Child* the adults betray the children.

38–39   * The sacrifice of Abraham is a decided obsession in my theatre.

84:4   * For man, his only real sons are spiritual ones.

8   Children degrade. ('The Master of Santiago')

84:9   . . . the family by blood is accursed. ('The Master of Santiago')
  11   . . . by election and the spirit ('The Master of Santiago')
  18–19   * the love of the idea he has formed of himself
  35–36   * Abstractions are nothing, people are all.
  36   * work

CHAPTER 5   ANOUILH

86:6–7   * old Sicilian sorcerer
87:4   * black plays—pure and mediocre
  16–17   * thirst for purity
  30   * happiness
  32–35   Happiness! Anyone would think happiness was the only
thing on earth! Yes, I do want to run away from it! I won't let it swallow
me whole. I have a right to go on suffering and crying with the pain of it.
(*Restless Heart*. London, Methuen, 1957)
88:4–8   of having reached the farthest limits of his pain. You may
not know it, but at the far end of despair, there is a white clearing where one
is almost happy . . . a frightful happiness. A foul, a shameful happiness.
(*Restless Heart*)
  10–11   * those who hanker after the absolute
  11–13   * I don't want to grow up. I don't want to learn to say yes.
Everything is too ugly.
  13–15   * an unfortunate, retrogressive evolution . . . the very theme
that inspired *Restless Heart* but unfortunately distorted and in a way
diminished.
  39–40   Oh, what is your name?—Orpheus. And yours?—Eurydice.
('Eurydice' in *Antigone and Eurydice*. London, Methuen, 1951)
89:4–7   To live, to live! Like your mother and her lover, maybe, with
their cooing and simpering and self-indulgence; then the fine meals, and
afterwards they make love and everything is all right. Oh no. I love you too
much to live. ('Eurydice')
  16–18   I am not here to understand . . . I am here to say no to you,
and die. ('Antigone' in *Antigone and Eurydice*. London, Methuen, 1951)
  30–31   * Antigone is right, but Creon isn't wrong.
  41   * these are not two opposed affirmations, but two negations.
Hence a feeling of gratuitousness.
90:1–2   * a psychological drama bordering on tragedy
  11–15   Tragedy is clean, it is restful, it is flawless . . . That makes
for tranquillity. There is a sort of fellow-feeling among characters in a
tragedy: he who kills is as innocent as he who gets killed . . . Tragedy is
restful; and the reason is that hope, that foul deceitful thing, has no part in
it. ('Antigone')
  17–20   Well, here we are.
These people are about to act out for you the story of Antigone. That thin,

little creature sitting by herself, staring straight ahead, seeing nothing, is Antigone. She's thinking. [* She's thinking that she's going to play Antigone in a few moments.] ('Antigone')

30–37   The moment is come, Medea, when you must be yourself. O Spirit of Evil. Mighty beast, alive, crawling over me, licking me, take me. I am yours this night. Penetrate me, rend me, swell and sear me to my inmost core. See how I receive you, help you, open up to you. Bear down upon me with your huge hairy form, grasp me in your great calloused hands; your harsh breath on my mouth, choke me. I am living at last, I suffer and I am born. This is my wedding feast. For this night of love with you it is that I have lived. ('Medea', in *Plays of the Year*, vol 15. London, Elek, 1956)

91 : 5–11   Then go your own way. Keep turning round in circles; lash and tear yourself to a shred, despise, insult, kill, reject whatever is not yourself. But I am calling a halt. I am questioning no more. Those appearances I accept with the same firmness and resolution as I once rejected them with you; and if there must always be fighting, it is for those things I shall fight from now on, humbly, with my back to this fragile wall, built, with my own hands, between myself and the meaningless void without. ('Medea')

22–23   * rose-coloured plays

32   * sensualists

35   * comedy ballet

38   * toughs

39   Spanish gentlemen (*Thieves' Carnival*. London, Methuen, 1959)

92 : 6–8   . . . a quick-step which does duty as a finale. The characters come in through all the doors, dancing and exchanging beards. (*Thieves' Carnival*)

93 : 7–9   You are terrifying, Isabelle.

I am happy, Georges. There's always something terrifying about happiness. (*Dinner with the Family*. London, Methuen, 1958)

12–20   Jacques: . . . You're an actor, I take it, sir?

Delmonte: I am.

Jacques: Well, you've just come in time to give us some advice. Our scene has just come to an end, you see: now how do you think we should make our exit?

Delmonte: Well, hm, an exit isn't as easy as all that, you know. Not a simple thing at all, an exit. It depends on the situation, the character, and so on. What sort of parts have you been playing?

Jacques: The villains. (*Dinner with the Family*)

32   * head waiter

94 : 8   * ice-cream vendor

9–16   An ice-cream! My dear young lady, it's two years since I last made an ice-cream. I doubt if I could remember how— Just as I expected. Thank you. You've set my mind at rest. I'm beginning to see a mad sort of sense in all this. I'd only have been worried if you'd had an ice-cream to sell— a real, freezing ice-cream. (*Time Remembered*. London, Methuen, 1955)

24	* Brilliant plays and Bittersweet plays
26	* refusal to compromise
39–40	* We're in the thick of the worst theatrical convention.
95 : 2–3	* True art is to conceal art.

6–8   Dear Aunt,—For reasons which you all know, I'm not able to appear among you to take part in the general rejoicing. There's nothing I've ever regretted more. (*Ring Round the Moon*. London, Methuen, 1950)

13   * master-showman

27–29   [* Life is very nice, but it has no shape.] The object of art is to give life a shape, and to do it by every conceivable artifice. (*The Rehearsal*. London, Samuel French, 1961)

30   * simple, unsophisticated

31–32   . . . you discover that life is vastly more simple, very much more serious—and very much better than you ever thought it could be. (*The Rehearsal*)

96 : 9–14   Silvia and Harlequin are really in love. The Prince desires Silvia—perhaps he loves her, too? Why should princes always be refused the right to love as deeply, as simply, as Harlequin? The whole court, that is, the rest of you, will conspire to destroy the loves of Harlequin and Silvia . . . In short it is the story of an elegant and sophisticated crime. (*The Rehearsal*)

38   * a great actress

40–41   * I have made a world of my own in which everything is more difficult and purer.

97 : 14–15   * walking-on parts, cardboard figures, a confidant as in a tragedy

17   * cuckold

17–20   * It isn't all that easy, Monsieur Julien, it's a real role, full of nuances. There's a whole ritual, a dance . . . you need know-how to enter into the part . . .

32–33   Oh, love is real enough; you will find it some day, but it has one arch-enemy—and that is life. (*Ardèle*. London, Methuen, 1951)

98 : 8   * between a trio composed of

12   * comedy

21   * *belle époque*, first years of the 20th century

99 : 20   * extravagant

30–36   Toto: Oh, I know. I've seen a puppet show.
General: Well, Toto, you'll see when you grow up, that life, even when it seems real and earnest, is still only a puppet show. And it's always the same play too.
Toto: But isn't it all right to laugh then?
General: Yes. That is the engaging thing about man, Toto. He laughs regardless. (*The Fighting Cock*. London, Methuen, 1967)

38–39   * Aglaé . . . in the arms of a young man in a mask who is kissing her.

100 : 5–10   * A shadow still hovers over Aglaé. Women will never cease to be a source of peril. But Jean Anouilh is no longer waging war against

them: he is offering them peace ... Jean Anouilh has looped the loop. He has reconciled love and life in a love of life—far from categorical imperatives, in the face of La Sauvage and her motto of all or nothing.

101:5   * Fancy-dress plays

13–14   You have a right to hit at me with all your power. And my right is to say No, and go on believing. (*The Lark*. London, Methuen, 1961)

22–35   [* As they enter the characters take down their helmets and certain props which had been left on stage at the end of the previous performance. They straighten up the benches and sit down on them.]

Warwick: Well now; is everyone here? If so, let's have the trial and be done with it. The sooner she is found guilty and burned the better for all concerned.

Cauchon: But, my lord, before we do that we have the whole story to play: Domrémy, the Voices, Vaucouleurs, Chinon, the Coronation.

Warwick: Theatrical poppycock! You can tell that story to the children: the beautiful white armour, the fluttering standard, the gentle and implacable warrior maid. The statues of her can tell that story, later on, when policies have changed. We might even put up a statue ourselves in London ... (*The Lark*)

101:40 to   The true end of the story is a kind of joy. Joan of Arc: a
102:1   story which ends happily. (*The Lark*)

103:6–7   * to make an exit. He had made a mess of it the first time.

9–12   * My dear friend, we're not in the theatre. Or rather we are there ... not in the tragic theatre but in that of melodrama, as on the boulevard du Temple. I'm an actor in an historical drama.

14–15   * post-war political scene

27   * a dinner party at which each of the guests has been instructed to wear wig and make-up representing an historical character from the period of the French Revolution

104:4   * purge

13–15   * It has been said that this is a political play: it is a play against politics of any sort. It has been said that it is a play full of hatred: it is a play against hatred.

16–20   * To forget this 'every man for himself' atmosphere we've all lived in, to return home, to marry ... to have children ... Once that was a man's life. Before the French started dabbling in politics and taking life theatrically ...

41   * sophisticated conversation pieces in the manner of Marivaux

105:28   * detective story

31   * to step back in order to spring all the farther

35   * virtuoso performance

106:1   * man-servant

15–16   * the double record of technical illusion and moral disillusion

20   * script-writer

26   * with a complete identity

106:42 to   * At base, the trouble with Antoine was that he could only
107:1   believe what he imagined . . .
     24   * son of the people
108:9–10   * The performance that is going to take place tonight is of a
play I've never been able to write . . . .

CHAPTER 6   SARTRE

110:2–4   * The technique of a novel always reflects the author's metaphysical views: the critic's task is to discern the latter before offering an
appreciation of the former.
     10   * simultaneism
112:20   * didactic play, play with a moral
113:26–27   * there is this war to be fought and I shall fight it
114:39   a moment of independence (*Loser Wins*. London, Hamish
Hamilton, 1960)
115:20–21   * I should do it again if I had to.
117:11   to lie as I must (*Crime Passionnel*. London, Methuen, 1961)
     17   . . . the real taste of coffee is in his mouth (*Crime Passionnel*)
119:10   . . . values . . . in an intelligible heaven. (*Existentialism and
Humanism*. London, Methuen, 1948)
121:30–31   * Beyond those hills another Orestes and another Electra
are waiting for us . . .
124:34–36   The century might have been a good one had not man been
watched from time immemorial by the cruel enemy who had sworn to destroy him, that hairless, evil, flesh-eating beast—man himself. (*Loser Wins*)
124:39 to   * Nothing indeed—neither wild beasts nor microbes—can be
125:3   more terrible for man than an intelligent, cruel, flesh-eating
species which could understand and outwit human intelligence and whose
aim, indeed, would be the destruction of man. This species is obviously our
own, achieving self-awareness through each man in a human context against
a background of scarcity.
125:9–13   If he had lived, my father would have lain down on me and
crushed me. Fortunately he died young; among the Aeneases each carrying
his Anchises on his shoulders, I cross from one bank to the other, alone,
detesting those invisible fathers who ride piggy-back on their sons throughout their lives . . . (*Words*. London, Hamish Hamilton, 1964)
126:8   * loser wins
     30   * the hell of the pratico-inerte
127:37–38   * he has written what he has written
     38–39   * author's authority

CHAPTER 7   CAMUS

128 : 3–4   * It isn't my view. They are as much an expression of me as any other of my writings.

27–29   * to explore the artistic value proper to all mass literature and to show that art can sometimes emerge from its ivory tower

130 : 6–7   * break all records

10   * absurd man

16–17   'Only one is just and justifiable'

'All can be justified, no one is just'

('The Future of Tragedy' in *Lyrical and Critical*. London, Hamish Hamilton, 1967)

30–38   After having deified the human reign, man is once more turning against this god. He is struggling, at the same time both a warrior and a refugee, torn between absolute hope and final doubt. Thus he lives in a tragic climate. Perhaps this explains why tragedy is seeking to be reborn. Today, man is proclaiming his revolt while knowing that this revolt has limits, is demanding liberty and undergoing necessity, and this contradictory man, torn apart, conscious henceforth of human and historical ambiguity, is the essentially tragic man. ('The Future of Tragedy')

40–41   * the limit which must not be overstepped

131 : 7–8   Psychology is action, not thinking about oneself. (*Carnets.* London, Hamish Hamilton, 1963)

11   * notice, note

13–23   * Although I have a passionate love of the theatre, I am unfortunate in only liking one sort of play, whether comedy or tragedy. After fairly lengthy experience as producer, actor and dramatist, I feel that there is no theatre without language and style, and that to be worthwhile a dramatic work must, following the example of our own classical theatre and the Greek tragedians, deal with the whole of human destiny in all that is most simple and majestic. Without hoping to equal them, these are at least the models one must take. Psychology or at any rate ingenious anecdotes and piquant situations, while they often amuse me as a spectator, leave me cold as an author.

132 : 1–4   * . . . the great problem of modern tragedy is one of language. Characters in lounge suits cannot speak in the manner of Oedipus or Titus. Their language must be both simple enough to be ours and great enough to be tragic.

23   * principal private secretary

37–39   * And it is enough that this action should lead to death, as it does here, for it is to attain a certain form of grandeur which is peculiar to men : absurdity.

133 : 11   * Snow

36–37   * Apart from the fantasies of Caligula, nothing here is historical. His words are authentic, the use made of them is not.

135:10–14   * *Caligula* is the story of a superior suicide. It is the story of the most human and the most tragic of mistakes. Breaking faith with man through fidelity to himself, Caligula consents to die for having understood that no man can save himself alone and that one cannot be free in the face of other men.

136:2   * He makes one think.

136:40 to   * I have looked in vain for a philosophy in these four acts. Or, 137:6   if it does exist, it is to be found in this assertion of the hero's: 'Men die and they are not happy.' No, my intention lay elsewhere. The desire for the impossible is, for the dramatist, a field of study as valid as avarice and adultery. To show it in its fury, to illustrate its ravages, to bring out its failure, that was my purpose. And it is with this in mind that one must judge this work.

    9   * play with a moral

    11–14   * With *Cross Purpose* and *Caligula*, Albert Camus uses the theatrical medium to develop a line of thought of which *The Outsider* and *The Myth of Sisyphus*—in novel and essay form—had marked the beginnings.

    17   * philosophic theatre

    18   * theatre of the impossible

    37   * an attempt to create a modern tragedy

139:18   * my son

    42   * to suppress

140:14–19   * The insurmountable obstacle seems to me to be the problem of evil . . . There is the death of the children which signifies divine despotism, but there is the murder of the children which reveals human despotism. We are caught between two forms of despotism. My personal belief, in so far as it is tenable, is that if men are not innocent, they are guilty only of ignorance.

140:40 to   * from lyrical monologue to collective theatre, via mime 141:1   simple dialogue, farce and chorus

    15   * *autos sacramentales*, mystery plays

    27–28   * the great cries which today bow down or liberate crowds of men

142:39   * man in revolt

143:14–20   * I have tried to achieve dramatic tension through classic means, that is the confrontation of people equal in strength and reason. But it would be wrong to conclude that everything balances and that concerning the problem examined here I recommend no action. I only wished to show that action itself has limits. There is no good or just action that does not recognise these limits and, if they have to be overstepped, does not at least accept death.

145:5–9   * There remains a classical theme, still relevant, which is perhaps the only tragedy in the world: the blind man, stumbling between his fate and his responsibilities . . . A secret then. And a conflict. That which sets the protagonists against their fate and which is resolved in their acceptance of this fate. This is the key to classical tragedy.

CHAPTER 8   GENET

147 : 20   * the Renault car of the police
148 : 37–38   * *poète maudit*
149 : 12–13   * poetry in space
150 : 26–29   * In every sentence one cannot fail to notice a bitter rancour, the wish to debase, hatred of society, of established order . . . of everything !

      31–35   * It is the denial, not just uttered but thrown up and belched out, of all that has contributed to the honour and dignity of the Christian West; a denial made possible by a deliberately upheld confusion between what is undeniably good in civilising action, and certain of its abuses and excessses that no-one would think of denying or excusing.

151 : 29   * lime-blossom tea

      35–36   And you've poured it into the best, the finest tea set. (*The Maids*. New York, Grove Press, 1954)

152 : 1–4   As for Armand's immodest attitudes, I cannot quite say that they were the cause of my decision to write pornographic books but I was certainly flabbergasted by [them] . . . (*The Thief's Journal*. London, Anthony Blond, 1965)

      28–31   If I were to put on a play in which women had roles, I would insist that these roles be performed by adolescent boys, and I would so inform the audience by means of a placard which would remain nailed to the right or left of the sets throughout the performance. (*Our Lady of the Flowers*. London, Panther, 1966)

      38   . . . my belching sink (*The Maids*)

153 : 1–5   Avoid pawing me. [* Move back.] You smell like an animal. You've brought those odors from some foul attic, where the lackeys visit us [sic] at night. The maid's room ! The garret ! . . . that notorious skylight from which a half-naked milkman jumps to your bed ! (*The Maids*)

      20–25   * My play, *The Balcony*, takes place in a brothel, but the characters belong no more to the real world of brothels than the characters in Hamlet belong to the world of royal courts. The world of the cottage, the factory, the palace carry their own moral significance. The description of a 'brothel' can have an immoral meaning which must be transposed.

      37–38   From his nostrils he plucks acacia and violet petals. (*Our Lady of the Flowers*)

153 : 39 to   My spurt of saliva is my spray of diamonds ! (*The Maids*)
154 : 1

154 : 35 to   Jojo: (very gently) Of course . . . he won't be on French soil,
155 : 4   but even so we can . . . . Since that's all we've got . . . the Lieutenant'll have the illusion of dying on home soil. (*He hesitates.*) Nestor, if you've got any spare gas, and the others too . . . we could shoot him a whiff of it . . .

        Nestor: All I've got left is my ration.
        [* Jojo: Not long ago, you said . . .]

The Lieutenant: (in a dying voice) Water...

Jojo: [* It's a duty we must carry out.] If he's not buried in Christian soil, at least let him die breathing some air from home. (*The Screens.* London, Faber, 1963)

5   * It is sweet and noble to die for one's country.

30–32   *Archibald:* I order you to be black to your very veins. Pump black blood through them. Let Africa circulate in them. Let Negroes negrify themselves. (*The Blacks.* London, Faber, 1960)

156:1   * unsurpassed stupidity

2   * a poetic art, not a spectacle

3–4   * are meant to exalt—and I mean exalt—the greatest virtue of the Army, its capital virtue: stupidity.

6   * My plays are written against myself.

13   * dazzling intelligence

38–39   * He is a traitor to the revolution.

157:3–7   ... angel of the flaming sword, virgins of the Parthenon, stained-glass of Chartres, Lord Byron, Chopin, French cooking, the Unknown Soldier, Tyrolean songs, Aristotelian principles, heroic couplets, poppies, sunflowers, a touch of coquetry, vicarage gardens... (*The Blacks*)

22–23   * profession of political faith

25–26   * events of May 1968

37   * Militia

157:41 to   * an apocalyptic manichaeism ... a revolt against history
158:1

158:38–40   * One thing must be said: this play is not meant to plead the cause of domestic servants. I imagine there exists a trade union for household servants—it doesn't concern us.

159:5   * commitment

8   * Why are you on the Algerian side?

10   * Because I'm always on the stronger side.

11   * committed in spite of himself

15–18   * The religious ideal has in any case been perhaps the greatest influence on me and indeed I don't think all is lost because I am still naïve enough to hold to my faith. God gives it to children. And besides, hasn't he, as Mauriac says, saved what was lost?

38–39   And this, in effect, is saintliness ... to live according to Heaven, in spite of God. (*Miracle of the Rose.* London, Anthony Blond 1965)

160:26   * orthodox, right-minded

28   * behold the man—you are the man

32–34   *Green Eyes:* ... I didn't want anything—do you hear me?—I didn't want what happened to me to happen. It was all given to me. A gift from God or the devil, but something I didn't want. (*Deathwatch.* London, Faber, 1961)

39   * Litany of the Livid—Day of Wrath

41   * the big Balcony

162:18–19   * Beneath the poetry of texts there is pure poetry, without form and without text.

29–30	* the naïveté of having faith
33	* the real
34	* the angels

163 : 35–36   * At one and the same time one has to believe and refuse to believe.

37–38   * Any performance is worthless if I don't believe in what I see, although it will cease—it will never have been—when the curtain falls.

40   * entertainment

164 : 3–15   * A young writer told me how he had seen five or six children playing a war game in a public park. Divided into two sides, they were preparing to attack. Night was approaching, they said. But it was midday in the sky. They therefore decided that one of them would be Night. The youngest and most delicate, now elemental, was put in charge of the battle. He was Time, the Moment, the Ineluctable. From afar, it seems, he came upon them with a cyclical calm, made weightier by the sadness and pomp of twilight. As he approached the others, the Men, these became nervous, disturbed . . . But to their mind the child was arriving too soon. He was in advance of himself : together the troops and their leaders decided to suppress Night, who reassumed the role of a soldier belonging to one side . . . It is theatre based on this theory alone that can enthrall me.

25–26   * a sad frivolity

166 : 34   * Excrementalism

166 : 38 to   * For if scandal must come—and it goes without saying that
167 : 6   the interminable, multiple scandal that the war in Algeria was, happened and lasted independently of Genet—the main thing is that it should cease. So that a term might be put to this tidal wave, there is no point in allowing oneself to be borne along, but one must get to the bottom of the scandal and attack at base the mysterious and often monstrous forces that create it. Now, *The Screens* reaches these depths and thus proves that there is today no dramatist morally better qualified to exorcise the ghosts of the Franco-Algerian drama.

CHAPTER 9   IONESCO

168 : 5   * short stories

168 : 30 to   For me every play is an adventure, a quest, the discovery of a
169 : 3   universe that's suddenly revealed, and there's no one more surprised than I am to find that it exists . . . ('Improvisation' in *Eugène Ionesco: Plays III*. London, John Calder, 1960)

7–9   The dialogue and movement of the stage are the author's particular way of exploring reality, of exploring himself, of understanding things and of understanding himself. (*Fragments of a Journal*. London, Faber, 1968)

170 : 1   * anti-play

F.M.F.—8*

171:4   * potatoes in their jackets
    6   puss ('Jacques or Obedience' in *Plays I*. London, John Calder,
    1958)
172:20–21   Human beings saturated in meaninglessness cannot be anything but grotesque, their sufferings cannot be anything but derisively
tragic. (*Notes and Counter-Notes*. London, John Calder, 1964)
173:1–5   . . . these two elements do not coalesce, they coexist: one
constantly repels the other, they show each other up, criticise and deny one
another and, thanks to their opposition, thus succeed dynamically in maintaining a balance and creating tension. (*Notes and Counter-Notes*)
    8–11   The tragic and the farcical, the prosaic and the poetic, the
realistic and the fantastic, the strange and the ordinary, perhaps these are
the contradictory principles (there is no theatre without conflict) that may
serve as a basis for a new dramatic structure. (*Notes and Counter-Notes*)
173:24   * Punch and Judy show
    28–29   . . . sincere and grotesque. . . , both pathetic and absurd. ('The
Killer' in *Plays III*. London, John Calder, 1960)
174:7–8   I have travelled in search of an intact world over which time
would have no power. (*Fragments of a Journal*)
    14   * nothingness
    23–24   I have solved nothing; I am still questioning. (*Fragments of a
Journal*)
175:1–2   A world that is new, a world that is for ever new, a world
that is for ever, young for ever, that is Paradise. (*Fragments of a Journal*)
    14–16   A song of triumph rose from the depths of my being: I *was*,
I realised I had always *been*, that I was no longer going to die. ('The Killer')
    23–25   * . . . to express this deviation, this fall, this surrender in spite
of ourselves of the primordial state which is so close to the paradisiac state.
    31   * burning nostalgia
    37–40   I told myself that on the days I felt sad and nervous, depressed
and anxious, I would always remember that glorious moment. It would help
me to bear everything, give me a reason for living, and be a comfort to me.
('The Killer')
176:6–7   * in time, in flight, in the finite
    10   * existential malaise
    26–31   Year after year of dirty snow and bitter winds, of a climate
indifferent to human beings . . . streets and houses and whole districts of
people who aren't really unhappy, but worse, who are neither happy nor
unhappy, people who are ugly because they're neither ugly nor beautiful,
creatures that are dismally neutral, who long without longings as though
they're unconscious, unconsciously suffering from being alive. ('The Killer')
177:9–14   Look, Madeleine . . . all the acacia trees are aglow. Their
blossoms are bursting open and shooting up to the sky. The full-blown moon
is flooding the Heavens with light, a *living* planet. The Milky Way is like
creamy fire. Honeycombs, countless galaxies, comets' tails, celestial ribbons,
rivers of molten silver, and brooks, lakes, and oceans of palpable light. . . .

('Amédée or How to Get Rid of It' in *Absurd Drama*. Harmondsworth,
Penguin Books, 1965)

    21–22   A damp dark valley, a marsh that sucks you down until you
drown . . . help! help! I'm suffocating, help! . . . ('Amédée')

    37–39   * brooks of molten silver, lakes, oceans of palpable light

    39   * the ocean of the sun . . . the ocean of the sky

179:15–16   * geometrical progression…the incurable disease of the dead

    17–20   Speed is not only infernal, it is hell itself, it is the Fall,
accelerated. The present has been, Time has been, neither present nor Time
exist any longer, the geometrical progression of our fall has flung us into
nothingness. (*Fragments of a Journal*)

    22–23   * The corpse is for me error, original sin. The growing corpse
is Time.

180:22   * man in revolt

    23–24   What can we do . . . What can we do . . . ('The Killer')

181:16–19   * All ideologies, marxism included, are only justifications and
alibis for certain feelings, certain passions, instincts also, all of a biological
order.

    35   * terrible farce—fantastic fable

182:18–19   . . . myself on one side, everything else on the other? Everything is alien . . . (*Fragments of a Journal*)

    25   * elsewhere

    38–41   I had written the work so that I might learn to die. It was
to be a lesson, a sort of spiritual exercise, a gradual progress, stage by stage,
towards the ineluctable end, which I tried to make accessible to other people.
(*Fragments of a Journal*)

183:19–20   * . . . a short walk along a flower-lined path . . .

    34–39   The Empire—has there ever been another empire like it?
With two suns, two moons and two heavens to light it. And there's another
sun rising, and there's another. A third firmament appearing, shooting up
and fanning out. As one sun sets, others are rising—dawn and twilight all at
once. (*Exit the King*. London, Samuel French)

        * It is a realm that stretches beyond the reaches of the oceans,
beyond the oceans which engulf other oceans.

184:33   * cable railway

    37   * happiness—joy that bubbles over, ecstasy

185:1   * delirious with certainty

    4   * nothingness

186:4–10   Which is the right way? Indifference, perhaps. That's not
possible; since we are here, we can't help participating; . . . Let's assume,
then, that everything is comic; let's laugh at it. That would be an insult to
God or to the world. . . . Let's have a sense of humour. We cannot reject the
world. Then let's take everything seriously; that's equally ridiculous.
Earnestness is fatal; being earnest means taking sides, falsifying issues.
(*Fragments of a Journal*)

16–17   * Nothing. Beyond there is nothing more, nothing but endless depths . . . abysses.

21–26   These walls that rise up, these impenetrable walls which I so doggedly seek to bring down or to break through may perhaps represent reason. Reason raised these walls to preserve us from chaos. For behind these walls there is chaos, there is nothingness. There is nothing behind these walls. They are the frontier between what we have managed to make of the world, and the void. On the other side there's death. Keep this side of those walls. (*Fragments of a Journal*)

187:9–11   I personally would like to bring a tortoise onto the stage, turn it into a racehorse, then into a hat, a song, a dragoon and a fountain of water. One can dare anything in the theatre and it is the place where one dares the least. (*Notes and Counter-Notes*)

CHAPTER 10   ADAMOV, BECKETT AND ARRABAL

188:5   * family likeness
    6–7   * typically French dramatists
    26   * grammar school—civil service
189:23   * boulevard theatre
190:3   * revival
    8   * staging
    18–19   * a schoolboy's caricature of one of his teachers who seemed to him to incarnate all that is grotesque in the world
    21–22   * a lesson in false sentimentality and false aesthetics
    23   * the stupidity of the fake natural
    35–40   * for there is such energy in the humanity of today and among contemporary young writers that the greatest misfortune is immediately seen as having its purpose and as being comprehensible not only from a point of view of benevolent irony which allows one to laugh at it, but even from a standpoint of true optimism which brings immediate consolation and allows hope to develop.
191:6–7   * This art will be modern, simple, swift with all the necessary short-cuts and amplifications.
    9   * vulgar idealism
    10–11   * this fake naturalistic theatre which makes up the bulk of today's dramatic art
    13–14   * a round with two stages, one at the centre of the other, making, at it were, a ring round the audience
    15   * renewing a neglected tradition
    19   * early years of 20th century
    23–24   Jarry's *Ubu* and Appollinaire's *Les Mamelles de Tirésias* are both symbolic dramas and dramas *à thèse*. (In *The Infernal Machine and Other Plays*. Norfolk, Connecticut, New Directions, 1963)
    31   the good absurdity (in *The Infernal Machine*, etc.)

31–32	* a logical sequence of illogical circumstances
39–40	. . . I try to paint *more truly than the truth.* (In *The Infernal Machine*)
41	* stage business, disguises
192 : 2–4	. . . will keep the Grail at Camelot, that token which is simply the very rare equilibrium with oneself. (In *The Infernal Machine*)
193 : 5–6	* actor's exit
32	* Punch and Judy
38	* committed dramatists
194 : 13	* Employee
14–15	* a real town where life would be gay and people good-natured
28	* admission of failure
41	* the firstcomer, anyone
195 : 6	* comedy of manners
17–19	* convenient . . . to place back to back the adversaries who are confronting each other, thus immediately supposing the struggle to be derisory, and applying in all circumstances the lofty philosophy of 'it's all hopeless'.
20–21	* one always knows what one is fighting and why
31	* refugees
196 : 24–25	Why tell me now, after all these years? ('Professor Taranne' in *Adamov—Two Plays*. London, John Calder, 1962)
31	. . . and I often write as I walk . . . ('Professor Taranne')
39–41	* . . . on the very simple, very justifiable wish not to pass the buck to the human condition already weighty and terrible enough in itself.
197 : 9–11	* the simplest words, those made most colourless by use, in appearance the most precise, and give back to them their share of innate imprecision.
18	* the objects which were on the right are now on the left and vice-versa.
25–26	* he often spoke of destroying his papers . . . but it was in terrible moments, when everything seemed futile in advance.
30	* whistles, noise of buses, horns
31	* unbearable brightness
33	* to create a feeling of unfamiliarity
36	* to underline the element of parody in the play
198 : 13	* of its own kind
199 : 23–24	Well, shall we go? Yes, let's go. (*Waiting for Godot*. London, Faber, 1965)
201 : 4–6	But we breathe, we change! We lose our hair, our teeth! Our bloom! Our ideals! (*Endgame*. London, Faber, 1958)
34	all the dead voices (*Waiting for Godot*)
202 : 10	Christ have mercy upon us! (*Waiting for Godot*)
203 : 20	Me—(. . . .)—to play. (*Endgame*)
28	Inspiring prospects. (*Waiting for Godot*)
205 : 11–12	* 'to be is to be perceived'

30–31   * You have fire and dawn in your belly. It's as though your hips rocked a tear that fills you with storm.

40–41   * I think my plays come from wilder horizons

206 : 1–3   * Theatre is essentially a ceremony, a celebration, which is at the same time sacrilegious and sacred, erotic and mystic, ritualistic putting to death and exaltation of life.

4–5   * the humanoid dreams that may well haunt the nights of an IBM machine

34   * half religious, half obscene

36   * bad taste and aesthetic refinement

41–42   * beneath the apparent disorder, it is indispensable that the staging be a model of precision.

207 : 20–23   * spectacles thus produced have brought about a renaissance of the theatre of today and have made the stage the ideal means of expression for the man of today.

32–33   Why ever did I come into this mad-house? ('The Grand Ceremonial' in *Plays III*. London, Calder and Boyars, 1970)

35–37   Being a gentleman he knows how to keep calm but being a stupid bastard gentleman he keeps calm in a stupid bastard manner. ('The Grand Ceremonial')

208 : 14–15   * It is the epoch of theatre that lives in the forefront of action, challenges and dreams. Fascinating dawn !

209 : 4   * the age of Louis XIV

Material assembled or translated
by Beryl S. Fletcher.

INDEX

Titles of published English translations are given within parentheses; literal versions of untranslated originals are given within square brackets.

List of published translations of plays and other works mentioned in this book. Only French authors are listed here.

ADAMOV, ARTHUR
  Paolo, Paoli, the Years of the Butterfly   London, Calder, 1959
  Professor Taranne (in *Two Plays*)   London, Calder, 1959
ANOUILH, JEAN
  Antigone (in *Five Plays*, vol. 1)   New York, Hill & Wang, 1958
  Ardèle (in *Five Plays*, vol. 2)   New York, Hill & Wang, 1958
  Becket, or the Honor of God   New York, Coward McCann, 1960
  Catch as Catch Can (in *Seven Plays*)   New York, Hill & Wang, 1967
  Cécile, or the School for Fathers (in *Seven Plays*)   New York, Hill & Wang, 1967
  Dinner with the Family   London, Methuen, 1958
  Ermine, The (in *Five Plays*, vol. 1)   New York, Hill & Wang, 1958
  Eurydice: Legend of Lovers (in *Five Plays*, vol. 1)   New York, Hill & Wang, 1958
  Fighting Cock, The   London, Methuen, 1967
  Lark, The (in *Five Plays*, vol. 2)   New York, Hill & Wang, 1958
  Mademoiselle Colombe (in *Five Plays*, vol. 2)   New York, Hill & Wang, 1958
  Medea (in *Seven Plays*)   New York, Hill & Wang, 1967
  Ornifle   New York, Hill & Wang, 1970
  Poor Bitos   New York, Coward McCann, 1964
  Rehearsal, The (in *Five Plays*, vol. 1)   New York, Hill & Wang, 1958
  Restless Heart (in *Five Plays*, vol. 2)   New York, Hill & Wang, 1958
  Ring Round the Moon   London, Methuen, 1956
  Romeo and Jeannette (in *Five Plays*, vol. 1)   New York, Hill & Wang, 1958
  Thieves' Carnival   New York, Macmillan, 1965
  Time Remembered (in *Five Plays*, vol. 2)   New York, Hill & Wang, 1958
  Traveller without Luggage   London, Methuen, 1959
  Waltz of the Toreadors, The   New York, Samuel French, 1958
ARRABAL, FERNANDO
  Architect and the Emperor of Assyria, The   New York, Grove, 1969
  Automobile Graveyard, The   New York, Grove, 1969

Condemned Man's Bicycle, The   London, Calder, 1967
Fando and Lis (in *Four Plays*)   London, Calder, 1966
Grand Ceremonial, The (in *Plays 3*), London, Calder, 1970
Labyrinth, The (in *Guernica and Other Plays*)   New York, Grove, 1969
Picnic on the Battlefield (in *Guernica and Other Plays*)   New York, Grove,
     1969
Solemn Communion, The (in *Plays 3*)   London, Calder, 1970

ARTAUD, ANTONIN
     Cenci, The   London, Calder, 1969
     Theater and Its Double, The   New York, Grove, 1958

BALZAC, HONORÉ DE
     César Birotteau   London, Elek Books, 1956
     Duchesse de Langeais, The (in *Great French Romances*)   London, Pilot
          Press, 1946
BARRAULT, JEAN LOUIS
     Rabelais   London, Faber, 1971
     Reflections on the Theatre   London, Rockliff, 1951
BEAUVOIR, SIMONE DE
     Force of Circumstance   New York, Putnam, 1965
     Prime of Life, The   Cleveland, World Publishing Co., 1962
BECKETT, SAMUEL
     Acts without Words   (1) London, Faber, 1958; (2) London, Faber, 1967
     Endgame   New York, Grove, 1958
     Waiting for Godot   New York, Grove, 1954

CAMUS, ALBERT
     Caligula (in *Caligula and Three Other Plays*)   New York, Knopf, 1958
     Exile and the Kingdom   New York, Knopf, 1958
     Fall, The   New York, Knopf, 1957
     Just Assassins, The (in *Caligula and Three Other Plays*)   New York, Knopf,
          1958
     Misunderstanding, The (in *Caligula and Three Other Plays*)   New York,
          Knopf, 1958
     Myth of Sisyphus and Other Essays, The   New York, Knopf, 1957
     Notebooks   New York, Knopf, 1963
     Nuptials (in *Lyrical and Critical*)   London, Hamish Hamilton, 1967
     Plague, The   New York, Knopf, 1957
     Rebel, an Essay on Man in Revolt, The   New York, Knopf, 1957
     State of Siege (in *Caligula and Three Other Plays*)   New York, Knopf, 1958
     Stranger, The   New York, Knopf, 1958
CLAUDEL, PAUL
     Book of Christopher Columbus, The   New Haven, Yale University Press,
          1930
     Break of Noon (in *Two Dramas*)   Chicago, H. Regnery, 1960
     City, The   New Haven, Yale University Press, 1920

Correspondence 1899–1926 between Paul Claudel and André Gide   London, Secker & Warburg, 1952
Crusts (in *Three Plays*)   Boston, J. W. Luce, 1945
East I Know, The   New Haven, Yale University Press, 1914
Hostage, The (in *Three Plays*)   Boston, J. W. Luce, 1945
Humiliation of the Father, The (in *Three Plays*)   Boston, J. W. Luce, 1945
Letters to a Doubter   New York, A. & C. Boni, 1927
Satin Slipper, The   London, Sheed & Ward, 1931
Tête d'Or   New Haven, Yale University Press, 1919
Tidings Brought to Mary, The (in *Two Dramas*)   Chicago, H. Regnery, 1960

COCTEAU, JEAN
Eiffel Tower Wedding Party, The (in *The Infernal Machine and Other Plays*)   Norfolk, Connecticut, New Directions, 1964
Infernal Machine and Other Plays, The   Norfolk, Connecticut, New Directions, 1964
Intimate Relations (in *From the Modern Repertoire*)   Bloomington, Indiana University Press, 1958
Knights of the Round Table, The (in *The Infernal Machine and Other Plays*)   Norfolk, Connecticut, New Directions, 1964
Orphée (in *Five Plays*)   New York, Hill & Wang, 1961

CORNEILLE, PIERRE
The Cid (in *Chief Plays*)   Princeton, Princeton University Press, 1957

DUMAS, ALEXANDRE
Edmund Kean, or the Genius and the Libertine   London, G. Vickers, 1847

FOUQUÉ, FRIEDRICH FREIHERR DE LA MOTTE
Undine   New York, Rhinehart, 1959

GENET, JEAN
Balcony, The   New York, Grove, 1960
Blacks, The   New York, Grove, 1960
Deathwatch   New York, Grove, 1958
Funeral Rites   New York, Grove, 1969
Letters to Roger Blin   New York, Grove, 1969
Maids, The   New York, Grove, 1958
Man Condemned to Death, The, pirated edition   British Museum, 1960
Miracle of the Rose   New York, Grove, 1966
Our Lady of the Flowers   New York, Grove, 1963
Screens, The   New York, Grove, 1962
Thief's Journal, The   New York, Grove, 1964

GIDE, ANDRÉ
Fruits of the Earth, The   New York, Knopf, 1949
Immoralist, The   New York, Vintage Books, 1960
Lafcadio's Adventures   New York, Vintage Books, 1961

Oedipus (in *Two Legends*)   New York, Knopf, 1950
Prometheus Misbound (in *Marshlands and Prometheus Misbound*)   New York, New Directions, 1953
Return of the Prodigal Son   Logan, Utah State University Press, 1960

GIRAUDOUX, JEAN
Amphitryon 38 (in *Three Plays*)   New York, Hill & Wang, 1964
Apollo of Bellac, The (in *Four Plays*)   New York, Hill & Wang, 1958
Duel of Angels   New York, Oxford University Press, 1959
Electra (in *Three Plays*)   New York, Hill & Wang, 1964
Enchanted, The (in *Four Plays*)   New York, Hill & Wang, 1958
Judith (in *Plays*)   New York, Oxford University Press, 1963
Madwoman of Chaillot, The (in *Four Plays*)   New York, Hill & Wang, 1958
Ondine (in *Four Plays*)   New York, Hill & Wang, 1958
Siegfried (in *Three Plays*)   New York, Hill & Wang, 1964
Tiger at the Gates (in *Plays*)   New York, Oxford University Press, 1963
Virtuous Island, The   New York, Samuel French, 1956

IONESCO, EUGÈNE
Amédée   New York, Grove, 1958
Bald Soprano, The (in *Four Plays*)   New York, Grove, 1958
Chairs, The (in *Four Plays*)   New York, Grove, 1958
Colonel's Photograph, The   New York, Grove, 1969
Exit the King   London, Calder, 1963
Fragments of a Journal   New York, Grove, 1968
Hunger and Thirst   New York, Grove, 1969
Improvisation, or The Shepherd's Chameleon (in *The Killer and Other Plays*)   New York, Grove, 1960
Killer and Other Plays, The   New York, Grove, 1960
Jack or the Submission (in *Four Plays*)   New York, Grove, 1958
Lesson, The (in *Four Plays*)   New York, Grove, 1958
New Tenant, The   New York, Grove, 1958
Notes and Counter Notes   New York, Grove, 1964
Stroll in the Air, A   London, Calder, 1965
Rhinoceros   New York, Grove, 1960
Victims of Duty   New York, Grove, 1958

JARRY, ALFRED
The Ubu Plays   New York, Grove, 1969

LENORMAND, HENRI-RENÉ
The Dream Doctor (in *Three Plays*)   London, Gollancz, 1928

MARITAIN, JACQUES
Art and Scholasticism (and *The Frontiers of Poetry*)   New York, Scribner, 1962

MARIVAUX, PIERRE CARLET DE CHAMBLAIN DE
  Double Infidelity (in *Seven Comedies*)   Ithaca, New York, Cornell University Press, 1968
MOLIÈRE, JEAN BAPTISTE POQUELIN
  Don Juan, or The Statue at the Feast (in *Five Plays*)   Baltimore, Penguin, 1968
  George Dandin, or The Husband Defeated   London, J. Watts, 1732
  Learned Ladies, The   Great Neck, New York, Barron's Educational Series, 1957
  Misanthrope and Other Plays, The   Baltimore, Penguin, 1959
  School for Wives, The   London, Elek Books, 1960
MONTHERLANT, HENRY DE
  Civil War, The (in *Theatre of War*)   London, Penguin, 1967
  Desert Love   New York, Noonday Press, 1957
  Malatesta   London, Routledge and Kegan Paul, 1962
  Master of Santiago and Four Other Plays, The   New York, Knopf, 1951
  No Man's Son (in *Master of Santiago and Four Other Plays*)   New York, Knopf, 1951
  Queen after Death (in *Master of Santiago and Four Other Plays*)   New York, Knopf, 1951
  Selected Essays   New York, Macmillan, 1961
  Tomorrow the Dawn (in *Master of Santiago and Four Other Plays*)   New York, Knopf, 1951

PASCAL, BLAISE
  The Pensées   Baltimore, Penguin, 1961

RACINE, JEAN
  Berenice (in *Five Plays*)   New York, Hill & Wang, 1960
  Phaedra (in *Five Plays*)   New York, Hill & Wang, 1960
ROMAINS, JULES
  Dr Knock (in *From the Modern Repertoire*)   Bloomington, Indiana University Press, 1958

SARTRE, JEAN-PAUL
  Age of Reason, The   New York, Bantam Books, 1959
  Being and Nothingness   New York, Philosophical Library, 1956
  Communists and Peace, The   New York, G. Braziller, 1968
  Condemned of Altona, The   New York, Knopf, 1961
  Devil and the Good Lord, The   New York, Knopf, 1960
  Dirty Hands (in *No Exit and Three Other Plays*)   New York, Knopf, 1960
  Existentialism and Humanism   London, Methuen, 1957
  Flies, The (in *The Devil and the Good Lord*)   New York, Knopf, 1960
  Ghost of Stalin, The   New York, G. Braziller, 1968
  Kean (in *The Devil and the Good Lord*)   New York, Knopf, 1960
  Nekrassov (in *The Devil and the Good Lord*)   New York, Knopf, 1960

No Exit and Three Other Plays   New York, Vintage Books, 1956

Reply to Claude Lefort (in The Communists and Peace)   New York, G. Braziller, 1968

Reprieve, The   Modern Library, 1967

Respectful Prostitute, The (in No Exit and Three Other Plays)   New York, Vintage Books, 1956

Room, The Wall and Other Stories, The   New York, New Directions, 1948

Saint Genet, Actor and Martyr   New York, New American Library, 1964

Situations   New York, G. Braziller, 1965

Troubled Sleep   New York, Knopf, 1951

Victors, The (in Three Plays)   New York, Knopf, 1949

Words, The   New York, G. Braziller, 1964

VILLIERS DE L'ISLE, COMTE DE

Axel   Dublin, Dolmen Press, 1970